# A FLY FISHERMAN'S
# BLUE RIDGE

# A FLY FISHERMAN'S
# BLUE RIDGE

## CHRISTOPHER CAMUTO

HENRY HOLT AND COMPANY    NEW YORK

*36226 24*

Published by Henry Holt and Company, Inc.,
115 West 18th Street, New York, New York 10011.
Published in Canada by Fitzhenry & Whiteside Limited,
195 Allstate Parkway, Markham, Ontario L3R 4T8.

Library of Congress Cataloging-in-Publication Data
Camuto, Christopher.
A fly fisherman's Blue Ridge / by Christopher Camuto.—1st ed. p.   cm.
Includes bibliographical references.
ISBN 0-8050-1466-7
1. Trout fishing—Blue Ridge Mountains. 2. Fly fishing—Blue Ridge
Mountains. 3. Natural history—Blue Ridge Mountains. I. Title.
SH688.U6C36 1990
799.1'758—dc20                                    90-4790
CIP

Henry Holt books are available at special discounts
for bulk purchases for sales promotions, premiums,
fund-raising, or educational use. Special editions
or book excerpts can also be created to specification.
For details contact: Special Sales Director, Henry Holt and Company,
Inc., 115 West 18th Street, New York, New York 10011

First Edition

BOOK DESIGN BY CLAIRE NAYLON VACCARO
MAPS BY CLAUDIA CARLSON
Printed in the United States of America
Recognizing the importance of preserving
the written word, Henry Holt and Company, Inc.,
by policy, prints all of its first editions
on acid-free paper. ∞
1   3   5   7   9   10   8   6   4   2

FOR MY MOTHER AND FATHER

Lakes and the sea have great secret depths quite hidden from man and often almost barren of life. A river too may have its deep and secret places, may be so large that one can never know it properly; but most rivers that give sport to fly-fishermen are comparatively small, and one feels that it is within the range of the mind to know them intimately—intimately as to their changes through the seasons, as to the shifts and quirks of current, the sharp runs, the slow glides, the eddies and bars and crossing places, the very rocks of the bottom. And in knowing a river intimately is a very large part of the joy of fly-fishing.

—RODERICK HAIG-BROWN,
*A River Never Sleeps*

In the night I dreamed of trout-fishing.

—HENRY DAVID THOREAU,
*The Maine Woods*

# CONTENTS

# CONTENTS

# CONTENTS

# ACKNOWLEDGMENTS

Books, like rivers, need friends. First thanks to Ted Leeson, who reminded me about the rivers, and to Bill Strachan, who invited me to write the book. Thanks to John Randolph at *Fly Fisherman,* Tom Pero at *Trout,* Marty Sherman at *Flyfishing,* Jonathan King at *Sierra,* and Virginia Shepherd at *Virginia Wildlife* for providing me with earlier opportunities to write about trout and the environment. I am also grateful for Debra Manette's excellent copy editing of the manuscript. In the field and in their offices, members of the Virginia Department of Game and Inland Fisheries, the North Carolina Wildlife Resources Commission, the U.S. Forest Service, the National Park Service, and the Department of Environmental Sciences at the University of Virginia were always eager to share their knowledge about land use practices and fisheries management. The Nature Conservancy, the Sierra Club, Trout Unlimited, and The Wilderness Society deserve general thanks and support for their work to preserve what is left of wilderness and wildlife in the Blue Ridge. Thanks to the Thomas Jefferson Chapter of Trout Unlimited in Charlottesville, Virginia, where I first learned about the trout in the mountains. Most thanks to those with whom I have shared memorable days on Blue Ridge rivers—especially Mary Camuto, Pat Camuto and Doug Bilinski, James and Kathi Dubovsky, Elizabeth Campbell, Bill Rowland and Andrea Fisher, Greg Leeson, Dabney Stuart, and Tim Good and Jacquelyn Fox-Good. This book is dedicated to my parents, but it was written in some respects for the children in my life, a wonderful gaggle of nieces and nephews—

# ACKNOWLEDGMENTS

Elizabeth, Michael, Kevin, Cheryl and Katie—and my best friend, Annie Good. I hope good rivers flow through their lives and that wild trout rise in their evenings.

—CLOVER HILL
*Winter 1990*

PENNSYLVANIA

N

Gettysburg

Potomac River

MARYLAND

Harpers Ferry

GEORGE WASHINGTON
NATIONAL FOREST

Shenandoah River

WEST VIRGINIA

B
L
U
E

R
I
D
G
E

Washington, D.C.

Potomac River

Luray

Rappahannock River

Rapidan River

VIRGINIA

SHENANDOAH
NATIONAL PARK

Staunton

Charlottesville

Waynesboro

St. Marys
Wilderness Area

Lexington

GEORGE
WASHINGTON
NATIONAL
FOREST

James River

Buena
Vista

James River

Lynchburg

JEFFERSON
NATIONAL
FOREST

Northern
Blue Ridge

©Claudia Carlson

Roanoke

Roanoke River

Smith
Mountain
Lake

VIRGINIA

Smith River

Dan River

Galax

NORTH
CAROLINA

Yadkin River

Jefferson

South Fork New R.

B L U E   R I D G E

Grandfather Mountain

*Highest Point in Blue Ridge* →

Lenoir

Linville Gorge Wilderness Area

PISGAH NATIONAL FOREST

Asheville

French Broad R.

PISGAH
NATIONAL
FOREST

Brevard

Central
Blue Ridge

©Claudia Carlson

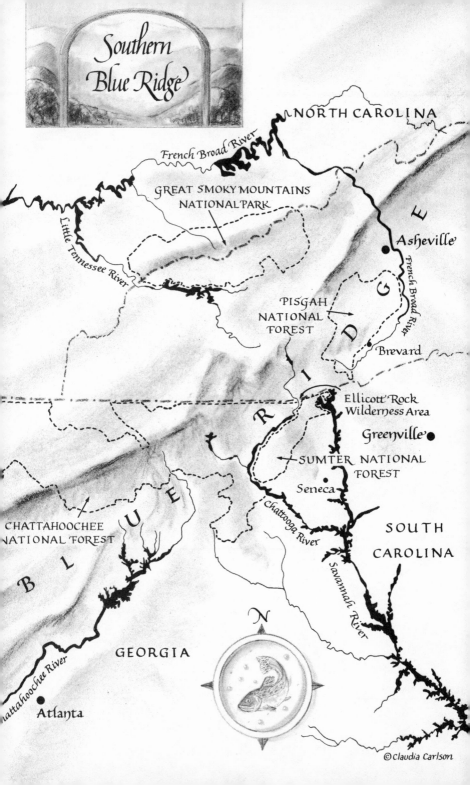

Southern
Blue Ridge

NORTH CAROLINA

French Broad River

GREAT SMOKY MOUNTAINS
NATIONAL PARK

Little Tennessee River

Asheville

French Broad River

PISGAH
NATIONAL
FOREST

R
I
D
G
E

Brevard

Ellicott Rock
Wilderness Area

Greenville

SUMTER NATIONAL
FOREST

Seneca

CHATTAHOOCHEE
NATIONAL FOREST

B
L
U
E

Chattooga River

SOUTH
CAROLINA

Savannah River

GEORGIA

N

Chattahoochee River

Atlanta

©Claudia Carlson

# SOLSTICE

Time has worn the old mountains to modest heights and gentle profiles. Some days you barely notice them. Still, the blue horizon draws the eye.

The mountains often make me wish I were a painter. The effect of winter daylight on their softly contoured watersheds produces impressions I try hard to hold in my mind. But the colors of the Blue Ridge in winter, a continuum of undramatic changes, won't stay within the discrete compartments of my words—the uninspired grays, greens, and browns I have at my fingertips. Language is one thing, but morning light slanting into the abrupt eastern slope of the Blue Ridge quite another. And evening light leaving the gentle western ridges, that too moves just ahead of the reach of a sentence, like a deer you are trying to photograph in the woods.

From a distance the Blue Ridge is uniformly gray in winter, but the gray darkens to brown as you approach the mountains. At streamside the brown is laced with the greens of eastern hemlock and white pine, as well as the waxy sheen of rhododendron and mountain laurel. The gray that was only a haze from the interstate solidifies as outcropped bedrock—neutral tones of quartzite and granite, the stuff of ridgelines and riverbeds. This gray and brown world that underwrites the green world—the world of bedrock, bare trees, and leaf litter—has a skeletal clarity about it that is easy on the eye and seems to offer some depth of perspective.

The blue for which the mountains were named is rare in winter, but there are evenings in late December when, viewed from the east against a salmon sky, the enfolded ridges take on an indigo hue that makes them appear larger than they are, higher and cut more deeply into the horizon.

Rivers run quietly, steadily through the gray and brown world, and the rivers, more than any other feature in the landscape, tempt you to make sense of the scene. But it is hard for words to follow water flowing over a staircase of moss-covered greenstone, or trace the pleasing abstract of sycamore bark at streamside, or depict the attitude of a junco keeping its distance in the winter understory. The near sound of rivers, like the far sound of geese in flight, plays on one's consciousness without resolution.

In winter trout are nowhere to be seen, but you know they are there. They inhabit a cold within the rivers that is older than the mountains themselves.

I move tentatively through the year's shortest day, as if I'm on the edge of something. I do not like the brief, dark days when the silent turn of the year in the dead of winter seems to stall. In early January I drive north along the eastern flank of the mountains twenty miles to get my fishing license at Wolftown in Madison County, Virginia. I buy it at the old post office and general store there, because I believe that somehow brings me luck. The locals wonder where I come from.

This year it was so cold I didn't bother to drive on three miles to the Rapidan, past Graves Mill, to start the year's fishing. The leaden sky seemed to get lower by the minute, as if it were packing the frigid air deep into fields of corn stubble and snow-dusted pastures, and I was glad not to be wading what I knew would be a gray, uninviting river.

But back home I was as restless as the wintering Canada geese that flew about the county in undisciplined vees from frozen cornfields to freezing farm ponds all afternoon. My house wasn't as warm as I thought it would be, and I kept moving from room to room, looking out the windows.

# I

# THE TROUT IN
# THE MOUNTAINS

In winter the North Fork of the Moormans River flows implacably gray, as if it had been dyed a granite shade by the eroding mountains. Even on overcast days a cold glare shimmers off the unbroken slicks in its currents.

The river runs coldest now, chilled by occasional snow and by freezing nights in the mountains. The cold gets into the river, which keeps up its inexplicable flow, and chases the trout, it has come to seem to me, into the mountains. At least no trout stir beneath the ovipositing stoneflies that dance slowly in the hard morning air just above the surface of the river in early January. Trout in water this cold might just as well be stones.

I watch the slant of the line in the water for a sign of life. Peering upstream in a show of concentration, hunched over and keeping the rod low, I strip line to the speed of the river. A heavily weighted nymph rides somewhere beneath the gray surface, untempting. Too cold. I cast awkwardly, swinging the fly into the whitewater at the head of a deep run, but the line keeps coming back to me evenly, meeting no resistance. I come out of the river when I am too cold to wade without stumbling. I walk the fire road for warmth and listen to the sound of the river underscore the silence of the woods.

I didn't always fish the river in winter, and I don't recall why I began seeing the year through as a trout fisherman several seasons ago. One year, I suppose, the importance of the river seemed not to be diminished by the graying of fall into December, or by the increasing reluctance of its trout to take a fly. Though the fishing had to be fit to winter circumstances, done in moments rather than days, I learned that the river was no less a river during the brief days of January than it was during the infinite days of late spring or on evanescent autumn afternoons. Even absent, the trout that I knew would appear in late February or early March were somehow still the heart of a landscape that, in all seasons, does them peculiar justice.

Given the progressive effects of an obsession with wild trout, it takes no conscious effort to one year fish a long fall that stretches into an early spring. Eventually you fish through the winter as a matter of course, keeping to the river and watching its signs. If, during the rest of the year, the Blue Ridge has shaped your taste in landscape and your need for character of place, you've really nowhere else to be. One year you never stop working your way upstream, reading currents and casting to likely holds, and you never think of the trout season as a season again.

I work slowly up the river, trying hard to be methodical in the cold. The lower stretch of the Moormans has a lot of good-looking water, quick deep runs that sluice quietly between large, undercut boulders where winter trout might hold. I fish those dark gray wedges and the good cover in slow water as best I can. Perhaps a hold-over brown has come upriver from the reservoir down-stream. Perhaps a brook trout will rouse itself from the mountain.

I cast a stonefly nymph into the whitewater at the head of a pool with enough slack in the tippet to let the fly sink quickly. With a mend, the fly tumbles toward the promising bulge of water in front of a snag, a dead hem-lock angled out into the river. I let it drift as far into the tangle of branches and current as I dare, waiting for the water to boil around the fly.

Nothing.

I keep on up the river, fishing the deeper riffles and the tails of pools as carefully as my numb legs and feet allow, shuffling as quickly as I can manage through water that doesn't look right for the season, bearing down at those deep, inscrutable runs where I keep seeing trout that don't materialize.

In half an hour the thirty-five degree water has eroded my concentration and turned my legs to stone. Less than halfway to the first ford I give up and slowly stumble to the bank. I stamp my numb feet on the frozen ground as I snip the dark brown nymph from the tippet. An unfeeling hand fumbles for the fly box. The vest feels awkward, humped over layers of wool and down, but the gear is reassuringly familiar. I pat the pockets. Every-thing is where it should be. I break down the rod and log the day in the back of my mind.

Walking the fire road brings blood stinging back into my legs and feet. The river is still the only sound in the woods, except for an occasional eddy of wind that rattles the bare, loose branches of oak and hickory and, high above me, clicks softly through the empty crowns of yel-low poplar. Now and then a ground wind kicks at dry leaves and then rises through hemlock and pine boughs,

an almost imperceptible susurrus that leads my ear back
to the river.

The awkwardness of peeling off clammy waders at the
truck makes the fishing seem absurd. The coffee in the
thermos is lukewarm, metallic, but I don't yet feel like
heading for home. I take the insect net I've fashioned out
of window screening and sawed-off broom handles down
to the river. Standing in the tail of a pool, I shove the
ends of the supports into the gravel to get the net down
to the bottom. The screening bellies toward me, full of the
river.

After ten minutes there is not much to see. Detritus
mainly, decomposed leaves and twigs. A drowned caddis.
Some immature mayfly nymphs I cannot identify. And
stoneflies. *Plecoptera.* Little black stones mostly, a
subspecies of *Allocapnia,* that, having evolved a trick of
winter emergence, have the river to themselves in January. They crawl out into the midday sunshine, and are a
sign both that the fishing is over and about to begin
again.

I no longer mind not catching trout in winter, but I
like to see the stoneflies whose half-inch-long bodies—
dark brown rather than black if you look at them
closely—long black antennae, and thickly lined folded
wings I try to re-create at the fly-tying vise with thread
and fur and bits of black goose quill. Fly fishing is as
much an affair of gestures as tactics, and tying an imita-
tive stonefly pattern carefully and fishing it below the
gray winter water during the first weeks of the year puts
me in touch with the life of the river with a degree of
precision I feel that life merits.

I rinse the net off in the flow above the lip of the pool.
On top of one of the boulders around which the current
divides a stonefly dries its folded wings under my gaze,
the detailed ribbing of its wings looking oddly artificial,
its faintly moving antennae curved expectantly. A still
life. Little black stone on basalt. One image in a scene in

which details seem endless. The gray river draws my attention upstream and down. Downstream, past seasons seem to gather in the marbled flow; upstream, I can see the year ahead. Simple enough, the larger symbols in the landscape.

Fishermen, it has often been noted, are a product of their home water, and a fly fisherman, in particular, is shaped by the character of the country toward which he or she is drawn. This relation is more practical than aesthetic, though no less significant for that. Tackle and physical stamina, as well as expectations and attitude, must adapt by degrees to the demands of the land and the turn of its seasons. The signs of adaptation are often prosaic. The dents in the rim of a fly reel, the torn bag of a landing net, and the ache in one's knees will reflect where a fisherman has been as well as any more lyric detail from a day on a river.

A river is a fact before it is an impression. A cold mountain trout stream may seem to be a work of art, an almost formal perfection in the landscape, but it is first and foremost an inevitable effect of orogeny, its form and flow a function of the size of its catchment basin, the geology of its streambed, and the amount of rainfall it receives. Even the seemingly miraculous mayfly, which it is the prestigious obligation of the fly fisherman to imitate, emerges from the chemistry rather than the poetry of a river. Neither Pliny nor Ovid could do better.

A fly fisherman's home water harbors, of course, the trout he seeks, but the trout are a focal point not always in view. Most fly fishermen think more in terms of rivers than fish. Even in hand, a trout or salmon or char remains an unknown. A river may, over time, be understood. And if you understand a river, the deepest prejudice of the fly fisherman has it, you understand the land. Topography is a matter of watersheds, the contours of the earth that determine the flow of water into the gathering of rivers. Rivers are a clear consequence of the

underlying character of the land, the truest map of the
country. However single-minded and predatory a fly
fisherman may be, entering a river is an act of subordination to a larger scene, to the life of a watershed and the
lay of the land.

From central Pennsylvania's lush farmland to the
forested wilderness of north Georgia, the Blue Ridge ex-
tends five hundred miles as the eastern flank of the
Southern Appalachians. The mountains rise as a single
ridge just west of Gettysburg, traverse Maryland from
Catoctin Mountain to the Heights overlooking the confluence of the Potomac and Shenandoah rivers at Harpers Ferry, gradually ascending across Virginia in a
southwest diagonal. Near Roanoke, the Blue Ridge
broadens from a ridge to a mountainous plateau, a band
of mountains thirty miles wide that rises into North Carolina. These mountains crest just north of Asheville,
where they confront the jumble of Southern Appalachian
ranges that stretch west toward Tennessee. Finally the
blue mountains spill into South Carolina and Georgia,
where the long arc ends north of Atlanta. Hundreds of
small coldwater streams form in these mountains and
flow down to the big rivers of the piedmont to the east or
the valleys and plateaus to the west—the Shenandoah
and Potomac, the James and the Roanoke, the New, the
Yadkin, the French Broad, and the Chattooga.

The small mountain streams that drain the short,
steep watersheds of the Blue Ridge from Pennsylvania to
Georgia are the headwaters of this country's first rivers,
those watery roads inland from seventeenth-century
tidewater settlements that drew Elizabethans slowly
through the unaxed American woods. Men who might
have stayed in London, where Shakespeare's green world
was unfolding onstage for the first time, instead worked
their way tentatively up the big rivers that "falleth from
the mountaines," in the plain words of John Smith's
1612 reconnaissance. Reconnoitering Chesapeake Bay,

Smith quickly understood the lay of the land, knew that rivers were the heart of the country: "From the head of the Bay at the north, the land is mountanous, and so in a manner from thence by a Southwest line; So that the more Southward, the farther off from the Bay are those mounetaines. From which fall certaine brookes which after come to five principall navigable rivers."

Of course, the principal rivers, in Virginia and elsewhere, are much changed from what the first English saw and what the Indians had known for centuries. Most now flow sluggish and warm through tamed, unforested land to the suburban impoundments where their character as rivers has been dammed forever. Even in the mountains, at best second-growth forests now stand in place of the absent majesty of old growth that once shaded half a continent, and whose fragrant blooms and pungent resins wafted hundreds of miles out over the Atlantic, awakening the senses of drowsing sailors—the penumbra of a real green world, a landfall beyond Europe's imagining.

The sublime eastern forest that surprised the imagination of botanist William Bartram during his travels through the Southeast from 1770 to 1776 exists now only in his pious, overwhelmed prose. But, along with the gentle profile of the long blue horizon itself, the small, uncivilized headwaters of the lost eastern rivers remain, in places, something like what they were before European history stepped foot into the American forest. Certaine brookes still fall from the mounetaines.

Those brooks, in which wild trout still rise to mayflies in the spring, remain. If eastern buffalo and elk and cougar are gone along with the big trees, *Salvelinus fontinalis* still holds in cold currents near the crest of the Blue Ridge, an Ice Age relic, the shy shadow of one hundred million years. Like the spruce and fir that spread south during the long Pleistocene winter when the great ice advanced, the brook trout is a vivid boreal presence in the Blue Ridge, a gift of deep time.

A fly fisherman's home water is not a region but a single river, often a particular stretch of that river, and his sense of that water is likely to be personal rather than historical. If that stretch of river is close enough to home or work, he may end up seeing more varieties of morning light and twilight there than he contemplates anywhere else. His understanding of the progress of a year will have a great deal to do with the seasonal life of that river's watershed. He will note more changes there, and observe more things that remain the same, than he takes account of elsewhere. His eye for detail will be sharpened down to the venation on a mayfly wing and his sense of significance enlarged to include the structure of a caddis case. His concept of drama will be scaled to the minimalism of a stonefly struggling from its shuck.

Because of all the time he spends there, the fly fisherman is likely to see things happen on his river that he witnesses nowhere else, casual events in the natural world he has been privileged to see: the cocky strut of a bobcat taking a kill to its young, a red-tailed hawk perched over a river, a white-tailed deer, unaware of the fisherman's presence in the shadows, nervously extending its neck in a vulnerable arc in order to drink from the edge of a pool. When he fishes, he fishes as an expert, if only in the sense that he has learned the subtle differences between his river and the rivers in books.

Ultimately a fly fisherman's sense of self may be shaped by the quality of his presence on that river and the clarity of his understanding of it. Every other river he fishes, however large or far distant, will be a tributary of his home water, a variation of it. Far-gone fly fishermen have a distant look, a blue swirl in the iris of their fishing eye left there by the currents of the river they know by heart and to which they relate all other moving water. A fly fisherman returning from his home river looks as if he knows something.

The North Fork of the Moormans River is my home

river, a small, unheralded stream, full of native brook
trout, around whose constant and constantly changing
flow my fishing mind is mapped. The North Fork of the
Moormans has become the heart of a quiet, remnant
country into which I wandered, pool by pool, ten years
ago, a slender blue province of gentle mountains and
fast-flowing streams that still hold a promise of native
trout, from modest Carbaugh Run in Pennsylvania to the
wild headwaters of the Chattooga along the northern border of Georgia and South Carolina.

The North Fork of the Moormans drains a narrow
north–south watershed in the southeastern section of
Shenandoah National Park, a preserve established in the
1930s that has been a godsend to a small part of the Blue
Ridge. The river was named for its first patentee, one
Thomas Moorman, an English Quaker who acquired land
along the upper Moormans in 1742 "near the Blue Mountains" but who did not, apparently, dwell along the river.
The Via family, in Albermarle County by 1784, did live
along the river and gave their name to the gap and hollow
they settled.

The river begins inauspiciously as a gathering trickle
at 2,700 feet in an old clear-cut on private land midway
between Pinestand and Cedar Mountains, near a cemetery in Via Gap. For six miles the North Fork of the
Moormans staircases down ledgerock of Catoctin greenstone, a grayish-green basalt that gives the small river its
monumental character. Mosses and lichens have added a
vegetative green to the Catoctin rock, a green that shades
in turn toward the darker hue of the eastern hemlocks
which occupy much of the riverside. The river flows
along a local fault in a perfect sequence of room-size
pools and deep runs, relaxes in chattering riffles, and
gathers itself in cascades and small waterfalls that spill
its momentum down the mountain. To the west, boulder-
strewn ground rises steeply to the crest of the Blue
Ridge; to the east the river faces the modest escarpment

of Pasture Fence Mountain, once valued for its sweet blue pasturage, a four-peaked ridge extending south from Cedar Mountain on the eastern flank of the river and parallel to the Blue Ridge. Second-growth hardwoods, oaks and hickories mostly, sort themselves out, competing for light and space on the slopes above the river that, fifty years before, held nothing but slash and stumps.

At several places along its eastern bank, greenstone cliffs jut out and overshadow the river, creating cool, dark stretches where the flowing water echoes disconcertingly. I fish a little tentatively through these sections, hurrying casts in the shadows. You notice the dark greenstone face of the escarpment more on overcast days, particularly in winter, when the gray daylight makes it seem as if darkness is about to fall all afternoon. An early dusk waits over your shoulder while you fish the lonely upper stretches of the river. The surrounding ridges close ranks in the gloom, and it feels as if a backcast might hang up on the side of a darkening mountain a half mile away as easily as it might snag an alder branch at the back of the pool you are fishing. On bright days the ridges and the greenstone walls recede and nothing hurries the fishing.

The North Fork of the Moormans has carved a bed in the mountains a sculptor would envy. Whitewater pours effortlessly over beveled lips of ledgerock, gathering the momentum that grinds pools out of fractured bedrock. At the heads of pools boulders are slowly undermined and ground to substrate that is fanned out in shallow tails where trout will spawn in the fall. Pools broaden into riffles full of oxygen where mayfly and stonefly nymphs cling to the bottom of the river and where, in protected pockets, caddis spin their nets. Water-loving hemlock, poplar, and sycamore lie fallen across the riffles, damming and diverting water around the rocks their roots have split, widening the river into the soil in which they once grew.

The river changes constantly and is changed by everything it touches. There is the cascading whitewater and the deep blue water of the big pools in spring, bluer than the mountains themselves. There is the brown low flow of summer, when the river simmers dully, and the bright green flow of autumn when the water starts to deepen against the backdrop of the changed woods. By the end of November, when the woods are bare, you will find the gray winter river flowing coldly again at your feet. All year there is the sound of the river, which is the voice of the mountains, a mother tongue like Sanskrit, the speech of bedrock. If you fish the North Fork of the Moormans often and in all seasons, you will remember the sound of the river and the shadows cast by the surrounding greenstone as vividly as you remember the trout you bring to hand. You may even try to remember the quality of light that seemed to hold certain moments in place.

At the southern end of the Pasture Fence escarpment, with the Blue Ridge at its back to the west, the North Fork of the Moormans turns sharply to the east into the gap between Pasture Fence and Bucks Elbow Mountain, where it is joined by the northward-flowing South Fork of the river. The breach between the mountains was opened by the final shrug of the earth that wrinkled the Blue Ridge into place near the end of the Appalachian mountain building, creating what geologists call a prominent local unconformity—the minor but well-defined thrust faults from which the river got its being. As the big pieces of the world drifted apart, carrying the Blue Ridge's sister mountains off to Mauritania, the gap became a drainage for the eastward-facing slopes of the newly formed mountains. Over time the Moormans River eroded the greenstone and wore through the older shales and quartzite beneath it. Eventually the river exposed the plutonic core rock of the Blue Ridge, its gray, Precambrian heart of coarse-grained Pedlar granite, half as old as the earth.

The gap in the mountains was dammed just below the

confluence of the two rivers in the 1920s, flooding the window the rivers had carved in time. I imagine there was once a perfect pool where large brook trout held over basement rock in the deep, cold flow where the rivers met. When they built the dam, they left a boulder of Pedlar granite, twice the height of a man, along the road where it still sits, split in half like some prehistoric egg, a stony piece of the heart of the mountains toward which the rivers once flowed.

If you look beyond the refuse at the water's edge and keep the dam beyond the periphery of your vision, the reservoir has the look of a remote tarn. Reflecting the waning brightness in the sky and drawing color from the mountains that surround it on three sides, its surface can take on astonishing hues in the evening when the sun begins to drop behind Thomas Moorman's blue mountains and the early dusk of the eastern slopes sets in. Except for the waterfowl that nest on the lake, the water is undisturbed, an invitation to the eye and mind.

For better or worse, the road to the Moormans has been getting smoother each year. During the last ten years I've watched uneasily as more of the dirt portion has become gravel, and the gravel been graded and then paved. One year I passed a work crew from a state prison sullenly prying at the bigger boulders in the road with wrecking bars under the nervous gaze of a guard cradling a twelve-gauge and trying hard to look like someone in *Cool Hand Luke.* Most of the interesting old homesteads along the way to the river have burned down or been abandoned, sold, and razed. The precious orderliness of small suburban estates has replaced the ramshackle hazards and sweet rural chaos amid which the hollow folk once lived. Fluorescent joggers are scaring the black bear.

Every year I resolve to fish the Moormans continuously mouth to source, covering every foot of it and thereby coming to know it perfectly. I imagine I will wade patiently upriver all year and fish every riffle, run, and pool. I will note every detail and notice every change. I will keep meticulous records on stream temperature and insect life and write detailed narratives of everything I see. I will resist the attractions of all other rivers, and by the end of the year I will know everything about this one.

This resolution may hold for the first few forays in January, but before I've covered a half mile of stream, a sunny day toward the end of the month will bring to mind the big pools and deep runs above the third ford where I have caught good trout and all the familiar, promising water above Big Branch, halfway up the mountain to Via Gap, where the dark cliffs border the river. The years have structured my expectations as irrevocably as the river has structured its bed. I know where the end of winter waits.

Although each year winter seems to break at the end of the month, in the mountains the January thaw is more illusion than reality. The remote sun and the warm, southerly wind may be convincing enough to shrink the ice sheet that has crept out over the south side of the reservoir, but the sullen river, not much warmer for a few bright days, shrugs along emptily. Its surface still reflects the slick gray glare I see in my sleep all winter, a blankness toward which trout don't rise and within which they rarely stir.

Snow remains in the creases of shaded slopes. Stalactites of ice hang from the lichen-blackened greenstone cliffs at the first ford and on the large shoulder of greenstone that marks the pronounced bend in the river just above the second ford. You can feel the deep cold of the mountain pulse from the ice and stone as you walk past. An infinite regress of gray tree trunks recedes up the rocky slopes on either side of the river. The largely dormant understory opens the watershed to the long view you get of it in winter, an abstract of bare branches through which a grackle occasionally flaps, adding to the emptiness with its raspy, heartless call.

Even on a bright day in January, it takes an effort to get in the river. The still shallows of some pools have a thin covering of ice, and every now and then a small, disheartening chunk will break off and float through a pool. Egg-laying stoneflies bob up and down over some riffles. If you lean close to them, you can see tiny egg masses detach from their abdomens and sink into the cold water. It's hard to imagine life emerging from such an unpromising start. A dark caddis, wings tented sleekly over its back, perches on a boulder, immobile and unreal in the sunlit cold.

For a few hours in the early afternoon the river looks promising. My eyes are drawn to the smooth slow water where trout might be stirred by stoneflies crawling over the streambed toward the river's edge. I cast a black stonefly nymph to midpool, guide it toward the dead spot at the base of a boulder, and then let it drift into the stillwater off the broadening fan of current at the tail of the pool. As I watch the leader I think I can feel the small, weighted fly ticking along the bottom of the river, a remote but reassuring progress. With short casts and steady retrieves I cover each pool easily, but no trout sucks in the nymph. No telltale pause or shift of the leader where it enters the water starts the inference that lifts the rod against the sleepy, uncertain pull of a winter trout. In places I fish the fly downstream, letting it tumble out of riffles into slow, deep eddies where a sluggish trout might be waiting for a stonefly that had lost its purchase on a stone.

I move upstream awkwardly in the incongruous winter sunshine, balancing my concentration between the warmth it offers and the cold in which I am immersed. The near-freezing water gnaws at the pleasure I usually take in wading. On numb feet and legs the resistance of the river seems antagonistic. Gelid currents grab and push. The stoneflies that chug occasionally through the air keep me fishing, but my hopes narrow steadily in the cold. Casting becomes a way of keeping warm. Despite all the gear packed into my vest, I rarely think of changing flies or tactics. In an hour I clamber out of an unfamiliar river, unsure of why I'm there.

Walking upstream along the Moormans on a late-January day, I can remember when I used to be more determined in my fishing. Not that long ago I would fish the worst days of winter, thinking to move trout by grimly sacrificing all hope of comfort. My stream notes record many bitterly cold days on the lower Rapidan River, above and below its confluence with the Staunton, a beautiful stretch of water I used to haunt in winter like a bear that refused to den for the season. At the time I was scratching an itch to be scientific, to get at the river with warm-blooded willpower and book-length expertise. Those old notes show absurdly long lists of flies tried and long reaches of water covered each time out.

I can still see my gray, numb fingertips sticking out of wool millarmitts, trying to work monofilament into clinch knots. I bit split shot onto tippets to help weighted nymphs sink and fought the ruined action of the fly rod when I cast. Some narrow ambition to prove I could catch trout every week of the year kept me on the river. I remember tugging a fly line in a jerky retrieve through iced-up guides on days so cold the water in my felt-soled wading shoes would turn to ice within moments after getting out of the river. More than once I skated to a fall trying to shuffle too quickly back to the warmth of the truck.

The elaborate notes I kept at the time confirm I caught trout, but I don't remember much pleasure in it. I do remember the deep, green January water of the Rapidan foaming white around gray, ice-capped boulders and the luminous silence of the snow-covered hemlocks that soaked up the sound of the river. I remember the lonely, inviting curve of the freshly whitened fire road receding up into the mountains.

Of all the trout I caught, I only remember the one I thought to set briefly on the snow before I released it, to see its brilliant colors set off against a white background. Its black undermarkings had faded, but the trout retained the orange flank of its autumn spawning. Its scarlet spots, ringed in pale blue, fairly glowed in the cold. Its tiny lower jaw was still fiercely kyped, which gave the small fish the determined look of a salmon or steelhead.

And I remember stopping one prematurely dark afternoon to watch the snow fall thickly on the millpond at Graves Mill as a blizzard piled into the mountains. Drinking coffee in the cab of the truck, I was glad to be pointed home, but glad, too, to be caught at the edge of the oncoming storm watching the dark oval swallow the snow while the river and the mountains whited out behind me. I stayed until the snow fell so fast that the oval disappeared. As it got dark, I made deep tracks home.

I eventually learned not to be overly eager for trout best left alone and that catching trout every week of the year, or every day of the year, was a meaningless quest. I learned, too, that there was more art than science to fishing in the mountains, and more craft, really, than art. Winter, like all seasons, would keep. The trout were there, suspended at the bottom of the river dimly dreaming some vague holarctic dream, a reverie best left undisturbed.

Now when I am stirred by the false promise of a late-January day, I am as content to watch as fish. So I walk upstream along the Moormans, keeping one eye on the river and the other on the sunlit winter woods. Walking begins to put the year underfoot, and looking into the gray latticework of the watershed sharpens my sight.

I stop where a shattered greenstone wall lies in the river, in the form of twelve wedge-shape boulders arrayed like an arrowhead pointing downstream. Above this point the river flows quietly. Below the breach in what was once part of the greenstone escarpment on the east bank, the river charges loudly through the stone gauntlet it has created, seeming to gather momentum from the friction created by its descent. The large-scale rubble, once all of a piece, has been abraded to separate shapes that now seem to fit perfectly the flow of the water around them. Of all the Blue Ridge rivers I know, none looks so much to be doing the slow work of time as does the North Fork of the Moormans in winter, especially where it trumpets through that arrow of broken green-stone and falls loud and white into the big pools that ladle it downstream through its sharply faulted land-scape.

I walk back down the fire road, which puts the river below me in the middle distance. In winter you can see exactly how the Moormans inhabits its landscape. By late afternoon the remote January sun has slid away. The sunlit emerald pools vanish and the leaden surface of the winter river returns. A stiff, cold wind circles down into the hollow from the ridge tops like a hawk. Trees creak. The gray air smells like snow.

The trout stay hid, as if they weren't there.

# MIMESIS

I was tying trout flies one evening in February when the rains came, long overdue. Winter had been dry, and everyone worried that there would be no good spring water. I watched with satisfaction as rain beaded on the hood of the truck and formed puddles in the garden. The insistent drumming on the tin roof helped me concentrate at the vise where Quill Gordons were slowly emerging.

After a few hours the flies seemed to tie themselves.

Pale yellow wood duck flank feathers, banded lightly with gray, bunch and cock upright, set for flight by figure-eight wraps of cream thread. The thread winds on to cover the hook shank to its bend, where it fixes in place a tail of stiff hackle fibers. A quill from the eye of a peacock, gently stripped of flues, wraps bands of light and dark body segments forward to where dark dun hackle winds through the wings, giving the fly enough life to sustain a minor, imperfect illusion. Mimesis, poets call it, imitation of nature.

As I tied imitations of the Quill Gordons I knew would soon be emerging in the mountains, I could see each fly on the water, riding on hackle tips and tail, breaking river light into opaque and translucent patterns, outlining for a waiting brook trout the perfectly balanced proportions of a mayfly drying its wings for flight.

I listened to the drumming overhead and hoped it would rain all night because the sound was almost as good to sleep to as the sound of a river. I tied Hares Ear wet flies to use as an early-season emerger, blending fur from a hare's mask to get a dark brown mix. My fingers dubbed the rough fibers studded with bristly guard hairs to a loop of thread that I twisted and then wound to a wet fly hook. I ribbed the body with gold tinsel and then set two wisps of gray mallard wing quill sweeping back behind brown hen hackle folded and tied in at the tip.

I scraped blue fur from a patch of muskrat skin with a razor blade, easily dubbing the fine hairs tight to the waxed thread with which I wound the slender, tapered body of an Adams. I reluctantly took the first hackle from a supple new grizzly neck whose checkered sheen mesmerized my eyes when I bent it to hunt the right sizes in the glare of the desk lamp. I tied Black Gnats and olive Elk Hair Caddis because they are good searching patterns. I tied Little Yellow Stonefly nymphs because I knew yellow stoneflies were in the rivers.

I was going to start tying March Browns, which were still a month away, but the rain kept up convincingly, so I reached for light and dark patches of deer hair and started to tie big bushy flies that float well, hackling Wulffs and Humpies heavily for fast water.

By midnight spring was arrayed on my desk.

I knew the rivers were rising. Even the dry feeder streams were coming to life. Handfuls of water trickled toward one another forming tiny pools that deepened until they spilled together and flowed. The busy sound of working water enlivened the woods.

It rained all night, sweet sound, and I thought of the big dry flies dancing at the edges of the white and blue water I saw quickening in the mountains. As the rivers rose in the dark, trout shifted in their currents, taking up positions I could see in my sleep.

# II

# BLUE RIDGE
# COMPLEX

If trout rose freely all year, there would be few fly fishermen. In the mountains, where rivers reflect the seasons as subtly as moving water reflects daylight, trout wait out the end of winter stirring, if they stir at all, in deep stillwater pockets out of sight. The fly fisherman, too, must wait while the year slowly straightens out under its own momentum, like a fly line during a backcast. There is in winter, as in other seasons, a critical pause during which a portion of the year unfolds.

The psyche of the fly fisherman is structured around important pauses—moments when something is about to happen—and a year in the field is mostly a matter of watching the edges of those moments carefully. Spring will emerge, in the guise of a mayfly or a black bear, when everything seems to stand still around a focal motion—a fluttering on the surface of a river, a sudden movement in the woods.

Although I know the fishing will be slow, I am drawn to the North Fork of the Moormans on warm February days when I sense the river might have slipped the season a degree or two. But despite slowly lengthening afternoons and the gradual browning of the gray mountains, the contracted mercury in my stream thermometer reflects winter's continued hold. The river is as likely to be colder as warmer from one trip to the next, but I dutifully chart its temperature from week to week: 38°, 37°, 39°, 37°. Until the water warms above forty degrees and stays there, I know I am going through the motions, fishing a cold shadow of last year's river.

On a given foray in early February I will nymph a familiar stretch of river for an hour or so, probing inside the cold, gray water for the edge of the season. On those brief winter afternoons I am, at best, remotely tethered to the river. My legs feel solid on its bottom, and the cork grip of the fly rod feels right in my hand, but from rod to line to leader, and then to tippet and fly, my senses diminish. At the fly, where a trout might be, I barely exist. In winter life in the river doesn't come to meet you, but I like to think as I wade upstream that each cast and well-mended drift brings trout toward me and urges the year on.

When I stop to change flies or tie on a fresh tippet, I find it hard not to watch those places where I know trout will be waiting in a month, eager to break the surface under an escaping mayfly. When sunlight filters through hemlock branches, brightening the flat slicks of slow water, I can't resist casting a dry fly. Even in February a Grizzly Wulff looks encouraging as it drifts at midpool or bobs on a standing wave in front of a boulder.

As I move upstream, I study the flow and structure of the river more carefully than I do at any other time of the year. I read its furrowed surface closely, as if each gray wrinkle in the current was a rune from a language by means of which rock and water and trout understood one another. Each boil and pillow and funnel of moving water is a sign worth noting. Possibilities circle slowly in each eddy. Had I not spent time trying to think through the signs on the water's surface to the remote whereabouts of winter trout, I would never have learned what the river looks like. I would never have noticed the miniature rivers within the river, the minute strands of finely structured current that have a life of their own and that represent the world to a trout. It was in winter I learned to take a trout's perspective and to see that a tiny spill of water over a cleft in a rock is far more significant than the picturesque cascade upstream that I might mistake for the center of the scene.

Whatever feel I have for unseen trout comes mainly from winter sessions of waiting, watching, and gently slip-striking barely perceptible differences in the dance of the line downstream to me. As I follow the line through a drift, I try to picture the nymph swimming toward a trout, wet body glistening with the tiny air bubbles trapped in the dubbed fur, long guard hairs feeling the current like legs. More often than not, I suspect, the fly moves unnaturally, dragged across conflicting currents by the leader or line, and reveals my wooden presence.

A fly fisherman would be hard put to describe the subliminal difference between the slight shift of a line that has just been taken by a trout and the movement of a line that is being toyed with by a river. The life in a sine wave of current and the sinuous life in a trout are, after all, formed by the same forces. Each is an afterimage of the other. But compared to a trout, whose shocked particularity on the end of a line is unmistakable, the flow of a river is a generalization that, for all its subtlety, will never swim off the other way. So as the line comes toward me, I throw my vision a little out of focus and watch. Some differences seem animate and come to hand as trout. But these are sullen, dull fish—December trout— not the bright fish of a new season.

Life in the drift changes slowly in winter, but the

closer I look into the river, the more I see. Even when I capture nothing but bits of leaves in the seine, the ragged edges of the leaf fragments show that stoneflies have been at work, shredding and munching away on the bottom of the food chain, turning trees into trout food. More often than not, there will be a half dozen drowned stoneflies in the screening and perhaps an immature mayfly nymph or a pale green caddis pupa dislodged from its case.

Since I am a fisherman, the farther I get from a river the fewer names I have for things, but I have learned to recognize the evergreen life forms that brighten the winter landscape and make the still, gray woods seem less empty. I like seeing Christmas fern and common polypody growing at the base of the greenstone boulders that litter the woods. Miniature fir forests of club moss thrive in boggy sloughs sheltered by stands of hemlocks. Here and there galax and wintergreen shine in shafts of winter sunlight. Except for the river, there is little activity in the woods. Occasionally I will surprise a gray squirrel rifling a cache of hickory nuts. Or I will look up from fishing, surprised myself, to see a thick-coated whitetail watchfully browsing along the riverbank.

Toward the end of February the river loses its leaden look. Ice still glazes logs and boulders sustained sunlight hasn't reached. Patches of snow lie in the woods, and there is a barely restrained bluster in the wind. But before the month is out the river loses its frigid grip, and the current begins to feel less like an adversary and more like a guide. Signs of life, which come slowly and singly in the dead of winter, begin to accumulate. A large brown stonefly chugs through the cold air. A few caddis hatch. Small clouds of midges appear on the water. Then a shadow glides upstream. The movement is unmistakable.

This year I was working my way through the sequence of long pools between the third and fourth fords on the Moormans when I saw the shadows move upstream for the first time. Every so often a trout dislodged from the stretch of water in front of me, swimming out from underfoot when I loomed into view only to disappear into the depths of a pool. When I saw the shadows move, I fished more deliberately.

I nymphed each large pool slowly, fishing the tail and then the pronounced tongue of current at midpool with a tight line. Then, casting from out of the shadows along the bank, I laid out long lengths of line on the water to cover the slow seams in the current at the throat and head of the reach, watching for the tip of the line to tug forward. When I had covered the water thoroughly, I climbed carefully through the boulders, keeping out of sight until I was in position to put short, blind casts into the tail of the next pool. I hunted trout this way for more than an hour, changing flies several times and thinking about nothing except the mechanics of casting and the structure of the river in front of me.

At one point I peered between two boulders looking for trout at the bottom of a deep, narrow run, where the water funneled together before pouring over and down into the next pool. I saw no trout at first. I did see an algae-covered boulder, a foot below the surface of the river, to which a dozen or more nymphs clung, dark flat-bodied mayfly nymphs gleaning nutrients from the vegetation on the rock. They crawled about slowly, antennae wavering uncertainly, two stiff tails angled out behind. *Epeorus.* Quill Gordon nymphs. They were careful to stay downstream of a little ridge on the boulder that sheltered them from the immediate force of the current. I watched them move cautiously about the niche they had found in the river.

When I turned my head to the left, I saw that a trout, too, had found its niche, a depression in the river-bed two feet downstream of this boulder where it could hold below the funneling water without much effort. Under the ruffled surface of the river the trout was dif-

ficult to see. The slender dark wedge of its body was broken up by the vermiculation on its back, black and olive
lines that played the light in all directions and broke its
form into patterns as random as the substrate on the riverbed beneath it. But the gleaming white edges of its orange fins, underlined in sharp jet-black lines, gave the
trout away.

I watched the trout and the boulder of nymphs upstream of it for some time, but I could not tell whether
the trout knew the nymphs were there. I wanted to see
one of the insects swept off the boulder by the current
into the trout's feeding lane. When this did not happen, I
couldn't resist trying to close the connection.

I cast a Quill Gordon nymph upstream of the boulder,
keeping the line in the shadows and letting nothing but a
long tippet flick out over the water. The nymph fell quietly into the river and drifted alongside the boulder on
the side the trout was favoring. As I quickly stripped in
line, a palm of current slipped the nymph behind the
boulder, leaving it for a moment looking helplessly without a purchase in the enclave sculpted out of the mainstream by the rock. The nymph looked as if it had been
swept there by the river. The trout came forward as if it
had been waiting for this all along.

I waited a fraction of a moment and then lifted the
fly rod.

The line tightened upstream. The rod bowed toward
the trout.


In midwinter I'm as likely to have a map as a trout in
hand. United States Geological Survey maps hang on
every wall of my study, some of the quadrangles a little
ragged from their life in the field, creased wrong and
burned here and there by cinders from campfires.

On Saturday mornings when rain or snow slants
across the windows and hides the mountains from view, I

haunt the map room at the University of Virginia's Alderman Library, laying out quads of places I haven't yet seen on the dark oak tables amid the detritus of snoozing undergraduates. Over the years I've pieced the Blue Ridge together in seven-and-a-half-minute chunks and searched the most promising rectangles for blue lines where clean, cold water might still filter through the crimson gill rakers of wild trout.

No doubt it is an accident of design, but the convoluted ribbing of contour lines on the topographic maps reminds me of the vermiculation on a brook trout's back and makes some important connections between land and trout clear. When I let a trout slip from my hand back into a river, I like to watch it lose itself slowly in the geometry of its habitat. The wormlike tracings on the olive back of a trout, refracted by the complicated play of daylight on the surface of a river, dissolve it in place. If a released fish doesn't dart away because of some sudden movement on my part, it will slowly transform itself under my gaze into something else—an algae-covered stone, a weed waving in the current, a shadow beside a rock.

The contour lines on the maps lead me back to the trout camouflaged in the landscape. Even in Alderman Library you can make some reasonable guesses about where topography suggests trout. Appealing blue lines follow the folded bases of ridges, descending through notches of closely spaced brown contour lines characteristic of the hollows and coves that structure the Blue Ridge. The size of a watershed gives me an idea of a stream's volume, and its gradient is a readable function of the spacing of the contours across which a blue line spills. Blue lines begin as bogs in saddles or springs in broken slopes, or simply from an accumulation of rainfall over a large enough area. The folds and slopes direct each blue line until it becomes a river and starts, in turn, to shape the land.

The thin blue lines are as vulnerable in the field as they look on the maps, each one a few precious miles of cold, flowing water and perhaps an enclave where wild trout thrive the way life tends to thrive on unexploited land.

There is only one way to find out.

Fish the blue line just after spring high water recedes, when the fishing is easiest. Get knee-deep in the line and wade upstream across the brown contours. Watch each shadow and weed and stone carefully, as if it might be a trout. Some blue lines pan out, surrendering wild trout to a fly. Others can no longer manage the transformation.

Although the modern USGS quads will lead me to the trout left in the mountains, the most interesting map hanging in my study is an old one, a reproduction of the Joshua Fry-Peter Jefferson map of 1751—"A Map of the Most Inhabited part of Virginia, containing the whole province of Maryland with Part of Pensilvania, New Jersey and North Carolina." The Fry-Jefferson map was one of the first to show in fairly accurate if stylized detail the relationship between the country's rivers and mountains. The easternmost ridge is clearly labeled "The Blue Ridge," and it is possible that this widely used map settled the name of the mountains. For more than a century prior to this, settlers indiscriminately referred to the first blue line of mountains as the Blew Ledge, the Blue Ledges, the South Mountain, and the Blue mountains. Before rumors of the Rocky Mountains filtered east, they called the Blue Ridge the Great Mountains.

Although no one bothered much about the name of the mountains, almost every early explorer and commentator, as well as their Indian informants, mentioned the rivers to which they gave rise. In the late seventeenth century, John Bannister, the first trained naturalist in Virginia, summed up the importance of those rivers in terms as clear as the streams themselves: "If there be nothing that does so much conduce to the fertility of the soyle & wholesomeness of the air, & consequently to the health, profit, & pleasure of the Inhabitants: as clear running waters, & navigable rivers well stowed with fish: I know no country can boast of more or better than Virginia and Mary Land."

To me, the beauty of the Fry-Jefferson map is the detail with which it renders the free-flowing rivers that the country then boasted. The rivers on earlier maps tended to fade away uncertainly before they reached their source. The thin black lines on this map wend their way up into the mountains, as if the steep, cold headwaters were important. Some of the names have changed, and the map has its topographical inaccuracies, but many of the rivers I search for wild trout appeared there, drawn with some care, for the first time.

The past, of course, is another country, and neither modern nor old maps can take you back to what the mountains and the rivers once were like. Even in the field, it is hard to conjure up a useful sense of the past. One October several years ago I explored a stream that drops abruptly through the small gorge it has cut in the Blue Ridge escarpment near the Virginia–North Carolina border. I backpacked several miles down from the crest of the Blue Ridge through brilliant fall foliage, stopping to fish where the cascading water formed pools too irresistible to pass. I caught native brook trout in the upper reaches of the river, and then a mix of brook trout and handsome, streambred rainbows as I descended. By the time I stopped to camp, I was catching only rainbow trout, descendants no doubt of hatchery fish planted downstream.

I made camp and an early dinner, gathered wood, and then watched the river and the trout until dusk. When it got dark, I bundled up against the fall chill and built a fire. While I nursed the fire to life and felt the welcome heat and the familiar, mesmerizing effects of the flames, I

tried to forget how close I was to the Blue Ridge Parkway on the ridge above and to a state highway not far
downstream. I tried to forget that the watershed was a
rare pocket of public land along a stretch of the Blue
Ridge where very little land has been preserved for its
own sake, and where few streams still supported a natural population of trout, brook trout or otherwise.

I stoked the fire until there was enough light to read
by. I was reading a lot of history that year, trying to get
an idea of what the Blue Ridge was like before Indian
trading paths became interstate highways. There is little
mention of trout in the early exploration literature, but
the mountains and the rivers are almost always in view. I
had brought along a copy of William Byrd's *History of
the Dividing Line Betwixt Virginia and North Carolina.*

The book read well in the field, perhaps because I was
camped near the ground toward which Byrd and his sur-
veying party had made their way in October of 1728. The
land, of course, was nothing like what it had been in the
early eighteenth century, but the wild trout in the stream
beside me seemed proof of some connection that had not
been completely broken.

William Byrd was more politician than poet, and far
more of a land speculator than an explorer, but even his
profit-seeking planter's eye was drawn, at times, into the
beauty of the blue horizon toward which his surveyors
blazed the line. And although fording and detouring
around the innumerable streams that crossed his path
was the principal labor of the journey, the clear-flowing
rivers that led back into the mountains eventually eroded
the edges of Byrd's materialism, freeing his imagination
for short flights of appreciation of a landscape whose ul-
timate value, he seemed to discern, could be difficult to
quantify.

Increasingly frequent halts to search out fords across
rivers forced Byrd to look around. The closer he got to
the mountains, the more he admired the bright, fast-

flowing waters that tumbled from them. Temporarily stopped by dense canebrakes along the upper Dan River, Byrd remarks on its extraordinary clarity. But when he thinks he sees something shining in the sunlit gravel of a broad riffle, his eye is dazzled by the old dream of gold that, two centuries after DeSoto's feverish march through the Southern Appalachians, still distorted the European view of the American landscape. "All our Fortunes were made," he remembers thinking. When closer inspection reveals the gold to be an illusion, Byrd is content to let the beauty of the river stand for its value: "However, tho' this did not make the River so rich as we cou'd wish, yet it made it exceedingly Beautiful."

However much a pragmatist Byrd may have been, the beauty and bounty of the land seems to have become, by journey's end, no small consolation for his trouble. The Dan keeps crossing his path, and Byrd's admiration grows: "It was Still a beautiful Stream, rolling down its limpid and murmuring waters among the Rocks, which lay scatter'd here and there, to make up the variety of the Prospect." In the private version of the *History* he frankly declares: "This seem'd the most beautiful River that I ever saw." Two miles farther, over "Broken Grounds and troublesome Underwoods," Byrd sees the mountains for the first time, thirty miles away to the northwest, at a point not far from where I was camped. "They seem'd to lye off at a vast Distance, and lookt like Ranges of Blue clouds rising one above another."

Byrd is not prone to be lyric, and his lyricism, when it emerges, is always conventional. But the few metaphors lodged in the matter-of-fact prose of his *History* stand out as brief, tentative moments of growth in his regard for the land. Like his countrymen, Byrd never stopped looking at the land as something to be used for profit, but when he stops to ford a stream and looks up to contemplate the mountains from which it flowed, the blue ledges on the western horizon seem to elevate his thoughts and enrich his language: Blue mountains were like blue clouds. Riverbeds were golden, not full of gold. A "Chrystal Stream" is crystalline. Eventually Byrd hears a kind of speech in the sound of rivers and remarks on the pleasure of being lulled to sleep by a cascading mountain stream.

By the time Byrd crosses the Dan for the last time, he seems genuinely attached to the rivers that get in his way and to the wild land that impedes his progress: "In the Evening we quarter'd in a Charming Situation near the angle of the River, from whence our Eyes were carried down both Reaches, which kept a Straight Course for a great way together. This Prospect was so beautiful, that we were perpetually climbing up to a Neighbouring eminence, that we might enjoy it in more Perfection."

Under the spell of the blue mountains and their rivers, Byrd is capable of seeing wildlife as something other than game. He seems to sense that elk and bear and passenger pigeons are worthy of interest for their own sake. He admires the stately passage of migrating geese overhead, which he knows have made an epic journey from Hudson Bay. He notes that the Indians call them *Cohunks,* after the sound they make, and that the Indian calendar begins with the month when the wild geese return. If Byrd cannot quite see the beauty in that, because he considers the Indians' contentment with "Nature as they find Her" a "purblind Tradition," at least he senses that such a practice is worth recording.

Perhaps reading Byrd by firelight that night on Rock Castle Creek softened and distorted my view of him. Byrd's materialism and aristocratic hauteur are rarely far from view. But it seemed to me that by the time his men blazed a red oak beside Peters Creek to mark the end of the survey, Byrd had been, if not transformed, at least educated by what was then unknown, unspoiled wilderness.

I broke camp the next morning and backpacked and

fished my way back to the crest of the Blue Ridge in
what felt like bracing football weather. The small,
quartz-studded gorge was beautiful and, if you followed
the river, quite rugged in places. The streamside foliage
was half shed, and as I worked my way upstream, shut-
tling the pack along, I found small trout holding under
colorful pods of floating leaves. The trout leapt for any
kind of small dry fly. When I found a thriving colony of
rare walking fern, whose swordlike tips had traveled the
length of a rock ledge that bordered the river, I got a
sharp sense of a fragile, untouched world.

In a few miles I ran out of river and gorge and was
back on the Blue Ridge Parkway, where traffic broke the
spell. The pristine wilderness that William Byrd and his
cohorts approached in October of 1728 was gone beyond
recovery, but there had been a tangy wildness in the crisp
fall air and in the vivacious trout, as well as in the graceful presence of the walking ferns. Of course, Byrd was
part of the vanguard of a culture that proved to be far
from content with nature as they found it. Three centuries later, when the benefits and costs of that discontent
have become apparent, only vestiges of wildness remain
in the Blue Ridge—a few stands of virgin timber, some
uninterrupted vistas, a remnant black bear population,
some bobcat and timber rattlers, a few undisturbed habi-
tats where rare flora and fauna persist, and the most subtle form that wildness takes—the quicksilver presence of
wild trout.

As trout country the Blue Ridge is a Balkan affair.
Trout survive where forested mountain land is preserved,
where highland watersheds are left to function as their
ecology dictates. Very little of the Blue Ridge is so preserved. You will no longer find wild trout everywhere
in the Blue Ridge, but if you search out wild trout, you
will eventually come upon everything else of value in
the mountains. Wild trout are a sign that the land is
doing well.

I once asked a geologist friend in Asheville if the Blue
Ridge could be defined. She smiled and showed me *her*
maps. They bore less resemblance to mine than did the
old Fry-Jefferson map. The maps on the walls of her office were geologic maps on which oddly shaped zones of
dominant bedrock type were overlaid on the topographic
features with which I was familiar. She pointed out what
geologists call the Blue Ridge Complex, bands of ancient
igneous and metamorphic crystalline rock that underlie
the geographic Blue Ridge. I knew the basaltic greenstone belts in the northern Blue Ridge because my favorite rivers flowed over greenstone, and I knew to
distinguish between granite and quartzite watersheds because the former weathered into a more mineral-rich riverbed. The rest of the puzzle was lost on me, and I was
glad to hear that the closer geologists looked into the
folded and faulted strata of the Blue Ridge, the less sure
they were about how the pieces got together. *Terra incog-
nita,* she called it.

My own Blue Ridge complex is a simpler affair, more
a matter of personal geography shaped by two-hearted
rivers, mountain trout streams that flow out of the past
into the present, bringing wild trout with them. I have
fished some of the classic trout water in the Catskills and
New England. I have patiently worked the mesmerizing
flows of the great spring creeks in central Pennsylvania,
just north of the Blue Ridge. I have humbled myself on
the big western rivers that have come to be the mainstream of the fly fishing world. I dream occasionally
about fishing Alaska and New Zealand and all the exotic
places you see on the covers of the fishing magazines,
places that seem to get farther away each issue. Sometimes I imagine myself fishing for large brook trout in
Labrador, on the Minippi or the Eagle, with a far wilder,
far less compromised country around me.

But for the most part I've followed the blue lines into
the Blue Ridge until the Blue Ridge became for me an-

other country, a slender remnant of an almost lost world enveloped in a fading blue haze and filigreed in places with bright streams where wild trout come to a fly with pleasing frequency. Each year I have wandered a little farther north and a little farther south from the North Fork of the Moormans until I've gotten fairly far afield.

On the North Fork of the Moormans, the year lengthens upstream, pool by pool. During March, brief winter forays become long afternoons, half days paced slowly up the river from noon to dusk. The river comes alive in spurts, cascading ahead into spring and eddying back toward winter by turns. Warm days contend with cold ones, but even when the weather turns bitter, or a late snow throws the year on its back, the gray winter haze does not return. From a distance, the mountains are a warm, glowing brown.

In March everything is a sign: a stalked scarlet cup poking out of the leaf litter, a mourning cloak searching over a flowerless landscape, the white flash of a pileated woodpecker's wings clipping through the open woods. There are fresh beaver cuttings along the upper river. A half-dozen young sycamores lie felled aside one pool. Fresh toothmarks glisten in the soft heartwood of stumps around which are piled damp white shavings.

One by one fishermen appear like some strange species of wading bird that has migrated back to the river after wintering elsewhere. The same faces appear each year, in about the same sequence. They move slowly, fishing their favorite early-season reaches. Drowned and stillborn Quill Gordon duns appear in the seine, their wings crumpled around them. The early duns are small and very dark, almost black. The temperature of the river rises— 39°, 41°, 40°, 42°—and the river seems to loosen and flow more freely. The days lose their finite, winter feel.

I take March as it comes. The trout tend to take dead-drifted Hares Ears or anything similar. They bore into the river when you set the hook and jump out of your hand when you go to release them. You start seeing the scene you will see in infinite variations all year long: a fly line tight to a river, a fly rod bowed to a trout. The landscape will change behind that scene, greening in brightly and filling out until it matures and darkens into summer growth. Then it will brighten momentarily with the dying colors of autumn until you look up in late November and again see bare brown woods behind the diagonal of the fly line and the arc of the rod. I play March trout quickly into the shallows and release them back to the wintry water into which they disappear, full of fight and confusion.

Trout must lose their dim consciousness of man during the winter. They seem genuinely surprised each year by the predator who has learned to pretend he is part of the river, who seems to be both in and above the water, a little like a bear the way his form looms into the brightness over the river and the way his shadow darkens the riverbed, but a bear that can sting and tear at a jaw from a distance, invisibly applying a force that pulls with the threatening authority of the sky, a leverage that angles like nothing else in the river's current. The sensation is far stranger than the sudden grab of a raccoon from around a rock or the bewildering smash of a kingfisher from above.

Day by day my casting settles down. Eventually my wrist and forearm get a feel for the fulcrum between forecast and backcast where the line absorbs the energy of the rod and takes on a life of its own, quick and elaborately accurate. A long, light fly rod is a perfect tool on a small river. The long rod throws loops into the line and leader reminiscent of the curves in the current. The fly lights on the water out of nowhere, its graceful life in the air sustained by its drift on the surface of the river.

On a good day backcasts find space among the bare

branches behind me, and the line flicks quietly forward into the cool air that flows over the river. It must be the alternate rhythm of wading and casting that makes fly fishing seem like searching. All day I am poised between the resistance of the river and the pulse of each cast, at the end of which a tippet unfurls and brings a fly to the water. Days tick forward with the rhythm of casting, held up only by the brief pause during which the line loads the rod.

Each year one trout in particular seems to start the year's fishing. This year I was a half mile below Big Branch, where the fire road is thirty feet or so above the river and long rays of mid-March sunlight slant into the water from downstream in the early afternoon, putting all the features of the streambed in sharp relief. The depth of the water is lost from this perspective, but the cover and feeding stations in each pool come quickly to the eye, as do quirks in the current imperceptible from stream level. You can see where the trout should be, where they will be as soon as winter lets go of the river.

I was resting and studying the bottom of a green, sunlit pool when I saw the first good trout of the year. I was staring at a slot of deep water between two undercut boulders near the head of a pool and thinking that if I was a trout I would be there, looking for the stoneflies and mayfly nymphs that I knew were in the drift. I would position myself right where that slender green stone was.

Details resolved and the slender green stone became a trout. I remember seeing it turn to the right and drift back with the current, rising discreetly to something floating in the film, but not breaking the surface to take it. A muted riseform circled over the point where the trout took the insect. The expanding concentric circles vanished downstream. With each rise there was a sunlit flash of enlivened water and then the slender dark form darted back upstream.

The trout held itself in the cold flow, its sleek green body quivering, tail to head it seemed, when it sighted waterborne prey approaching. I could see how it used its streamlined body to catch an edge of the current to move back and how it slipped the river with a twist to slide forward. Occasionally the fish would follow its prey downstream to the lip of the pool, taking the insect with a lunge just before fast water grabbed it. Then it would drop to the bottom, out of the flow, and return to its feeding position. Sometimes the trout responded to something in the current but did not take it, having made some final judgment against what it saw.

I was going to move on and leave this first rising trout of the year to feed in peace in that run between the boulders. But the weight of my fishing vest and the awkward feel of waders and heavy stream boots, as well as the fly rod in my hand, urged me down toward the river. And when I felt the sunlight on my face and neck and looked into the quick, sparkling water, I remembered the hand and foot-numbing days of dead-drifting nymphs through slate-gray water I barely believed held trout.

I walked downstream fifty feet and worked my way down the embankment to the river. I approached the pool slowly, sidling along the near bank, trying to keep myself blanked against the trees. The riseform continued to pulse in place as I made my way into casting position.

I cast sidearm to keep the line out of the sky and managed to put a small Adams into the current above where the trout was holding, snaking enough slack into the line to get a good drift. I lost the fly in the glare but struck at the rise to which the drift was timed.

In hand, the first bright trout of the year always seems a bit unreal, almost abstract, as extravagant as a cockatoo. Taxonomically the brook trout is a char—a distinction without a difference to the fisherman—except that the word *char* has interesting roots, deriving obscurely from Gaelic and Welsh words for red, red-blooded, red-bellied. Whatever its lineage and taxonomic status, the Celtic etymology suits the bright, passionate fish. The scarlet spots on the flank of the trout, surrounded by their arctic blue aureoles, are the most exquisite detail in a landscape full of excellent design.

I fished through several more pools without success. Spring does not come on all of a sudden. The trout stayed hid, but I could not bring myself to go back to nymph fishing. I wanted winter behind me. The brown woods, bathed in sunlight, seemed to simmer with life, but a thin layer of cold air lay compressed over the river like a shadow stream, a winter soul.

I did not feel like coming in, so I hiked the fire road two miles to Tobacco House Hollow to see the head of the watershed and catch the end of the season. A winter chill clung to the mountains, but occasionally warm arms of air reached down the watershed from Via Gap. This was Shenandoah Valley air that, having simmered in the sun over freshly plowed fields, rose and flowed east through Blackrock Gap. As I walked I could feel spring pulling at the late-winter afternoon, feeling with long, intermittent breezes for a purchase on the year. The seasons seemed to be changing hands in the air overhead.

Where sunlight reached the river, I watched for trout. Occasionally I saw slender olive shapes holding in slow water and flashes of white when trout turned. Here and there rises bloomed on the surface of the river. At one point I stopped to watch a trout rising regularly, much like the one I caught. When the trout paused, I tried to make its slender olive form look like a stone, but I could not take the life out of it.

I sat and watched the river near an old homestead at Tobacco House Hollow. All around me signs of a vanished mountain culture were tangled in the understory— the remains of a school and a church and, farther upstream, the cemetery at the head of the river. With the sun off the water, the river went gray and looked cold again. Spring seemed to be losing its grip.

I thought about the people who used to live along the river. I wondered what lessons they taught at Via School and what prayers were prayed at the Wayside Church. And who was buried in that enviable spot at the head of hollow near the source of the river? What had they thought about when they sat here, as they undoubtedly did, listening to the river, watching for trout, and waiting for spring?

As you come down the road from Via Hollow, you are far above the river for a mile or so. The watershed of the North Fork of the Moormans is laid out clearly before you. A large, exposed face of greenstone at the top of the Pasture Fence escarpment is the last feature in the landscape to catch the late-afternoon sunlight before the sun is lost behind the Blue Ridge. You can see it clearly at the top of the last steep rise in the road. For a few moments the rock face glows brightly, seeming to hold the sunlight in place. Then the greenstone darkens, and as you descend into the oncoming dusk the sound of the river rises, as if to replace the waning light.

# BLOODROOT

I see the same day every year. One day in late March
bloodroot appear on the trail to Bear Church Rock
along the Staunton River and I know the fishing will
be good.

The bloodroot are a predictable surprise, and a nov-
elty, until I realize the woods are full of color. There are
enough open buds on the hardwoods to put a green cast
in the brown slopes that surround the river. Catkins
hang like ornaments in sweet birch trees. Alders have set
their thick, green leaves along the stream. The flowers of
spicebush and red maple add to the impression of growth
and change. Each detail leads to another. Stoop to in-
spect the pistil of a bloodroot, and your eye will be led on
by the erratic flight of a Sooty Azure to the white and
blue hues of toothwort and liverwort. Bright groups of
rue anemone and periwinkle lead you to the river, whose
muddy banks are full of neatly cut raccoon tracks. The
blue remains of a crawfish lie scattered on a rock.

The same warmth that draws out the first wildflowers
has been working on the river. The contents of my early-
season fly box have come alive. A bewildering variety of
caddis hatch amid a confusion of stoneflies. Midges and
gnats swarm low over the water. Ground beetles and ants
crawl about everywhere. Before you've taken stock of the
changes you see a Quill Gordon coming off the river, and
then another, and you feel that the year has gotten ahead
of you.

By midafternoon trout are rising with abandon all
along the river. The first year I ran into this day I fished
hard and greedily until dark, catching fish almost at will.
I thought I was a genius. A deer-hair dry fly or an Elk

Hair Caddis, if the water is high, or an Adams or Quill Gordon in low water will take as many trout as you like. Each year I cast less and less to these eager, early-season trout.

This year I fished sparingly and stopped at a rising trout in the large pool below the long, mossy cascade that marks, for the fisherman familiar with the river, the divide between the upper and lower Staunton. I caught this trout, played it gently to the rock on which I was sitting, and released it. I so expected this fish to be a spring beauty that I barely looked to confirm the fact before slipping it off the fly. In early spring you can take the trout for granted.

I quit fishing by midafternoon but took my time coming down the river. I met a man coming up the trail, boot-foot hip waders hung around his neck, unstrung fly rod in hand. He didn't ask if I'd had any luck, which is what the hikers always ask. He asked where I had stopped fishing so he could start where the river was undisturbed. He knew the pool I meant. He looked around him at the day as I spoke, as if he'd seen that before too.

The Staunton is a small stream, never more than fifteen feet wide, much less along most of its length. There is a point a half mile or so above its confluence with the Rapidan, however, where the angle of vision you have from the trail gives the river a larger look. The flattering play of afternoon sunlight on the gentle bends in the river seems to broaden it, and the dignified sequence of ridges down through which it flows, brown and then blue in the distance in early spring, seems to deepen its character.

Coming down the mountain in the late afternoon with the sun over your shoulder, your shadow touches the river a hundred feet below you at one point. You have to look harder along the edges of the trail for the bloodroot, whose long white petals have folded in the waning daylight.

# III

# THE BLUE RIVERS

Perhaps the constant flow of a river or the loop of a fly line repeatedly flicking upstream induces an incurable restlessness, but the characteristic gesture of mountain fishing is to move on, to make the hours of a day flow through miles of stream, as if, with a fly rod on a river, you could transform time into space. By the beginning of April, it seems that not only the hours, but the days and weeks of the early part of the year have been laid out, ford to ford, along the North Fork of the Moormans. But before the greenstone cliffs along the upper river have lost the last cast of their winter pall, I am on the Rapidan, thirty miles north, fishing the fast blue water of early spring.

If you approach the Rapidan from Wolftown in April, fat Charolais will be grazing the pastures along the road to the river. You are likely to see a sturdy red-

tailed hawk drifting over the margin of a field, and perhaps the yellow flash of a warbler dodging in and out of
the cover along the road. Along the way, farm ponds full
of sluggish bass warm in the spring sunshine, but compared to the river ahead, they don't constitute much of a
temptation.

A winding, two-lane blacktop unfolds the brown over-
lapping ridges ahead and eventually brings you to the
hamlet of Graves Mill, whose few buildings have weathered to a shade of gray one winter paler than last year.
Just beyond the post office, the mill sits stolidly beside a
pond, its roof shedding shingles, its rusted mill wheel tilting off the end of its shaft.

Beyond the mill the blacktop becomes gravel, which in
turn gives way in a few hundred yards to a rocky, deeply
rutted dirt road where the head of the valley narrows to
a hollow not much broader than the width of the river.
When I dream about having a farm, I put it in this valley along the road from Wolftown, backed up against the
broad shoulders of the mountains down through which
the Rapidan flows loud and bright in the spring. Each
year I watch with anticipation and regret as For Sale
signs come and go.

The Rapidan flows southeast from the broad crest of
the Blue Ridge near the swampy Indian old field at Big
Meadows in the center of Shenandoah National Park.
Two beautiful headwater streams, Mill Prong and Laurel
Prong, join to form the Rapidan at Camp Hoover. Below
the former presidential retreat, the river drops southeast
out of the mountains for four miles until Chapman
Mountain turns it south along the slender foot of Fork
Mountain. Two miles below the bend, the Rapidan is
joined by the Staunton River. From the hill overlooking
their confluence, you can see some of the best trout water
in the Blue Ridge.

In early April deep blue currents pile up and split
around the pale granite through which the lower Rapidan

flows. If there have been good spring rains, the river charges blue and white off the mountains, filling its undercut banks. Whitewater fumes into deep pools, but the depth of the larger pools absorbs the flow, creating broad tongues of slow blue water. At the margins of the slow water, fingers of current eddy upstream and slack into stillwater pockets behind boulders and dead trees. Cascades connect pools. Each frothy run grabs oxygen out of the cool, bright air, as if the river needed to breathe. When a sequence of pools gives out and the gradient eases, the river broadens, distributing its flow into riffles where the small stones on the streambed seem to rattle in the heavy flow. Where the river meanders, it shifts substrate, digging into its dark banks and gathering detritus into the tangled cover where trout hide. Eventually the riffles constrict and the water descends quietly in deep runs nestled in bedrock. Then the river spills over a ledge and cascades into another deep blue pool.

If you fish a river often, it takes on a life of its own in your mind, and in my mind's eye this is the way I always see the Rapidan—as a cold blue river in early spring. Because I am waist-deep in it each year when March becomes April, I associate the promising look and sound of the Rapidan with the onset of spring in the Blue Ridge. I can't imagine the open slopes greening in, stroke by stroke, without the accompaniment of its currents. Brook trout shake off the ragged ends of their winter dreaming when they hear the thunder of the blue river around them. The first wildflowers bloom when the trout fan out into their early season holding positions around the margins of blue spring pools. Mayapples push their folded emerald canopies through the litter of brown oak leaves when the first mayflies emerge from the river. In April trout rise to an emerging world. Wild turkeys hide in the deep woods to nest, and sluggish timber rattlers and copperheads emerge from hiding to bask in the strong spring sunlight. Woodpeckers hammer roosts in snags. Groggy female black bear reconnoiter cautiously in the dark folds of the watershed showing their young the world for the first time. Life surrounds the river and tends toward it.

I, too, tend toward the river. Unlike winter, which seems like one slow, gray day, each early-spring day is a kind of season in itself. The character of the river changes almost from hour to hour—you must be there to see and feel those changes. So on some cool April morning, I wade into the Rapidan a quarter mile below its confluence with the Staunton. Despite the glimpses of spring I get on the Moormans during March, the year starts in earnest here, when I find myself standing in the riffles that chatter by an old stone bridge abutment built into the north bank of the Rapidan.

When I first get in the spring river, the water looks and feels too fast to fish. The blue water is cold, but the river does not pull the warmth out of me the way it does in winter. I turn sideways to the current and lean heavily on my upstream leg. Given the force of the river, I imagine trout pinned on the bottom, feeding on nymphs in the thin cushion of slow water along the riverbed or tucked in cul-de-sacs of cover impossible to reach with a fly—slots in ledgerock or tangles of drowned treetops. The overwhelming presence of the river gradually moderates as I get used to the combined effects of the boisterous sound around me and the force of the current. Eventually the din of rushing water blankets my concentration like rain, while the complicated flow directs my eye, bank to bank, upstream and down. I begin to break down the structure of the river until I start seeing all the promising edges in the blue currents.

Once I concentrate, it's as if I can hear the small silences around the still spots where trout might be. The din recedes and I no longer feel the river piling up around my stomach and pushing me around. If I fish directly upstream the way I like to, the line comes toward

me faster than I can strip it in. So I cover one half of the
river with quartering casts and a weighted stonefly
nymph on a short line and leader. I hold the rod high to
keep the fly line out of the conflicting currents, staying
tight to the nymph when it swings out below me. I lean
forward, trying to sense a soft take or a sudden grab at
the fly. I lift the rod tentatively at all the sweet spots in a
drift. The fast water plays tricks with the line that I re-
learn, one by one, to ignore. I strike at nothing, miss
what might have been takes. I reach with the long rod at
the end of each drift to get the nymph into what hints of
cover I can perceive through the water's broken surface.
I cover the riffle systematically—casting, holding, reaching center to bank, tail to head.

The featureless surface of the riffle is hard to de-
cipher, and as I step upstream to reposition myself, I try
to focus on finer signs, sensing that the trout have been
moving around the generalities in my habits of vision. I
mismatch a heavier nymph to a lighter tippet to help the
fly sink. The mismatch casts poorly but I think I can feel
the fly bump into the larger rocks hidden in the riffle, the
rocks where trout would be.

I change flies more frequently than I normally do because I know early-season brook trout can be choosy.
Their metabolism is still slow, and the river is doling out
insects in a studied way. I take some pleasure stopping in
midstream to rummage among flies I haven't taken a
close look at since the evening I unclamped them from
the vise. Like most fly fisherman, I tend to think about
trout and rivers when I tie; certain flies are for certain
rivers, or seasons, or situations. When I pull a Quill Gordon emerger from the nymph box in April, the time at
the vise seems vindicated. I am exactly where I thought I
would be when I tied the fly. When I get to the head of
the riffle, I look back over the water I have fished
through and tell myself to settle down. The river is fast
and reckless, but the trout are slow and deliberate. In
early April the mornings fish slowly.

However reluctant I am to wade out of the river, I know that I will notice more when I stop fishing. Caddis hang on rocks in the shallow water at my feet. The half-inch cases of fine-grained sand cemented into a tube look like pebbles caught in the filaments of algae to which the insects cling. When I look closely, I can see the black head and forelegs of the caddis larva busily gleaning the rock. When I lean over them, the pebbles turtle away. I don't think I've ever fished them, but in a fit of thoroughness I once tied some case caddis patterns. The caddis sometimes get swept into the flow, and a trout will munch one like an egg roll if it happens to float by.

Crayfish scuttle around in the shallow water where I see inch-long brook trout mingling with schools of dace. Water striders glide along, singly and humped awkwardly in mating pairs. Immature mayfly nymphs crawl over stones. These are strange, half-formed creatures. *Stenonema,* perhaps. March Browns. Their flattened heads look like the faces of miniature barn owls. Their gills are only tiny filaments sticking out like pins from their abdomens. Three short tails fan out at the end of their brown and white bodies.

When I wade back into the river, the insistence of the current is reassuring. The pocket water upstream of the riffles is easier to read. The flat slicks of relatively still water behind the boulders set out in the river like chess pieces are too tempting. I tune the leader and poke my finger into the crowded compartments of my one early-season dry fly box. Slipping the loop of a turle knot back over a plump Grizzly Wulff, I check with satisfaction the heavy tailing and hackling on a fly designed more for the water than the fish. Big and buggy. Buoyant. A fly for blue water and a boisterous, cold spring river. Cocky.

The pockets behind the gray boulders look like windows in the river. I want to tap on each one, peer into the patch of clear current, and see a trout holding in the light, expertly eyeing the margins of its small world. I move along the bright side of the river, where sunlight balances the spring chill in the water perfectly and throws my shadow back into the woods. I pop short casts into each dark pocket and then work out line and shoot longer casts into the trickier currents tangled in shadows and roots along the far bank.

I work the pocket water patiently because I know the trout are there. Each year the consistency of the river is reassuring. All the arcane practices of fly tying and fly fishing would be worthless without that. The river makes everything happen. Without letting the fly get soaked, I dance it out of the fast water into the standing chop behind a midstream boulder. A trout takes it. The appearance of the trout into the dark pocket plays slowly in my mind. I see it rise, a dark form at first and then pale when it turns. The rise is neither slow nor sudden. The fish simply appears from below without any apparent effort, planed up almost forty-five degrees to the surface of the river. The trout doesn't seem to have any momentum, and I don't quite see how it hits the fly. When the pocket breaks in a splash from below, I suppress a shout as I set the hook and feel the fish.

The trout takes a short radius of line in a semicircle upstream, forcing itself down into the river, tiring itself quickly against the damping shock of the rod, trapped by its impulse to pull against what pulls it. A little pressure with the rod brings the fish back in the slow current along the near bank.

The trout is cold and beautiful, like the river.

When I release it back into the water, it holds in the shallow flow at my feet. When I straighten up, it shoots away upstream.

The blue pools are the heart of spring and the reward for all the winter fishing. The pools on the Rapidan were built for fly fishermen. They are not so large the river loses its character in them, which can happen on bigger water, but they are substantial enough to force the swift spring currents to deepen and define themselves. Where the currents are well defined, trout are easy to locate. The pools are deep, but not quite still. In early April trout will slowly rise to a dry fly along every likely seam of current and from every likely lie.

By three o'clock the sunlight and warmth that have filled the woods seem to have entered the river. I cannot see them, but I can almost feel trout stirring at *Epeorus* nymphs shifting around on the streambed. While I concentrate on fishing an emerger across and downstream, feeling with difficulty for a trout grabbing at what it thinks is a swimming dun in the heavy water, I am suddenly distracted by life in the air around me. Mayflies. *Ephemeroptera.* Insects as delicate and ponderous as their name, at once airy and reptilian.

Gray upwinged duns escape the chill in the river, having made a dangerous passage toward their day in the sun. They pop out of the pocket water that surrounds me and fly straight up out of the river, slowly gaining altitude, their slender bodies and delicate tails arched with the effort. The cold river seems to pull at them. As I tuck the fly rod under my arm and assume the prayerful profile of a fly fisherman changing flies in midstream, I see duns drifting in the currents around me, some drying their wings, others drowning in turbulence. Others drift to boulders and crawl out of the river, so stunned by the change that I can touch them and they will not fly away.

Quill Gordons appear sporadically from late February on, but now they carry the day. Unseen trout are, no doubt, taking the insects on the streambed where they struggle from their nymphal shucks, or are intercepting them as they swim to the surface, but eventually enough duns are floating and twitching on the river's surface that the trout, who read the river from below, set up downstream of where the river conveniently funnels their prey.

Trout rise all around me.

When I see those first trout of the season rising regularly to Quill Gordons, I know the year has taken hold. The complex life of the watershed seems concentrated in the surface film of the river. I watch a gray, sail-shape dun floating downstream toward me, waiting for its wings to dry. I watch a trout waiting for a mayfly to float toward it. Everything seems to surround their encounter.

I cast long and short to rising fish, release them and move on, false casting sparingly as I go. The ring of each rise is exciting to see. Within each ring is a trout. I no longer have to reach into the river and grope for trout. I barely have to think. Trout hold and rise steadily, as if they were made for the fishing—to catch and admire and release back to the river. When I have caught enough trout and brought the feel of a living river back into my year, I sit on the bank and watch what is left of the afternoon's rise.

Hatches in the mountains are short-lived affairs. The idyllic hours of warm spring afternoons, when fly fishing gets to show off its perfection—when mayfly, trout, and angler all seem to be doing the same thing—are as evanescent as a pleasing pattern of shadow and sunlight on a forest floor. With so many graceful forms of life around me, I feel like an intruder.

Spring is easy to take and hard to fathom. In April I've had black bear cubs frolic toward me as thoughtlessly as Labrador retriever pups. I've parted the soft boughs of a stand of white pine to find a sun-dappled fawn staring up at me. The changing pastels of early-spring growth in shrubs and trees throw a cast of color and light into the woods during the lengthening afternoons that would make you swear that the world was as perfect as it must have been on its first day. You can't sit down on a rock to have a sandwich and a stream-chilled beer without some formal perfection of natural beauty tugging at your sleeve: the soft, mesmerizing sheen of bluets, the finely rendered detail in the throat of a violet,

the lacy young fronds just showing in the clenched fid-
dlehead of an unfurled fern. But all these things seem
static and self-contained, too innocent to understand.

A hungry brook trout rising to a mayfly struggling to
dry its wings in the surface film seems a sharper image of
the life of spring. The beauty of each is enhanced by its
need. The functional perfection of mayfly and trout, as
well as the critical flaws in their natural histories, are
revealed by their exposure in the ring of the rise. There
in the swirl of the trout beneath the fly, nature seems
redder, a bit more riveting. Your eye wanders everywhere during a long spring day on the river, but when
the trout start to rise, you watch the rising trout.

The tension between predator and prey increases depth of
field. Within that deepened field of focus, you see being leap
simply to its chances within the limits of one creature's fate:
A mayfly starts to break free from the surface film. A trout
rises toward a mayfly. A river flows indifferently around the
little drama to which it has given birth. When you cast to a
rising trout, you ride the indifferent currents into play, not
to play God, but to touch the play of being in a modest way.
Sometimes the fishing seems important.

When the ridge west of the Rapidan keeps the sun's
rays from reaching the river, I start fishing downstream.
The sky is still bright overhead, and the tops of the surrounding mountains are bathed in sunlight, but the
woods surrounding the river darken quickly, before evening. The river takes on a silver sheen, as if it had drawn
the late-afternoon light from the woods. But in April no
cold descends with this false twilight. Winter is gone,
and the day's warmth radiates from the ground.

I wade slowly downstream, fishing wet flies haphaz-
ardly into the backs of pools while the current pushes me
along. When fishing begins to seem beside the point, I
break down the rod and walk the open woods.

———

In April one river leads to another. North and south of the Rapidan, the Blue Ridge Mountains rise abruptly out of central Virginia pastures, as if they had grown there. The mountains wear a woolly look until the canopy closes and the hardwoods join the fullness of the evergreens in a seamless cover of green. In April the cool, lambent daylight won't hold a trace of haze, and the contours of the watersheds are as clear as they will be until the turn of the hardwoods recasts them in mid-October. Mountain trout streams with common names and local reputations flow at the base of the shaded folds where the slopes join.

Each time I break my concentration to change a fly, or to climb up over a ledge toward a new pool, days seem to have passed and the name of the river to have changed while I fished. In memory, the rivers flow together. The North Fork of the Moormans flows into Ivy Creek, which tumbles in turn into South River. South River falls into the Conway whose long, cool pools somehow become the thin trickle of the upper Staunton. The Staunton spills, in fact, into the Rapidan, but in my mind's eye I can fish far enough up the Rapidan to find myself on a stretch of the lower Rose I love in early spring.

There are others, but the names of these small mountain streams don't much matter. If you have a taste for such fishing, you will find that each has its own character and moods. Fish these rivers often enough, and you may discover some latent topography in the back of your mind to which a corner of the Blue Ridge corresponds. The greenstone rivers are dark, somber streams where trout fishing seems solemn and the days end early. Afternoons expand along the sandstone and quartzite rivers on the western slopes of the Blue Ridge, whose pale riverbeds have a bright, open feel. Eastern-flowing streams, like the Rapidan, are shadowed by large boulders that surround the fly fisherman with the dignity native to granite landscapes.

As April proceeds, the blue rivers subside. Eventually

they take on the color of the woods, olive and brown—the hues of the backs of trout. Whitewater retreats to the heads of pools and a complex but readable current fans out downstream. For two weeks or so the rivers look much like the diagrams you see in fishing books. You can see the small dark eddies, beneath which the larger trout often lie, swirling beside the cascading water at the heads of pools. You can see pools shift their weight into the bends in the river, where water runs quick and dark under eroding banks. The rubble of the river bottom and all but its deepest hiding places become visible. You can see the bulge of holding water in front of midstream boulders, as well as the slipstream on either side and the cove of quiet water behind. Still hard to make out are the depressions in riffles, which remain fast enough to be opaque. The river is full of good trout lies. When you approach it carefully, you can see trout holding over their shadows on the brown and yellow streambed.

Insects draw the season on, much as the books say they do. Once you learn the nomenclature, there is a pleasing formality to the life that takes to the air from a trout stream. *Paraleptophlebia adoptiva* joins *Epeorus pleuralis* and lasts until *Stenonema vicarium* and *fuscum* start hatching sporadically in the shallows. *Isoperla bilineata* come off the river with grace and pleasing frequency. All sorts of buggy cognates are about, far beyond your need to know the names of things.

The rivers put a far finer point on life than the carefully wrought contents of my fly boxes do. However hard I may have worked at the fly-tying vise, my offerings look a little foolish beside the real thing. A hungry mountain brook trout will readily grab a reasonable fake, but a close comparison of the flies studiously tied in winter with the insects that emerge in April reveals a few slender similarities and many wonderful, unbridgeable differences. The art of the fly fisherman pales in the field.

If peacock quill wound over a hook creates an un-

canny imitation of a Quill Gordon's body segments, dun
hackle and wood duck feathers hardly do justice to its
ovoid, slate gray wings. The light brown bodies I dubbed
for March Browns and Gray Foxes only generalize the
dark brown backs and pale yellow underside of the real
flies. And there was nothing to hand at the fly-tying vise
with which to fashion wings constructed of colored pan-
els like stained-glass windows fashioned in delicate folds.
The slender bodies, prominent eyes, and fragile legs of
the Little Blue Quill and Little Yellow Stonefly were impossible to duplicate beyond a fuzzy, inexact impression.
And the reddish-brown polywings I carry don't reach far
toward the beautiful form of the elongated and clear-
winged mayfly spinners that bring trout to the surface of
the river with such lack of discretion that my impoverished imitations work.

Life beneath the surface is even more intimidating.
Any rock from a riffle or the back of a pool teems with
nymphal and larval life forms well beyond the range of
my fly box. The latex strips and peacock herl I used to
imitate caddis larvae come close to the natural, but my
mayfly nymphs are crude approximations of the well-
formed creatures I find clinging to the bottom of stones.
Even my more realistically tied stonefly patterns lack the
detailed structure and extraordinary markings of these
complex insects.

But in the mountains you can generally fish with
whatever flies you have brought and connect often
enough with trout that are hungrier than they are careful. The fly fisherman, too, occupies a niche.

Sometime during April I make the year's first camp
on the triangular terrace of land that overlooks the confluence of the upper Rose River and Hogcamp Branch,
one of the many beautiful spots I know will be too
crowded later in the year to enjoy. I spend one day
slowly fishing up the Rose through a greenstone gorge
until I come to its upper falls. Each year I fish the

plunge pool beneath the long, thin cascade carefully, expecting to be rewarded for my efforts with an outsize brook trout, but I have never caught anything other than small trout in the spot.

I spend a day fishing through all the good ledgerock pools on the Hogcamp Branch, a sizable tributary of the Rose that survived the ill effects of a copper mining operation years ago and has good hatches of stoneflies and mayflies. The fishing on Hogcamp varies widely from year to year. Rivers have good years and bad, and I like keeping track, in the general way that a fisherman knows a river, of how my favorite streams are faring.

I used to kill two trout, one from the Rose and one from Hogcamp, at this camp. After I took up catch-and-release fishing, this was for several years a kind of ritual, a solemn celebration of the year's first nights in the mountains and of the trout fishing that, by the middle of April, had begun in earnest. It was also, I suppose, a way to honor trout as game and to remind myself that fly fishing for wild trout is not a sport.

I do not understand what is written in magazines and books that treats animals and fish as trophies and the pursuit of fish or game as a kind of contest. Perhaps that is simply because there are few fish in the mountains you could hold up with the fuzzy pride you often see displayed on the covers of fishing magazines, or because there is rarely an audience for your ego in the mountains. Even the current vogue of catch-and-release photographs continues to promote the strange idea of trout as status symbols. The "This is mine, I killed it" pose has been replaced by the "This is mine, I let it go" shot. This is an improvement, of course, because there are not enough trout left for the killing, but the gesture is still toward possession and self-aggrandizement.

So I used to kill two wild trout each year as if to remind myself that trout fishing is not, at the heart of the matter, a pastime. It is a predatory practice whose true object is killing. The knowledge of insect life, the deceptive art of the trout fly, the skill of casting, and the stealth of wading all evolved from that goal. I didn't want to wash my hands of that.

There is a pleasure one takes in killing game that is good to be reminded of and good to dwell on. When I fish to kill, I fish a little differently, not in the wading or the casting, but with an intent, gray feeling in the back of my mind that is as difficult to describe as it is to confront honestly. Killing puts an unfamiliar edge on the appetite and makes the subsequent meal unusually important.

On the last day out, I would kill two trout for breakfast, and those would be the only wild trout I killed all year.

This year I let the ritual go. I gathered a different breakfast and brought it down to the sunlit point where the rivers meet. A colony of yellow coltsfoot had taken hold in the embankment down which I scrambled to an inviting flat rock at the river's edge. I tore up half of them in my carelessness. In spring, it is difficult not to disturb things. Bright green shafts of false hellebore called attention to a mossy bog across the Hogcamp Branch that gives way to higher ground and a dark stand of old hemlock.

I ate and watched the rivers flow together. I remembered the way I poached the trout in lemon and butter sauce until their pink, translucent flesh just barely turned opaque and flaky, easy to lift off the fine, arched bones in an unbroken piece. I thought about the killing, but did not get beyond the usual impasse—that although it was important to face the unaccountable dependence of life on death, there was no longer enough wildlife left for repeating the lesson endlessly. And, too, it was hard to shake the simple truth in Thoreau's wry observation that most creatures were better off alive than dead. Still, I missed the chance to fish with the intent, gray feeling. I didn't abandon the ritual of taking a few trout to mark

another year in the field—it seemed important not to
wash my hands of the killing or to give into the commercialization of fishing as a sport—but, as I fished the
morning out, I was glad not to have killed any trout.


Before April disappears into May, I spend two or
three long days working my way up Whiteoak Canyon.
Everything about this steep, spectacular watercourse—
its broad cascades and deep-green pools half obscured in
billowing mists, the voice of the river lost over the precipitous basalt faces of its five falls, each of which forms a
bulge in the mountain like an unfinished Celtic sculp-
ture—is finished to a final dignity by some remnant old-
growth hemlock and spruce near the head of the river, a
rarity in Virginia's Blue Ridge.

Old growth. Even the phrase is beautiful. Old growth
is what nature intends land to come to—an extravagant,
aged, vegetative presence. A living final form. My guess
is that you never see a watershed quite right, never see it
fully enough to understand its underlying structure and
its potential reach, until and unless you see that watershed clothed in the mature forms of whatever life took
root to flourish there. There is an inexpressible dignity in
a gigantic, ancient hemlock impassively shading the evanescent life in a trout pool. And there is in the plumb,
branchless reach and perfect crown of the old yellow poplars, as well as in the detailed lineaments of their deeply
furrowed bark, a grace and a symmetry that ought to be
beyond reckoning. There are places in Whiteoak Canyon
where you can still fish in the company of the old trees.

Looking back, April seems like one long day. By the
end of the month I am back on the Rapidan casting into a
bad glare in the late afternoon, working my way through
the long straight stretch of river above the bend at Chapman Mountain. When the sun gets behind the ridge to
the southwest, the glare leaves the surface of the river

and for an hour or so the fishing is as good as it will be all year.

Pale evening duns rise into the diffuse light that lays over the river. The waning daylight seems to radiate from the pale surfaces of sycamore and hornbeam and beech bark. The big pools and runs are gray, their currents deeply furrowed and distinct. The duns rise straight up out of the water like spirits released from the riverbed. March Browns and Gray Foxes still attract trout into the shallows. You cannot take time to identify all the stoneflies and caddis coming off the river because this light that clarifies the river's currents so well, and which illuminates its insect life so clearly, is brief. For the first time all year the nature of the river is transparent. This is what you fish for—the river in the evening at the end of April.

When the river comes into focus this way, the rush of water sounds quieter, but you know that is an illusion produced by your own concentration. The resistance of the river is strong, but there is a boulder behind which to stand sheltered from the current and out of view of the big fish at the back of every run. You shoulder the rock and rest while you change flies, another pale dun to replace the mashed, soggy fly that took the big fish from the back of the pool in which you are now standing.

By the end of April you fish well, slowly, patient as a bear. You must be ready in spring to fish evenings like this at the end of a long day on the river. God knows where such evenings come from, but if you are on the river when the light begins to fail, and then holds for an hour, you know you have been offered a window on the year and you hope you have the energy left to do the occasion justice until dark.

Four or five casts cover most runs. Roll cast to the edge of the whitewater at the head of the run and watch the fly dance back toward you. Your mind's eye will bring a trout to the fly at the edge of every heartbreaking eddy or swirl. A small trout may splash to the fly at mid-pool, but that is not what you are after. The currents will deepen and darken at the back of the run in such a way that you watch that smooth funnel of water with a reverence beyond your regard for the rest of the river.

Somewhere in the back third of the run a good trout will turn. You will see a shapely arc of green and white in the water. The trout will come up confidently for the fly and take it turning. If the fish is at the lip of the pool, it will lunge for the fly just as you begin to draw it out of the chute of fast water into which the run gathers. Hooked, the trout will charge upstream and bore down into the river, which must seem to have betrayed it.

If playing such fish were not so riveting, and bringing them briefly to hand not such a crucial part of understanding the life of the river, the fishing would be almost sadistic. As every fly fisherman releasing a wild trout back to a river knows, the fishing is far from that, but it is very hard to explain the worth of the fisherman's intrusion into the river world. You can sense a trout in your river-chilled hand for a few moments after it has swum back to cover, and you have an image of it in your mind, tinged with wonder and guilt, that nourishes your sense of caring for what makes its passionate being possible.

On the Rapidan toward the end of April you can fish the pools and runs one after the other on these evenings when time seems to stand still and spring seems as infinite as childhood. However tired you may be, if you fish slowly, you will catch each one. The big trout at the back of each run will be quick and bright and strong. You will learn to play them with authority, but gently, and once you have schooled your own pride and excitement, you will learn how to release them without ever taking them from the river. One year you will refrain from casting to the last good holding place you see in the twilight, letting the trout you know waits there be the last fish of the day, a fish for the river gods or for your own future in the mountains.

If you are with someone, you can have a makeshift dinner beside the river with what is left of the day's provisions. You can watch it get dark and talk quietly until the fishing and even the mountains are unimportant. The sound of the river remains, and that is all you really need.

Later, you'll remember how all month the river seemed like a creature with a will worth learning to understand, and how the last few trout of the day seemed brighter than you had remembered trout being, each one more perfect than the last, like sparks struck somehow from the mountain by the rushing water, as in a myth.

# SHADOWS IN THE
# STREAM

I don't remember exactly where I was, but I remember evening was coming on and fishermen were rising to a river.

I was in the Blue Ridge southwest of Asheville near the end of a long trip, four feckless weeks on the road in North Carolina fishing for trout wherever I pleased. I sat on the tailgate of the truck eating saltines smeared with a tinned deviled ham that, although inedible at home, somehow becomes a delicacy on the road. I was tired of trout fishing, a rather wonderful way to feel on a balmy evening at the end of May. I still had my vest and hip waders on and a rod strung, but I was done. The occasional rings of rising trout that I could see from my perch moved me only to admiration. When I finished eating, I sipped an ice-cold beer and felt the trip pool pleasantly in the back of my mind.

I was parked at one end of a highway bridge that crossed a slow riffle maybe thirty yards wide. Sooner or later every trout stream in the country comes to such a bridge. It's where you pull over when you first reach the river to check it out, braking into the ruts other fishermen have worn into the weedy shoulder. It's the litter-strewn, often unappealing place where a name on a map begins to take on substance. Ultimately your image of the river will have nothing to do with that overfished stretch of water, but you start there. While a makeshift sulfur hatch unfolded, I watched a succession of fishermen pull over and start fishing the river.

The locals geared up and moved off quickly, disappearing into fisherman's trails that threaded along the brushy bank upstream and down. They had *spots*—memories to fish or mistakes to undo—and they strode off with a minimum of gear to do battle with whatever had eluded them.

First timers and the less obsessed took *the walk,* the nonchalant stroll to the center of the upstream side of the bridge that is no more casual than a baseball manager's hike to the mound, hands jammed into his back pockets, mind going like a buzz saw. Whether the river is a legend or a no-name, first looks from fishermen are sidelong and intense.

I remember in particular watching a fly fisherman from Colorado take the walk. He pulled up behind me in a dusty VW camper with those distinctive green and white mountains on the plates. My wisest friends have all gone west to fish and never come back, so I get uneasy when I see a jaded-looking westerner hop out of his vehicle to take a look at an eastern stream.

Colorado had the saunter to upstream center down pat. He stayed a bit back from the edge so as not to loom out over the water when he looked down into the river. He took in the flow and depth and the structure of the stream bottom, nodding his head as if mentally checking off details. He took a long view of the river upstream to see what the sequence of opportunities would be and then looked carefully along each bank. He watched for trout, of course, but he knew the good trout would not be visible and that he would have to fish them out of the shadows in the riffle and along the dark left-hand bank.

Finally he walked to the far side of the bridge and slid down the embankment to the edge of the river from which he picked up a few cobbles. He turned them over, looked at them closely, and then put them back. He climbed back up to the road and came across the bridge quickly, smiling slightly and making an abbreviated casting motion with his right hand.

# IV

# A MOVEABLE

# FEAST

Truth to tell, there is little romance left along the American road. In the east you are rarely treated to even the illusion of unruined space. The green breast of the New World has, for the most part, been franchised off to the beaming people who would have the rest of us make passionate distinctions between subspecies of cheeseburgers, or soft drinks, and for whom a trip to the mall is a solution to the angst that rears its head during nightly newscasts about toxic waste, world deforestation, and an Earth atmosphere that has begun to resemble Venus's.

Once a bucolic rite of spring, the gentle art of fly fishing has become more like an act of guerrilla warfare. I get on the road each year with some trepidation, and when I find the clear, cold, unpolluted water trout love, I fish with the pleasant if uneasy sensation that I have slipped behind enemy lines.

If the Blue Ridge suffers the indignity of a highway running along its crest for hundreds of miles, at least the CCC boys who built the Blue Ridge Parkway banked the curves and graded the dips and rises to fit the rhythm of the country music I prefer to listen to on the road. Get under way before the Winnebagos start to spawn during Memorial Day weekend and you can drive in time to the rockabilly that booms out of Winston-Salem and crackles up from Greenville. Or stash some tapes in the cab and let the perfect phrasing of Emmylou Harris's sweet voice lead you on.

The geography of the Blue Ridge helps sustain some useful illusions, and if you want the trout you catch to seem to be an enduring part of an untrammeled landscape, a modest illusion or two is worth packing along. If you follow the Blue Ridge's north–south axis and stay within its slender bounds, traveling as you would, say, in Chile, you can come away with a sense of endless mountains that give birth to an inexhaustible brood of rivers. Fly fishing is probably more a homage to the past than an act of faith in the future, but it is difficult to fish a region with expanding affection if you sense you are on the verge of using it up. It helps to be able to sense good water upstream and down, beyond the reach of a day's fishing, and rivers to fish beyond the rivers on this year's itinerary.

In short, there are enough miles of bright water in the Blue Ridge to support the fly fisherman's deep-seated need to believe in infinite possibilities. But only just. You can't get lost, physically or spiritually, in the Blue Ridge as you can in Montana or Alaska—for better or worse, you always know where you are. Some Blue Ridge trout streams flow within a hundred miles of Washington, D.C., and others within fifty miles of Atlanta. And although all the rivers eventually run unto the sea, most detour now through mall fountains from Fairfax to Spartanburg, jetting ignominiously for a few seconds into the greenish glow that keeps shoppers schooled at store counters like bream at the edge of a pond. The borders of the Blue Ridge are sharply drawn, and you know what to expect if you go too far.

By chance, my first trip to North Carolina was shrouded in minor visual illusions that gave the fishing a dreamlike cast, dampened as it was by a constant rain and enclosed in shifting mists. One May I drove two hundred miles south without escaping the nagging low front that pelted me with rain when I packed the truck at home. I had barely been able to glimpse the mountains as I drove, except for where the parkway descended into the wind gaps that dipped beneath the cloud cover. While concentrating on the soft white haze into which the yellow center lines curved back and forth, I could feel the dark bulk of the invisible mountains that surrounded the road and the bright empty spaces beyond the overlooks.

As I drove south into new country I couldn't quite see, I could feel the gradual rise in terrain and the broadening of the Blue Ridge as it gathered itself for its meeting with the Black Mountains just north of Asheville. I couldn't tell for sure, but I seemed to be getting somewhere. North Carolina was not New Zealand, but I had a week and two new rivers to fish.

After a night in an empty public campground, I backpacked off into the mist and rain within which I could feel dome-shape mountains and bowl-shape coves. Even half hidden, the horizon somehow projected the perfectly balanced succession of images and afterimages—mountain and cove, ridge and ravine, peak and saddle—that constitute the larger symmetry of Blue Ridge terrain. And although at first I couldn't see more than fifty feet down the trail or into the woods, I could feel the promising continuity of the mountains underfoot.

The constant rain and the steamy green warmth of the cove forest into which I descended seemed full of life, dense and various and growing at all points. The scale of growth was larger than I was used to. Hemlocks, pines, and the hardwoods I recognized grew much larger than they did in the hollows of Virginia. The woods were full of unfamiliar fern and wildflowers. The rhododendron that were mere shrubs along streams familiar to me were trees here, and the sound of water dripping and smacking on their thick leaves was louder than the incessant shushing of the rain into the dense boughs of the evergreens or its staccato pattering into the tender, half-grown hardwood canopy.

The trail followed a ridgeline for a half mile before switchbacking down the steep head of a cove. Visibility improved a bit as I descended and left the clouds on the slope above me, but the rain kept on and a shifting mist hung in the air. When the mist brightened or gusted open, I got a clearer glimpse of the contour of the cove, a two-tiered amphitheater of unbroken green that opened toward the east. Runnels of muddy water braided gullies into the trail, but elsewhere the dense vegetation held all the moisture in place, suspending it in a kind of natural reservoir. The incessant rain was distributed drip by drip from canopy to glistening understory and then into a rich, deep mat of mossy soil.

I was listening for a hint of the river at the bottom of the switchbacks that dropped me into the head of the cove when I came on a spike buck browsing alongside the trail. The deer stopped and looked at me naively for a full ten seconds, tilting its head as if to resolve me into focus, before it decided I was really there. When it turned and bounded off, the watershed seemed less empty, and I heard a murmur of running water in the silence the deer's departure made.

I shucked the pack and stashed it beside the trail, grabbed the rod and vest, and then threaded myself through a game trail that bent distinctly into the rhododendrons. The muffled sound I heard through the rain wasn't so much a stream as a dark tangle of water and rhododendron roots, an arm-wide ribbon of water that burrowed a faint channel through the vegetation. There at the head of the cove, the terrain seemed to be holding the river back, hoarding it in the dense undergrowth. Balked every few feet by dams of dead rhododendron leaves and diverted by tiny deltas of clayey soil flecked with quartz, the miniature river was perfectly clear and colder, much colder, than the rain.

The upper cove sloped so gently the stream barely grew for the first half mile, emerging from the rhododendrons only to bog down in a sunken old field of grass tussocks cut up by innumerable deer tracks and guarded by a raucous jay that harassed me as I sloshed along. One slope of the cove eventually came nearer and then disappeared beneath the emerging riverbed where the terrain folded sharply. Beyond the fold the upper cove dropped abruptly into the larger amphitheater of the main watershed.

The ribbon of water pooled above the drop and then arced twenty feet before catching itself in a long cascade down the broken bedrock exposed along the fold. A river took shape in the air, and from where I stood at the top of the drop I could see a series of inviting, dun-colored pools leading downstream from the foot of the cascade.

I once briefly dated a woman who thought all trout streams looked alike. The first one I took her to was lovely, the second interesting, the third a pleasant reminder of the first two. The fourth apparently began a redundancy that quickly led to trouble. If nothing else, this served to remind me that fly fishing for wild trout is an acquired obsession. If the obsession deepens on home water, where a fly fisherman learns the knack of successful return, it broadens on new water, which offers a chance to begin again—a minor excuse to start over that certain simple souls crave.

If the way a river slides darkly along an undercut bank, or purls through pocket water, or holds its breath in the still water of a pool is always and everywhere the same, those similarities hardly count as defects in the eyes of a fisherman. Nature is not the avant garde. Beneath the picturesque similarities are differences worth getting into a river to pursue.

I lost the first fish I hooked in this promising new stream, a stout twelve-inch rainbow that took a wet fly I fished from the bank into the tail of that first plunge pool. I looped a ropy cast across the pool without stopping to shake off the dulling effect of the rain and the walking. Although I saw the trout come out of hiding to follow the fly as it swung through the current, my damp reflexes were slow to fire. The fish was upstream of me and in the air before my mind had closed around the take.

The rainbow was beautiful breaking the water each time, and with each twisting rise and fall my heart leapt and fell and I knew I would lose it. But with each charge into the dark-green recesses of the pool, when I could feel the trout's firm intentions telegraphing through the graphite, I thought, *Yes, you've got him, just stay tight to the fish.* I started anticipating the jumps and deliberately leaned a bit of slack toward the commotion when the trout was in the air. I thought I had caught up to its moves when it jumped for the fifth or sixth time, silver and rose against the cascading whitewater. I can still see it at the apogee of its last leap before it collapsed into the froth—wet fly hung in the corner of its mouth, game as a billfish.

The slack felt terrible. I cursed myself and milled around stupidly, trembling with a spike of adrenaline I no longer needed. The worst part of losing good fish is that you cannot release them. They tailwalk across the back of your mind for days.

I left the rod and vest where I now knew the river began and bushwhacked back to the main trail to retrieve my pack. I made camp about a mile downstream of where I had started fishing and then threaded my way back upstream through the witch hazel and rhododendron that picketed the river. The ledge and the cascade where the river began was obscured by foliage. When I approached the spot from downstream, the river seemed to come out of nowhere.

All the way to camp the river was full of wild rainbows that came recklessly to the fly and fought hard once hooked. They grabbed flies like trout that hadn't been fished over, coming confidently out of hiding for buggy wets and emergers and for big hairwing dry flies I drifted and twitched on the rain-pocked surface of the river. I had only to work my way slowly through the archway of shrubbery and flick a short length of line downstream toward obvious lies. I had a pleasant sense that my knowledge of the river was growing exactly as the river grew.

Even in the rain the river ran clear, and the sound and feel of it rushing downstream led me through the obscure afternoon. I waded the stream for passage, lowering myself from level to level where it stepped abruptly down the mountain. Except for the deer and the jay at the head of the river, the woods were silent and motionless. Except for the trout, life seemed hidden.

In front of a smoky fire that evening, I traced the day's fishing in my mind. I was sorry to have found no brook trout in the river, but the rainbows I landed and released were beautiful streambred fish, their silver, black-spotted flanks brush-stroked with iridescent rose along their center line and dabbed on their gill covers. The younger fish were marked with inky ovals that looked like fresh fingerprints. *Salmo irideus.* I liked the obsolete classification. The taxonomists might have taken the *rainbow* out of the name, but in hand the fish fairly glowed with the vermilion iridescence that leaves such a distinct trace in the mind. Rainbow. Whitewater trout full of western zest. You could sense a deep determination in them.

The rain never stopped on that trip. I fished for five

days in the shifting mists and the foggy silence that was broken only by my own shuffling through the woods or the current and by the appearance of trout around the fly. To an observer I might have looked a bit forlorn wading and casting slowly in the rain, catching and releasing trout with such regularity that catching trout might have seemed not to be the point.

I was hardly in virgin territory, but for a few miles the river seemed untouched. I fished it down to its confluence with its sister stream and fished down the main stem until hatchery trout and the unmistakable signs of other fishermen began to undo the illusion. I flushed a pair of wood ducks from a pool at an old mill dam. The ducks rose low and fast off the water twenty feet in front of me and flew downstream, the male an unmistakable blur of color. I caught nothing but hatchery fish in the mill pool and killed three of these for dinner.

The next day I started back up the sister stream, a not-quite mirror image of the first, and for a day or two fished with the pleasant sensation that I had unbroken country before me, half a continent, say, of ridges and darkly forested coves and cold, clear-flowing streams full of wild trout.

There was, of course, no such expanse of unbroken country, but every May I have found good water to fish in the mountains of North Carolina between Blowing Rock and Brevard. The Blue Ridge reaches its greatest height and breadth there, and where those cove forests are left alone, pine and hemlocks and Appalachian hardwoods grow slowly toward their former grandeur, sheltering a world that has more variety of native plant and animal life in it than all of Europe. In the steepest, rockiest watersheds, irreplaceable fragments of trout streams drop over the rough terrain and flow quietly through forested river bottoms hidden in the quiet, cathedral depths of the coves.

The good trout water left in the mountains flows

through what used to be called "the back of beyond," an Irishism, I believe, for mountaineer country. Bright creeks and runs thread their way around small mountain farms and hamlets and flow through dark river bottoms between hogbacked ridges. Forest Service roads, graded and graveled for the lumber trucks that keep the mills at Lenoir and Hickory busy, follow the rivers as best they can, but you will inevitably find yourself hiking down a steeply pitched trail to get to the good water. You are likely to pass the remains of an old still or the shot-gunned carcass of an ancient Ford tucked away in the underbrush. You will see the remains of old cabins and homesteads as well as well-tended graves remembered with wildflowers or decorated with bits of pottery and quartz. The rivers are known locally more for the havoc they create when they flood, but in their headwaters they are fine trout streams. I know them mostly as late-spring streams, still flowing with a bite in their tumbling currents, but settled down from the high-water days of April.

I think of yellow birches, large *Ephemera* spinners, and rising brown trout when I think of Wilson Creek. There is a stretch of river I remember as much for a stand of yellow birches where I camp when I fish there as for the brown trout that inhabit the rocky pools bordered by the birches. I make a good trout camp there every year in the middle of May, and although the spot is three hundred miles from my house, when I get to that stand of birches and see the river sliding by I feel like I am home. In mid-May, when there are simultaneous spinner falls and hatches in the evening, the big browns, which are hard to catch during the day, come out of hiding to take the insect life coming and going.

I try to fish well on Wilson Creek because I know there are good trout in the river and because the river is so excellent it instantly commands a fisherman's respect. Certain rivers do that. You fish them as if someone were watching you. The Wilson Creek watershed has been logged and burned and flooded out during the last century in an almost biblical series of calamities, but nothing has ever broken the wild heart of the river or tainted its cold, crystalline flow. I have caught wild browns and rainbows in Wilson Creek, and I am told if you fish up far enough you will find a remnant brook trout population in the headwaters. I have fished pretty far up the river and not found the brook trout, but I believe they are there.

Perhaps there are no ideal rivers, but when I am watching a brown trout rise in the buttery water from the edge of my camp on Wilson Creek in the evening, I am not so sure. While dinner cooks itself and the trout rises in front of me, I can sit in the shadows, drink coffee, and wait for deer to appear in the half-light of the opposite bank. A belted kingfisher may chatter loudly over the river or a scarlet tanager flit silently through the understory. Pleasing colonies of wood fern grow profusely around camp, which, beyond the birches, is surrounded by Catawba rhododendron. The large purple flowers of the rhododendron put a subtle perfume in the warm evening air. The last long fingers of sunlight spotlight the painted trillium, fire pinks, and yellow lady's slippers that grow in open patches near fallen trees. As those last rays of daylight lift into the canopy, they briefly light the stately pink and white bloom of the tulip poplars that have flowered overhead.

A short walk would flush grouse, bring me to a bear-slashed tree, or bring to mind the stocky timber rattlers tucked away in the brushy slopes of the cove. Somewhere nearby wild turkey scratch for mast hidden in the leaf litter. As the woods lose light, raccoons slip from trees and make their way cautiously to the riverbank to fish while owls rouse themselves to hunt.

The brown trout rising in front of me is unaware of anything except the spent mayfly spinners drifting helplessly toward it. The spinners are plentiful, and so the trout's rises are timed as much to its hunger as to the availability of food. At no other time of the year does it have so much choice.

The trout's mouth breaks the surface of the river when it intercepts an insect. The white gape of the fish is odd to see. Sometimes it lifts itself high enough to bring its eye out of the water. When it slips back under the surface of the river it leaves a bubble in the spot. When the trout sinks beneath the opaque disturbance of its rise, the concentric waves of the riseform expand from that point, encouraging you to think of the trout's rise as a kind of center. If you keep watching that spot in the river, the rise will begin to seem like a pulse, as if the river were throbbing in the trout.

In the morning, before breakfast, I fish the stretch of river immediately below camp. The months collapse and fold in the coves, and there is an early April chill in the May morning. Sunlight comes late to the bottom of the cove. The river is dark, and its currents cold and confusing. Wading begins to wake me. I skirt the deep water, content to shuffle knee-deep through syrupy riffles. I don't like wading deep too early in the day—something about the river getting too much of a hold on me when the world is so quiet and I am only half conscious.

I move along slowly, casting myself awake. No insects are coming off the river. I cast too much at first, undoubtedly spooking trout I cannot yet see in the dark, wrinkled water. I strike slowly at takes and miss them, regretting without emotion each missed fish that tugs free. As I fish, I watch the line of sunlight advance slowly through the woods. I come out of the river when I see the line reach camp.

I cook breakfast and make a pot of fresh coffee on a backpacking stove perched on a mossy stump between the

tent and the river. The tedium of camp chores comple-
ments the tedium of fly fishing nicely. There is always
something simple to do—rebuild leaders, patch waders,
chop wood. Routines underwrite the general pleasure of
camp life. The line between work and rest vanishes.

I watch the river and the woods as I eat, thinking
only that the clarity of morning light is humbling to
thought. Along a river in the morning, the world meets
you squarely. My impulse is to watch and listen, as if I
might absorb the frankness that seems to hover in the air
around me. The river slides by, patient and insistent, as
generous and unforgiving as time.

A camp stakes a pleasant, temporary claim on a river.
The pack and the tent, the makeshift kitchen and the
small fire ring become a provincial capital from which
you venture out each day with a larger stake in the river
than the day fisherman. You've made a place on the river.
You are always fishing either out from or back toward
camp, and this gives a slightly more emphatic direction to
the day's journey. When you come back to camp, you see
familiar order in a strange place. Your time on the river
runs a little deeper because you eat and sleep there.

The longer you stay camped on a river, the more you
find yourself doing what any animal does: You sit still
and watch the world around you very carefully in order
to understand your place in it. You lean toward your
first response to things: What is that? Looking and listening come to dominate your thinking. You see the
order you have imposed does not extend far. You note
how the short, faint trails of your knowledge give out
when you look at the details of the world around you.
You try to sharpen your thoughts against a growing
awareness of the limitations of your senses, even while
those senses expand their customary reach. You watch
the river constantly.

The best water on the river is upstream of camp. I
save that quarter mile of deep, well-wrought pools for

evenings. Below the easy morning stretch of water, the river drops rocky and white and forms deep, green pools and narrow runs closely guarded by shelving of gray slickrock on one side and dense vegetation on the other. Below the rocky, mountainous stretch, the river flows more broadly and with a gentler gradient, like a quiet forest stream. The character of the river and the logic of its landscape has determined that a two-hour hike downstream will give me a full day's fishing back to camp.

A good stretch of river is never the shortest distance between two points. River time is slow and convoluted, and when I concentrate and fish deliberately hours disappear into pools, diffuse themselves in riffles, and contract in the eddies where I wait for good trout to show themselves. I don't think about it while I fish, but all day the river does what it will with my time. I know that all the studied, somewhat pretentious practices of fly fishing—the slow progress of wading, the metronomic beat of casting, the watching and waiting and fussing with flies and tackle—only serve to create the illusion that I am in control, making the moves and choices.

The practice of fly fishing is pitted against the resistance of rivers. The resistance you feel in a river all day is real, at times almost animate. Working upstream through rushing water and over jumbled, broken bedrock may just be an ordinary day's fishing back to camp, but some days the fishing becomes an odd travail only fishermen who wade rivers understand. No creature experiences a river the way a wading fisherman does. Some days you look up and see camp before you even thought about keeping an eye out for it. You notice the long, low angle of sunlight poking through the trees west of you, and you hear the changed sound in the late-afternoon woods brought on by the coolness that has crept back into the air. Perhaps a woodpecker starts knocking on a distant tree, or a wood thrush darts across the stream, its long, glossy tail catching the late light.

You didn't know the day was half over and all of a sudden you have an acute sense of how brief a day is. You are not thinking of yourself so much as the day and everything in it—the river, the life around you, even the sound and odor of things. Being in the river all day has put you inside of its sinuous, convoluted time, and suddenly you feel you have shared the day, and lost it, with everything around you. And even though the river worked against you and, in some sense, betrayed you, you miss the nagging force of its current when you wade to shore and suddenly feel alone, even though you have been alone all day.

If you get down in a cove forest in the back of beyond and spend a day wading up a mountain stream that hasn't lost its spring snappishness, quietly concentrating on your fishing, the river will make you feel time pass that way. But because the river is so beautiful and was so truthful when it whispered in your ear all day that time was going—that your time and all time was going— you do not begrudge whatever in you it has taken away and you do not take lightly whatever you have taken from it.

If there is, on certain rare occasions, a reason for killing a wild trout, perhaps it is to symbolize the way you feel time in the river. River fishermen do not talk about this among themselves because it is understood; they do not tell others about it, because it is something only rivers teach. But they teach others to wade and cast and do the menial things fly fishermen do so that some day they, in turn, might feel the insistent, mortal tug in a river and be educated to understand the beauty of being and time the way a heron, or a fox, or a trout might be thought to understand such things.

You do not feel time in the river every time you fish, but sooner or later you will feel it. Some day you will reel in and turn your back on a river to wade toward shore, and you will see, or hear, or smell something and a sharp sense of time passing will come on you like joy, or fatigue. It will send a little shiver up your spine, and you will feel grateful and afraid. Then you will busy yourself with some practical task, and the fear and the gratefulness will subside.

Once you have felt it, you will understand why it is important to fish a good river properly. The intensity of the feeling will recede, and its relevance will often seem obscure, but every time you hike through a forest to measure off a length of river for a day's fishing, you will take a deep, unconscious pleasure in every downstream stride. The day's way back is the river's way. It will take you longer, and you will be hard-pressed to say where, exactly, the time went. That is what the river is for.

So I mark off two hours downstream on Wilson Creek to give me a day's fishing coming back.

I skirt the river so as not to disturb it, following a vague network of trails around impenetrable rhododendron thickets. Moving quietly over soft mats of brown pine needles, I enjoy the cool quiet of morning in the cove. The forest floor is lit here and there by shafts of sunlight that highlight a seamless reach of growth and decay. I keep an eye out for wildflowers and timber rattlers. The terrain forces me back and forth across the river several times, and at each ford I'm tempted to start fishing.

By the time I wade into the shallow tail of a pool to start fishing, the morning coolness has dissipated and the world around the river has grown quiet and warm. There is a special kind of silence in the woods in May. Rivers have subsided from the boisterousness of April. The summer buzz of insects has not started. Fresh, intermittent breezes rustle the crowns of trees, but the air over the river is still.

Wilson Creek is wide enough so that the canopy does not close over it. The river seems to follow the blue strip of sky overhead, flowing olive in its shaded depths and amber through its sunlit riffles. I fish slowly all day through its cool, lively water, taking time.

Two separate cascades of water spill into the first pool, creating a double current. There is a vee of dark green water upstream of where the currents converge. An Elk Hair Caddis turns a pleasing length of brown trout in the notch of the vee. The fly rocks on the wake of the refusal.

I wait and eye the spot while changing flies. The trout is not rising, and nothing is coming off the river. I shoot a sidearm cast low over the pool. A small Adams appears on the water, drifting freely.

The amber arc turns up toward the surface again and comes back with the fly, taking it just before it washes out of the vee.

The trout feels like a part of the river broken free, a slice of current out on its own. The rod plays the fish, which has few options. One charge left, one charge right, then it holds deep. I bring it in green rather than let it sulk and strain at the bottom of the pool. When the brown stops swirling in the water around my knees, I see that the fish is unusually dark and stout—a little larger than I thought.

I hold the mahogany trout on its side in the water and slip it off the fly with the help of hemostats. I right the fish and gentle it back and forth until it shivers out of my loose grip and holds in the stillwater, balanced on flared pectorals. When I straighten up, it glides a few feet away and then holds at the edge of the current against which it seems to rub itself. When it noses into the main current, it is pushed back out until it finds the right angle of attack and shoots effortlessly forward to the head of the pool.

Unless you are a trophy hunter, a fourteen-inch brown trout represents a kind of perfection, the platonic form of what a wild brown should be. The color and markings of the fish complement its size perfectly, as if it had grown to just the right proportions. A fourteen-inch fish is large for a mountain stream, but not a gargantuan anomaly. You can't brag about it. The brown is old enough to be wily, but because it inhabits freestone water, it is not impossibly selective. The fish doesn't make you a hero for catching it. When you tell someone about it later, you will call it a "nice trout" with a precise degree of emphasis that another fly fisherman will recognize and appreciate. He or she will see it in the mind's eye with uncanny accuracy—a fourteen-inch brown. Yeah. Nice trout.

This brown trout turns out to be the best fish of the day. I fish Wilson slowly but steadily all day, taking the water on its own terms. I fish dry flies—Adams, sulfurs, caddis—on the flat, slow water, Zug Bugs and Tellicos—Carolina standbys—in the deep white slots. I drift black woods crickets into the stillwater around juicy cover, twitching them to entice sulking trout. Small rainbows charge almost anything I put on the water. They remind me of brook trout. The more numerous browns are more selective. They take a longer look and sip flies down a little fastidiously, sometimes forcing me to come back with a lighter tippet and a smaller fly.

I fish as well as I can, and the river doles out an unspectacular mix of success and failure. Camp slides into view before I think to watch for it. A breeze rises, and evening begins to close around the river.

Days on rivers end in pools. After supper I head upriver with a cup of coffee and a fly rod. I am tired of reading water and of wading against the river. I am tired of casting. I am even tired of paying attention to the world around the river. I want an easy fish to end the day, a decent trout from a still pool.

Stillwater. I rarely fish ponds or lakes, but a deep, still pool in a mountain stream is a different kind of stillness, like the stillness within a heartbeat. In the evening, a large pool in a trout stream represents pure possibility.

It is too early for the spinner fall, so there are no rising fish. I leave the coffee mug on a boulder and wade back into the river. The cup looks absurd sitting there. The sun is not a half hour set, but a murky twilight is already flowing out of the heavy timber of the bottom of the cove. I tie on a fly I can see, an Elk Hair Caddis or a light-colored hair wing.

No false casting. Quiet. I let the fly trace the imperceptible motions of the surface of the pool. A tuft of tan elk hair wanders around the dark water as if it were on its own. Wait. Tail. Wait. Near side. Now midpool. Wait. The dark water rumples.

The fish feels strong, but not large. When I try to force it to the back of the pool, it holds the fly rod trembling in a deep arc. I let it take line back into the pool. The reel makes a brief squawk. I hold the fly rod high and let the trout tire itself. The river feels like a stage. Perhaps it is the half-light, or my fatigue, or the urgent feel of the fish trying to get back into the river.

Back in camp, I shave dry heartwood from a split quarter of pine and nurse a handful of flame out of the curled shavings. I build a fire around the blackened coffee pot. Resinous smoke rises from the kindling. The pungent odor of the wet Carolina woods mingles with the woodsmoke.

Spinners come to lantern light while I tend gear, the large *Ephemeras* on which the trout feast at night. I find them crawling across the contours of the maps laid out under the lantern, deceived by their glossy surfaces. There are large reddish spinners, clear in the body and blackened in places, their tails and forelegs enlarged for mating. These have clear, diaphanous wings etched with fine black lines. And there are large yellow spinners with nearly opaque, sulfur-colored wings, which they hold slightly folded as they walk across the maps of the rivers I plan to fish. When I kill the lantern, the spinners fly to the dying fire.

When camp chores are done, I rebuild the fire. The

pitch of riversound changes randomly, as if the river was shifting around in the dark. A slosh of Jack Daniels in a Sierra cup takes the edge off the coffee and seems to set the day back in a frame. I can see the trout I released back to the olive water of Wilson Creek swim off behind the flames.

If you drew a circle with a radius that stretched from my campfire on Wilson Creek to the Linville Gorge, twelve miles away, you would capture some fine wild trout water within it. I can see those rivers in the fire: Harpers Creek below the falls, Gragg Prong above Lost Cove, Lost Cove Creek in the deep recesses of the darkest cove in the mountains, where outsize timber rattlers guard trout pools and send many a fisherman back up the trail. I can see the nameless tributary of a hard-fished river where the largest brown trout I have seen in the mountains swims like a lord in the small stream's one good pool. The pool is impossible to fish. There is no place from which to cast, no way to cast into it. The pool forces you to watch, as the good places on trout streams often do, and the large brown swims and feeds as if it knows it is beyond reach.

Farther south I can see Curtis Creek and Shining Rock and, beyond Asheville, the Davidson. Most years I end May on the Davidson. The river will be crowded, but I'll fish a late afternoon and evening through the riffles below Avery Creek, casting long for the pleasure of it. I like to work this stretch fishing downstream, covering the beautiful water systematically, reaching toward possibilities difficult to make out under the choppy surface. I swing nymphs and emergers through every inch of water. Every so often a good rainbow will grab the fly, and I will have a tight line to the river.

In the mornings I like to fish the Davidson above the hatchery, where it is a small mountain stream. I'll fish dry flies upstream until the ledgerock pools begin to look like the pools on the North Fork of the Moormans and I start to think about heading home.

On Wilson Creek I can see the fading coals from

where I lie in the tent. Occasionally a breeze rekindles the fire and small flames dance silently in the ring of stones. When the fire rises, I watch the glow of firelight on birch bark and listen to the river flow slowly in the dark.

# AIR AND RAIN

Fish far enough into what is left of the backcountry and you will end up at a meeting.

One evening in October of 1986, Dr. James Galloway addressed the Thomas Jefferson chapter of Trout Unlimited in Charlottesville, Virginia. A mile from Jefferson's stately university, where Galloway taught in the Department of Environmental Sciences, he set up a slide show in the glare of bad lighting and primary colors of the Ramada Inn's Meeting Room B. Two dozen die-hard trout fishermen sat on folding chairs, sipped beer, and listened respectfully to the professor's spiel.

"As a rule . . . rain is not acid far from town."

Galloway began his talk by quoting Robert Angus Smith, who coined the term *acid rain* in 1872 when studying the differences between urban and rural air quality around Manchester, England. Smith had been studying the presence of "free sulfuric acid" in the atmosphere and in rainwater for more than twenty years. He correctly attributed the presence of acidic sulfates to coal combustion, and noted that acid-laden precipitation downwind of Manchester's industry caused "the fading of colours in prints and dyed goods, the rusting of metals, and the rotting of blinds," as well as the disintegration of building stone. If "acid rain" had become a buzzword in the 1980s, it was a problem that had been waiting in the wings for a long time.

Galloway did not want to dwell on history, however. He had been studying the acid sensitivity of trout streams in the Blue Ridge since 1979, and what he found was worrisome. In the pristine, protected watersheds of

Shenandoah National Park, low-alkalinity streams were being subjected to increasingly high levels of acidic deposition. Rivers were acidifying. The principal difference between the world of Robert Smith and ours, Galloway implied, was that rain was now acidic—very acidic—far from town.

Galloway, who had helped to develop standardized international protocols for precipitation collection, had cast his research net wide. By 1986 he was collecting data on acid deposition from Poker Flats, Alaska, to Tierra del Fuego, from Kruger National Park in the Transvaal to Amsterdam Island in the Indian Ocean. Galloway had a ship collecting samples in the Atlantic from New York to Bermuda and atmospheric collectors onboard NOAA (National Oceanic and Atmospheric Administration) research aircraft flying between Virginia and Newfoundland. Now he wanted to know more about the Blue Ridge.

So he was talking to trout fishermen about sulfur dioxide and nitrogen oxide. He talked about upper atmosphere particle transport, dry and wet deposition, and the geology with which potentially sensitive surface waters were associated. He explained soil buffering capacities and made a pass at sulfate adsorption, cation exchanges, and what was generally known about the effects of decreased pH on stream life.

He showed slides of North America overlaid with wavy isopleths of the mean pH of rainfall and slides that showed the pH at which stream biota, from benthic organisms to brook trout, could no longer survive. He talked about sudden acid shock from spring snow melt and the slow leaching of toxic metals into stream water. He said correlations among all these factors were difficult to make, but that much was known. It was clear that the acid-buffering capacities of the thin mountain soils of the Blue Ridge were being depleted. Once what he called the "sponge" was full, the wild trout population in the mountains would likely suffer a significant decline.

Finally Galloway brought out the familiar USGS topo map for Virginia. Every mile of wild trout water in the state was highlighted in blue. Chairs scraped forward, and everyone's eyes fixed on that map and all the river miles of trout water in the mountains. Galloway said he wanted to get samples from those four-hundred-odd streams—taken at the same time—so that he had a picture, a snapshot he called it, of the alkalinity of all of Virginia's wild trout water.

No one knew the rivers better, or seemed to think more of them, than trout fishermen. He hoped, when the time came, they would help.

# V

# THE WEB

# IN THE RIVER

Looking for Green Pond became the joke of the week.
Price Smith's Bronco and Paul Bugas's Chevy pickup bounced up and down the Forest Service road through their own dust for more than an hour. Everyone took turns with a faded copy of the Big Levels USGS quadrangle that was falling apart at the folds.

Smith and Larry Mohn had done the last survey two years ago. Now they were driving up and down Flint Mountain in Augusta County, wondering where—exactly—they were. The badly rutted dirt road should have taken them right by Green Pond.

"They can't have moved Green Pond," Smith radioed ahead.

"Acid rain," the speaker cracked. Smith looked over at Rick Webb.

Webb hadn't been to Green Pond since he had ridden

his Honda 50 from Waynesboro up to the Blue Ridge Parkway and down this same road when he was twelve years old. That was twenty years ago. Now he was as bemused as the Virginia Department of Game and Inland Fisheries people about where he was.

Lunch was at the side of the road. Big Levels was bear and turkey habitat, pitch pine and chestnut oak stunted and warped to windward by the harsh conditions of a dry, windy, soil-poor sandstone ridge. A tangled understory of laurel slicks half choked by briers, vines, and dust seems to lead nowhere. Not especially pretty terrain on a hot June day.

Webb tends to notice things and name them: chestnut seedlings, a rat snake, some rare swamp pink. He picks up a piece of quartzite studded with cylinders an eighth of an inch in diameter.

"Skolithos."

Everyone looks around and finds a rock and looks at the white tubes embedded in them. Trace fossils. Worm borings in Cambrian mud.

After lunch Mohn marches off on a hunch and finds Green Pond. The Forest Service had rerouted it to get it out of the wilderness area that was established in 1984 to protect the St. Marys River.

Green Pond marks the trailhead down to the river. Fly fishermen familiar with the St. Marys smile when you mention it: six miles of wild brown, rainbow, and brook trout water in the George Washington National Forest. For ten years, however, good fishing stories about the St. Marys have been sliding into the past tense. The river used to be this and that. St. Marys rainbows, especially, were ghosting into local mythology.

While Fish and Game start to backpack their gear down the mountain, Webb stops to look at Green Pond, a small ellipse of standing water surrounded by a dark green bog of sphagnum moss fringed with sedge and cinnamon fern. Highbush blueberry on which black bear feast in late July ring the pond. The acre is unique, a water table trapped on top of a mountain, an impermeable shale cup perched on permeable sandstone, a feature left by some geological shuffling no one quite understands.

Webb smiles and nods at this interesting difference in the landscape.

"Boreal. Like something you'd see in Canada."

There is no discernible hierarchy on the trail, but the work at the first sampling reach at the head of the river a mile below Green Pond shakes out responsibilities. Fish and Game has done this before. The river at this point is a five-foot-wide trickle through a tunnel of mountain laurel. White laurel blossoms float downstream all day like little boats. Flame azalea burst out here and there along the riverbank.

Bugas and one of the summer interns set up to sample aquatic insects just above the lower end of the reach before anyone mucks up the river. Doing bugs, they call this. The intern lugs the heavy Carle sampler upstream, grunting a little at its awkward weight. Summer experience. The round, mesh-sided cylinder, two and a half feet in diameter, is set in the stream to cover a representative section of streambed. A small cloth collection bag goes on the end of a plastic funnel on the downstream side of the sampler. Bugas vigorously rakes the circle of streambed covered by the sampler with a garden trowel while the intern times him for a minute. The detritus and insect life raised by his raking flow into the funnel-shape end of the sampler and then into the collection bag. They do this three times, collecting three bags of benthics—bottom-dwelling macroinvertebrates. The bagged bugs go in a jar of alcohol.

When the bugs have been collected, Price Smith runs a tape upriver and measures off three hundred feet of stream. He sets a holding net across the upper end to keep the fish in the reach. Mohn shoulders the packframe with the battery and the shocking unit mounted on it, puts on rubber electrician's gloves, and takes up the prod plugged into his unit and the shocking net. Smith and another summer intern, also in cleated waders and rubber gloves, handle a net and a bucket. One will scoop, the other carry. They set current and voltage and disappear slowly into the tunnel of laurel, jostling and joking.

Webb and Bugas talk about the benthic sampling while they wait for the others to return. Bugas is doing one collection at each station. Webb favors a heavier sampling. More data, less extrapolation. Bugas doesn't disagree but mentions time, money, and the scope of their work. Everyone wants to do more science in the field, but there are limitations. At least on the St. Marys, they have some baseline data to work with. Someone was here before them.

In fact, Fish and Game is on the St. Marys partly because Eugene Surber was on the river more than fifty years before. Surber, at the time a biologist with the U.S. Bureau of Fisheries in Leetown, West Virginia, studied the St. Marys extensively in the 1930s. He was interested in the food production of trout and smallmouth bass streams, most especially the bottom fauna on which cold-water species depend for the bulk of their natural diet.

Surber worked at a time when public fisheries management was preoccupied with the hatchery production of trout for recreational put-and-take fishing. The sometimes uncertain fate of hatchery trout in streams led researchers, concerned at first only with the lost investment in planted fish, to become more curious about naturally productive trout streams. Charged with studying the best ways to maintain a stocking program, Surber, like some of his more farsighted peers, became increasingly fascinated by the natural history of native populations of trout and the complex, delicate web of aquatic flora and fauna on which such populations depended.

Surber's work on the St. Marys reflects this divided

interest. If his responsibilities as a public fisheries biologist tied his research to the recreational politics of hatchery trout distribution, Surber's passion seemed to be understanding the natural productivity of a trout stream from the bottom up. In fact, the Carle sampler Fish and Game was using to collect their benthic samples was a descendant of an invention of Surber's—a foot-square metal frame with a second frame attached to it at a right angle and trailing a fine-mesh cotton collection net downstream, as elegant and functional a piece of field gear as you will find. What was commonly called the Surber sampler became "for the stream-invertebrate worker a symbol of office almost equivalent to the butterfly net of the entomologist," according to H. B. N. Hynes, whose 1970 *The Ecology of Running Waters* gathered the fruits of a half century of field research by men like Eugene Surber. The Surber sampler has, for the most part, outlived its usefulness as a collection device, but Eugene Surber is still associated with understanding the natural life of rivers from the bottom up. Fisheries management specialists in and around the Blue Ridge remember him. Fish and Game seems to like following in Surber's footsteps along the St. Marys.

Like Paul Bugas and the summer intern, Eugene Surber collected macroinvertebrates on the St. Marys. Although his ostensible purpose in studying the stream was to determine its suitability as a put-and-grow fishery for hatchery fingerlings, he spent considerable time cataloging the river's aquatic fauna. He took monthly benthic samples from riffles all along the St. Marys from the summer of 1935 to the summer of 1937. He didn't sample in the dead of winter, but he sampled again for ten months in 1938 when he also took alkalinity, pH, and carbon dioxide readings. Although, as Surber suspected, the low alkalinity, slightly acidic stream was at best an average food producer, producing little more than one wet-weight gram of potential food organisms per square foot of riffle per year, it was one of the best trout streams in the two-million-square-acre George Washington National Forest.

The St. Marys' benthic life was wonderfully various. Surber found much of the Latin fly fishermen love to find clinging to the stones and detritus, or burrowed into the mud and substrate of a river: *Hydropsyche, Rhyacophilia,* and *Philopotamus* among the caddis larvae; several species of *Ephemerella* and *Baetis, Stenonema fuscum, varium,* and *pulchellum,* as well as *Paraleptophlebia mollis* and *Isonychia sadleri* among the mayfly nymphs; *Leuctra, Alloperla, Acroneuria abnormis* and *lycorias, Perla capliatoni, Peltoperla arcuata,* and *Pteronarcys proteus* among the stoneflies. The names sound ancient, as indeed the species are. And there was more: crane fly and fish fly larvae, snipefly, black fly, and midges; riffle beetles and crayfish. What Surber found was the delicate, various, and balanced array of life forms that are the foundation of a trout stream.

But his assignment was not to fathom the delicate web of life that held the St. Marys together as a trout stream. Surber was attempting to determine the fate of 11,107 hatchery brook and rainbow trout fingerlings planted in the river from 1935 to 1938. Since the St. Marys already had a viable population of native brook and rainbow trout, the plantings must have been a management gesture toward "enhancing the fishery." Would the river grow and support these artificially propagated trout so that fishermen might catch them?

Tracking the fingerlings was complicated by a major flood in March of 1936. Even discounting its effects, however, by 1938 the answer was clear. Although the fact that only 2.4 percent of the marked hatchery transplants were recovered from the river was striking, Surber's observations about the natural life of the river were more important. He noted that while the hatchery trout were disappearing from the river, where catches were closely monitored, "naturally spawned trout" were increasing as a percentage of the population. Despite dumping all that state-sponsored fish flesh in the St. Marys, Surber noted that by 1939 there was "a sharp increase in the abundance of naturally spawned or wild brook trout." He also noted that "the wild brook trout in the stream grew more rapidly than those planted," fish he couldn't help but note in passing that were "slim and colorless." In concluding his 1940 report, Surber urged "those in charge of the distribution of trout to pause and investigate further before wasting additional fingerling trout."

Given Surber's love for and interest in the natural productivity of rivers, one wonders if it was the waste of hatchery trout that was foremost on his mind or the potential waste of a trout stream that seemed to do just fine on its own. In this beautiful river where wild trout thrived under natural conditions, hatchery-raised fish demonstrated, he concluded somewhat archly, an unimaginable "unfitness for survival."

They finally did leave the St. Marys alone. The Forest Service kept stocking the river until hurricanes Camille in 1969 and Agnes in 1971 blew out the access road beyond anyone's desire to rebuild it. When the stocking finally ceased, the St. Marys settled in to being a wild trout stream, which had been its intention all along. Special fishing regulations were imposed in 1979 to protect the resource from angler mortality. Finally, in 1984, the watershed was included in the federal wilderness system.

Now the bad news was that after one of the best-loved and best-understood native trout streams in the Blue Ridge had finally been bronzed with wilderness status— six precious miles of freestone trout habitat protected and preserved for posterity, saved from inept management, from timbering, from mining and a railroad, from local political and economic shortsightedness—the river seemed to be in trouble again.

The electroshock team doesn't come back with much

from their first pass through the uppermost reach. There are six brook trout in the bucket: one four-inch adult, five young of the year. No forage fish. The young of the year are stunted, 50 millimeters long and maybe a gram apiece, a click on the scale. They don't look like much laying in the vee of the fish ruler.

Larry Mohn smiles habitually through his beard, but that doesn't mean he's happy. The St. Marys is in his district and this is his show.

The sweat-soaked crew makes a second sweep and comes up empty.

"We missed one adult and two, maybe three young of the year. There's nothing else in there."

"What did we get up here last time?"

Bugas looks up at Mohn and flips the metal clipboard shut. "About the same."

After two more passes through the reach, Fish and Game packs up to move downriver to where they will stash their equipment for an early start the next day. Rick Webb gets out his own maps and sampling gear.

Webb works for Galloway. When Galloway finished drumming up support among the Trout Unlimited faithful, he disappeared into his far-flung research and put Webb in charge of what became known as the Virginia Trout Stream Sensitivity Study. The study began with a massive collection of stream samples late in April of 1987. After two years of planning, three months of training, and two weather delays, Webb gave the go-ahead over the phone one Thursday night to his field coordinators, and more than two hundred trout fishermen recruited by Trout Unlimited took to the hills with maps, data sheets, and collection equipment exactly like what Webb was toting down the St. Marys.

By that Sunday night Webb was looking both grateful and amused as scruffy men he didn't know came in from all over the Blue Ridge and the western highlands of Virginia. They lug coolers full of stream samples up the winding stairs and through the narrow corridors of Clark Hall at UVA, shouting and joking, dripping melting ice water and tracking mud. Pickups and beat-up $4 \times 4$s hemmed the building in. The students wandering in and out of the library seemed to think something was wrong. Nothing was—the professor's spiel had worked pretty well.

A week later, when the last few samples from the boondocks in the extreme southwestern corner of the state had come in, 380 white plastic bottles were lined up in rows on slate lab tables awaiting analysis of pH, conductivity, and stream-water alkalinity, as well as measurement of concentrations of sulfate, nitrate, chloride, calcium, magnesium, sodium, potassium, and silica. There was a bottle for almost every one of those streams on the state topographic map with which Galloway had lured the fishermen. Bottled, they might not have looked like much, but Virginia's native trout streams now flowed through Clark Hall.

The cooperation and camaraderie of the collection generated an optimism that analysis of the samples quickly dissolved. Now, more than a year after that first massive effort, and with quarterly sampling of sixty-six sites continuing, the numbers in the opaque bottles were beginning to tell a tale. And the story on the St. Marys wasn't good. If Fish and Game was on the river looking for effects, Rick Webb was on the river looking for causes. Gene Surber's old beat had come alive.

Webb unshoulders his pack at his first collection site and goes through his own ritual: Take the stream temperature, put on plastic gloves, rinse the 750 milliliter nalgene sample bottle three times in stream water, take the sample without disturbing the river, label the bottle, put the sample in a Ziploc bag and then on ice in the pack, fill out the field data, photograph the site. He does this carefully, mechanically, like something he has done hundreds of times, which he has. These are the basic moves in his game. If this isn't done right, nothing counts. This is where his numbers come from.

Webb samples his way downstream. He has eight collection sites in the watershed. He knows the St. Marys is a stream at risk. The quartzite streambed has very low alkalinity, almost no capacity to buffer the acidic deposition borne on the winds that blow from the Tennessee and Ohio valleys, as well as from local sources.

The river and the watershed *look* good, and wilderness status gives the ten-thousand-acre enclave as much of a chance as possible to return to what it once was. But that is not enough.

Webb kicks at a chunk of black ore near the site of an old manganese mine. Trees are growing on a conical hill formed from mine tailings.

"You can stop the logging, close the manganese mines, pull up the rails, and let the road shrink back to a trail, but you can't keep the rain and snow from falling. You can't keep the clouds away."

When Eugene Surber took the pH of the river in 1938, he had no reason to be more thorough, or more suspicious, than he was. His one-time, one-site colorimetric reading was 6.8, which was probably a high reading. At the time the acidity of a river was thought to be a natural function of the geology and soil of its catchment basin, a given and a near constant. They might be choking on the Industrial Revolution in the cities, but no one thought that rain in the mountains might bring acidic gases and particulates from hundreds, even thousands of miles away.

When Surber worked on the river in the 1930s, the mean pH of rainfall in Virginia was probably around 5.0. By the late 1980s, the mountains were caught within the 4.2 isopleth.

Webb is soft-spoken, committed to research rather than rhetoric. In 1982 he was homesteading with his wife and two daughters in Braxton County, West Virginia, when he got involved in an acid mine drainage battle that threatened his own hundred acres. That cost him a way of life.

"I had this plan to grow blueberries and keep bees," he says with a laugh, but there is no self-mockery in his laughter.

"This was the '70s. You know. We wanted to leave civilization, at least civilization as we knew it. We saw an ad in *Mother Earth News.*"

He shakes his head and smiles. "We built a house, farmed with a horse, lived under kerosene light for six years reading Wendell Berry and Helen and Scott Nearing. We walked everywhere. Took care of ourselves. It was good. There were others. Some of them are still there. Some of them are doing okay.

"Once I got involved in fighting the mine drainage thing, that was the end of it. I had to spend too much time in town. We set up an office. I read law, talked to lawyers, got help from environmental law center people in Washington. I learned to do stream chemistry, started sampling streams, getting data. I had no scientific training yet. You can kind of see what's going on, but you need the numbers. I was sued for a quarter of a million dollars for libel, physically attacked at a public hearing. I guess we were back in civilization."

Webb is watching the river, talking in a quiet, neutral tone that has a controlled eddy of nostalgia in it.

"We won. Sort of. I'd like to go back some day. Maybe live in Elkin. Elkin would be a good place for a trout fisherman to live. I'd like to live on a river or on a mountain."

Coming down the river, Webb points out a pool where he caught a thirteen-inch brown trout. Fish and Game has to wait an hour at the bottom for him to finish his sampling. This makes a long day longer, but no one seems to mind much.

On the second day of the sampling, Larry Mohn is unusually talkative. He, too, tends to watch the river while he speaks, looking upstream and down, alternately nodding and shaking his head.

"I used to bring people who were visiting up here to fish. You know, let the river show off. Now I take them somewhere else. The St. Marys is still a good river, but it's not like it was."

Coming from Mohn, this does not sound like the typical fisherman's lament for the past.

"Fish populations fluctuate, but what's happening up here is different. The rainbows are going, the forage fish, mayflies are just about gone. I don't think we got a single *Ephemerella* last sampling."

Mohn loves the river but is cutting his ties. "Shit. There hasn't been a Quill Gordon hatch up here in years."

That fact, as much as any other, tells the story for the biologist in Mohn as well as for the fly fisherman.

"Given the alkalinity of the watershed and everything we know about acidification effects, it probably is the deposition Galloway and Webb have been talking about. Look at what they found up in Shenandoah National Park. Almost twenty-five pounds of sulfates *an acre* are being dumped on these catchments *every year.* All that shit has got to be doing *something.* But we can't say for sure. That's what this is all about."

He shakes his head at the river again.

"Takes time."

Three passes with the shocking unit through the second sampling reach yield four adult brook trout and seventy-one young of the year a little larger than yesterday's fry. There are two blacknose dace.

While he keeps an open mind about the sampling under way, which by itself doesn't tell him anything, Mohn is thinking about the indices of biological difference that showed up in the comparison of the 1976 sampling and the sampling two years ago in 1986. Those were the differences that got Fish and Game worried.

From 1976 to 1986 there was a significant drop in population and biomass of *every* species of trout and forage fish and in almost every species of invertebrate studied. Those invertebrates that increased their numbers were known to be acid tolerant and seemed to be taking advantage of niches left by declining species. There was a decline in the number of fish and invertebrate species in the river, as well as in the number of species.

The new year-class of brook trout was missing, but that was probably due to a record flood in 1985. Rainbow young of the year, which had done well in other state streams despite the same flood conditions, declined significantly. This was the most telling sign that acidification was getting a grip on the river. Among trout species, the rainbow is most sensitive to increased acidity. In the four upper reaches of the river, blacknose dace, another acid-sensitive species, were all but gone. Rosyside dace ditto.

The invertebrate population was reduced both in numbers and in numbers of species. Mayflies, less acid tolerant than stoneflies, were the hardest hit: *Epeorus* gone. *Stenonema* gone. *Ephemerella* gone. *Paraleptophlebia* gone. *Rhyacophilia* gone. *Baetis* had declined significantly, and some species seemed to be acid tolerant and perhaps thriving because of decreased competition. Among the stoneflies, *Chironomidae, Leuctra, Alloperla, Perla,* and *Acroneuria* declined significantly. Crayfish seemed to be declining but there were differences among species. No one knew what was happening lower down the food chain to the algae and other microscopic flora, but it looked like the web was unraveling.

The decline of trout populations, most especially poor recruitment among a once-legendary rainbow trout population, was only the most visible sign of many hard-to-detect changes. The net result was a decrease in stream biomass and a decrease in stream biodiversity. Less life. Less diversity of life.

This was not Gene Surber's river.

Lunch the second day is below the falls on the St. Marys, a series of three cascades that divides the upper and lower river, a popular destination for hikers and campers. Two couples are camped at the big falls, which create the best swimming hole in the river, a beautiful bowl of cold blue water. The campers watch the sweaty green and khaki Fish and Game crew troop over the log that serves as a bridge, carrying gear that looks a little too electronic and seems a little too awkward for the backcountry. The campers have pitched their brightly colored, futuristic nylon tents right beside the trail, but they seem annoyed at the intrusion. They are not curious about what's going on.

Webb isn't along on the second day, but he sent an assistant, a graduate student in hydrology, to help out. Mohn asks if Webb worked up yesterday's quarterly readings.

"5.2 up top," the assistant tells him nodding upstream, "5.9 down at the gate. Alkalinities are around what they were."

Meaning near zero.

No one is surprised, but Webb's numbers haunt lunch. The pH in almost every reach of the St. Marys is already below what is tolerable for rainbow trout; some sections have a pH that is troublesome to brook trout. The river seems to be acidifying from the top down. Along with the benthics, many species of forage fish are going or gone. And, in the long run, the pH of the river can't help but decrease further. Its future is a function of geology and air quality. Geology is a function of the nature of the earth. Nobody can do much about it. Air quality is a function of politics. Nobody wants to talk politics. For ten years the sulfur dioxide emissions reductions that would help the St. Marys, and rivers like it, have been held hostage in Michigan Congressman John Dingell's Energy and Commerce Committee.

Everyone familiar with the literature knows the litany: the salmon rivers in southern Norway as early as
the 1920s, the lakes in southern Sweden in the 1960s,
some of the salmon rivers in Nova Scotia, and the dead
lakes in the La Cloache Mountains in Ontario in the
1970s, the fishless habitat in the Adirondacks in the
1980s. In Massachusetts, Pennsylvania, Maryland, West
Virginia, wherever anyone looked carefully enough, fossil fuel air pollution was taking its toll on low alkalinity
watersheds. Salmonids have been choking like canaries in
coal mine birdcages for almost a century. Now the St.
Marys, so long a local concern, seemed about to join a
discouraging list. During the 1980s, when nothing was
done about reducing sulfur dioxide and nitrogen oxide
emissions in the United States, the wild trout in the Blue
Ridge and in western mountains of Virginia had become,
in the words of a preliminary report, "a resource at considerable risk." The first published article to come out of
the Virginia Trout Stream Sensitivity Study provided a
"quantitative assessment of acidification for the native
brook trout streams of . . . the mountainous portion of
Virginia." That June 1989 article concluded that the
"acidification of these streams is . . . a continuing phe-
nomenon." A paper submitted jointly by the UVA team
and the Virginia Department of Game and Inland Fisheries to Trout Unlimited's Wild Trout IV symposium in
September of 1989 added that "substantially more
stream water acidification may be anticipated in the future." Citing the St. Marys as its most significant evidence to date, this paper predicted that "a substantial
change in the fisheries status of these streams can be expected."

Galloway got his start on environmental studies in the
Adirondacks. Webb did his graduate work on sulfate retention under Galloway in the Blue Ridge. While Galloway began testing his models on a global scale, Webb was
poring over the mountains he knew as a kid, looking

closer and closer at what was going on there. He spent four years working in the Paine Run watershed in the southwestern section of Shenandoah National Park, forty miles to the north of the St. Marys. He studied the way the Paine Run catchment handled the sulfate deposited on it. Galloway had other graduate students doing thesis work in the mountains, studying the geologically sensitive watersheds that drain the western slopes of the Blue Ridge, catchments composed of base-poor sandstones and quartzites.

In the late 1970s Galloway suspected that many Blue Ridge and Southern Appalachian streams were acidifying, although there were no dramatic biological effects to help call attention to the chemical changes taking place. Except when flushed into the rivers by floods or sudden snowmelts, the acid that had been falling on the mountains was not yet in the rivers. It was in the soil. That, Galloway saw, was the only advantage the Southern Appalachians had over their northern cousins, whose soils had been raked away by glaciers. The older soils of the unglaciated southern mountains had delayed, and in a sense hidden for a while, the effects of acid deposition.

If sulfate retention in the soils was one half of the puzzle, the acid neutralizing capacity, or alkalinity of the mountain streams that drained those acidified though otherwise pristine catchments was the other half. The important number in the bottles the trout fishermen brought back from the mountains in April of 1987 wasn't so much pH as it was alkalinity. The alkalinity profile turned out to be much worse than Webb and Galloway had expected: 93 percent of the streams surveyed were sensitive to acid deposition; half were extremely sensitive—in grave danger of radical changes in stream chemistry and serious biotic decline. Ten percent were already acidic. Given the unalterable factors—the geology of a watershed and the finite buffering capacity of its soil—and the causal connection between sulfate deposition and decreased acid neutralizing capacity—the wild trout habitat in Blue Ridge and elsewhere existed on borrowed time. The only variable that could be altered—the amount of sulfur dioxide and nitrogen oxide put into the atmosphere from anthropogenic sources—had long been a political football. The reprieve the unglaciated soils of the Southern Appalachians had given its streams had been squandered.

A half mile farther downstream the third reach yields only twenty-two brook trout fry, delicate fish an inch and a half long, dotted with distinct black parr marks. Their translucent fins are pinkish, white-tipped, some with a trace of black underline. Some show the beginning of vermiculation on their backs, the principal camouflage of adulthood, a protection against natural predators but no armor against the shifting ion concentrations that now determined their fate.

Twenty-two young of the year from more than three hundred feet of stream. Halfway down the river no sub-catchable adults, no dace.

Mohn is hanging on to a thin smile. "A few years ago this was all good rainbow water." His arm sweeps up and down the river.

The discovery of the acidification of the Blue Ridge and the western Virginia highlands was as ironic as it was disappointing for Mohn and Bugas. In 1975 the Virginia Commission of Game and Inland Fisheries decided to inventory Virginia's native trout streams. Mohn and Bugas drew the enviable assignment to do the legwork. They expected to find 200 streams and maybe 600 stream miles of water left in the state, all of it in the mountains, that had self-sustaining populations of trout. What they found amazed them.

"We were shocked," Mohn remembers.

By the time they finished their exhaustive survey in 1981, they had identified 450 streams and more than 2,000 stream miles that had self-sustaining populations of trout. More than 1,300 miles of that was native brook trout water—more indigenous brook trout habitat than remained in the rest of the Southern Appalachians combined. The rest was water where rainbows and browns had established themselves, either by displacing the brook trout or by occupying marginal water from which the brookies had retreated.

Virginia had never been thought of as a trout state, and in a sense Mohn and Bugas's findings didn't change that. Most of Virginia's wild trout are small fish and easy game. They represent a biological and a historical resource more than a recreational one. But the men were excited by the environmental implications of what they found in the field. Based on their work, the state's fishing regulations and trout stocking policies were changed to enhance and protect the wild trout fishery so that what remained might be preserved.

Of course, while they were discovering this, Galloway's researchers were also in the mountains, and the numbers on *their* clipboards—the numbers on deposition, alkalinity, and pH—were starting to eat away at the miles of trout water Mohn and Bugas triumphantly brought back to Richmond.

All this was coming together on the St. Marys. If wider recognition of the acidification of the precious trout-bearing Blue Ridge streams had a beneficial effect, it was that some of the traditional barriers between agencies, each of which has its own political limitations and institutional inertia, were quickly being eroded in the interests of confronting a common problem, a problem that, by the mid-1980s, had fish, forest, and wildlife specialists frightened. And that is a word many of them used— *frightened.* Federal people, state people, academics—they were worried. Too much was happening that they didn't understand.

The "web of life" wasn't supposed to be a metaphor in a biology textbook. It was supposed to be a fact in the field.

More than trout were on the line. Wherever they

looked close enough, and whatever their specialization was, field botanists and biologists saw ecosystems from microhabitats to regional plant communities changing. And although the changes were always complex and often subtle, and would take years to document and understand scientifically, it was clear in many instances that the net effect of the widespread unraveling of ecological webs was a decrease in species diversity and that polluted air and water were the most likely causes. Acidification was at the heart of the pollution. Effects had been documented for terrestrial and aquatic insects, fish and amphibians, freshwater mussels, waterfowl. The spruce and fir forests of the Southern Appalachians were already doomed. A poisoned environment was becoming, in its own short-term defense, a biologically simpler one, but one with fewer and fewer resources for adaptation and survival in the long run. And most botanical and zoological communities had yet to be studied.

On the way down the trail to the vehicles, the talk is fishing. Everyone stops at the big pools to watch briefly for trout before moving on. In the field, talk about rivers rarely flows into talk about politics, but that is where all rivers eventually go—to Richmond or Raleigh or Washington—where their fate is determined by people who often seem to know, or care, little about them. Logging, development, industrialization, resort commercialization of the landscape—for four centuries the Blue Ridge has been losing ground. The pleasure of field work buffers everyone from cynicism, but there is a feeling in the air that concern for these headwater streams and their wild trout is a last-ditch affair.


You can see the St. Marys watershed clearly as you approach it from the Shenandoah Valley. The river has cut a deep notch in the mountains, having found a weak seam in the sandstone and quartzite that forms the backbone of much of the western slope of the Blue Ridge in Virginia. Bare cliffs, bleached in the sun, tower over the river. The ridge behind the river to the northwest marks the divide between the watersheds of the Shenandoah River and the James River. The St. Marys is one of the headwaters of the James.

If the Ice Ages pushed the trout arctic waters had spawned into chilled temperate zone seas, and the retreat of the Wisconsin glaciation stranded them in mountain streams, where a hint of arctic cold remained, then the acid that rains down on the mountains is the beginning of the end of a memorable odyssey. The trout in the mountains have nowhere to go. Their rivers are the most remote, and beautiful places left in a world given over to clear-cuts and concrete. Who would have thought they would ever try to head downstream again, chemically panicked like fish in laboratory tanks by the drop in pH coming down the mountains?

As a river acidifies, the habitable world trout know fluctuates strangely. Eventually, that world shrinks and disappears. The diurnal and seasonal rhythms of aquatic insects change. Acid-stressed predators become prey. Acid-resistant prey find new niches and thrive in the altered environment. Relations among fish species rearrange themselves; patterns of coexistence and competition break down. The life of the river is changed at all levels. Chemistry drives biology. Forced out of normal patterns of behavior, individuals do not have time to adapt to all the changes. A dearth of individuals eventually leads to the death of species. Biological diversity decreases; the ecology of the river simplifies.

The physiological functioning of a trout is altered by increased acidity. Delicate gill membranes, where critical oxygen transfer must take place, clog with heavy metals leached from the soil by acid run-off. Metabolism is stressed, growth altered, slowed. Behavior changes: Feeding, predation, spawning are all affected. Immature

trout, like children, are more sensitive than adults to tox-
icity and to untoward changes in the conditions of life
around them. There are fewer parr, young of the year,
and alevin. Female trout produce fewer eggs. Fewer eggs
eye and begin to grow. More developing eggs deform and
die. Finally, some females fail to release eggs at all due to
serum calcium loss. Intermittent spawning failure in a
stressed environment leads to recruitment failure and cyclical population decline. Eventually, biological replica-
tion fails to keep up with decreased life spans. One
generation of wild trout becomes the last. The web
shreds.

The St. Marys comes alive on the third day of sampling. Bugas is shocking out deep pools, reaching with
the probe under ledgerock. Mohn nets beautiful streambred rainbows and brook trout as they show themselves;
he reaches after them like a shortstop stabbing a bad hop.
Mohn and Bugas work well together, and the appearance
of more fish enlivens the routine of collection. After the
first pass, one of the interns brings back a bucket of fish
to be measured and weighed. Price Smith works up nine
adult rainbows, eight adult brook trout, eight brook
trout fry. But there are no young rainbows. Two more
passes bring in more adult rainbows, adult and juvenile
brook trout, and a handful of fantail darters.

The adult specimens from this part of the river are
extraordinarily beautiful. There are brook trout over
nine inches, brilliant males, touched perfectly with color
like finely painted porcelain, and pale olive females, more
softly rendered impressions of the same idea. Some un-
nameable continuum of artfulness is defined by the form
and detail of these rainbow and brook trout, a field of
expression hard to render. The black and olive vermiculation on the backs of the brook trout becomes a fine black
spotting on the pale olive backs of the rainbows. The minute red, yellow, blue, and sometimes green spots on the
flank of the brook trout become dark oval blotches over a

rose stripe on the rainbows. The rainbows show this rose boldly on their gill covers and faintly in the tips of their finely spotted tails. The brook trout sign themselves with orange ventral and anal fins scored with a fine black line and tipped in ivory.

No wonder Eugene Surber was indignant at the "pale and colorless" hatchery trout he found struggling to survive in the river.

Everyone takes time to look over the fish before they are released, even though they have seen thousands of such trout through the years. Questions about the river start turning over again. The picture is richer, more complicated now. The growth rate for adults of both species looks good, but where are the young of the year rainbows? There were heavy snows and fast snowmelts last spring. Perhaps an acid pulse took out the year class. The brook trout seem to be doing well among the rainbows, which usually drive them out. Are the brookies moving downstream ahead of an acid buffer that hurts the rainbows more than them? Is their increased presence in the middle stretch of river a temporary resurgence before they, too, begin to feel more directly the increased acidity of the river? There are still no blacknose dace. And no one can remember fantails this far up river. Webb and Mohn see no end to the local effects on fish distribution that the change in pH can have on the river.

Dace finally show up in the next reach downstream, but the rainbows are gone again. They seem to occupy very little of the river now. Price Smith shocks out good numbers of brook trout, adults and young, as well as blacknose and rosyside dace, torrent suckers, pretty fantail darters, mottled sculpins, and a smallmouth bass. This enclave of diversity in the river is refreshing, if not reassuring. If there are still brown trout in the river, they are farther downstream.

A bunch of kids come along while Fish and Game is gathering its gear at the ford that marks the head of the last sampling reach. The kids are carrying trash bags and an odd assortment of tools—shovels, picks, mattocks, fire rakes. The Forest Service has hired them for the summer to police trails and break down overused campsites.

They watch with intent amazement as the last bucketful of fish is being measured, weighed, and logged. They know the trout and the bass, but they ask about the other kinds and how many are in the river. Each one of them looks in the holding bucket for a long time and nods approvingly at the biggest brook trout.

The oldest, unimpressed with the fish, looks over the tangle of electro-shocking gear with admiration.

"You zap 'em with these, doncha?"

They say they're from Sherando, a hamlet tucked in the mountains just over Kennedy Ridge. This is home for them, their backyard.

Larry Mohn makes a joke about them leaving the town unprotected. The kids laugh, a little embarrassed.

"Shoot," the big one says, shaking his head. "Sherando. Nobody thinks anybody's from there. It's like fifty people maybe."

Each one of them stops to peer in the fish bucket one more time. Then they troop up the trail, motley locals, like the brook trout.

Bugas draws final duty. He releases the last bucket of fish, redistributing them carefully, one by one, throughout the sampling reach. Barely a week into the interrupted nights of first fatherhood, he looks tired. He has been admiring the trout a little more than the others all week, quietly watching them hold in the current at his feet when he releases them, muttering to himself about how beautiful they are. Sentimental, perhaps, with a new baby at home.

At lunch one day there was talk about the way the Blue Ridge used to be—when undisturbed forests shaded the rivers and the air and rain were untainted.

"Trout must have been everywhere," someone mused.

"It would be nice to go back, just for a day, to see what it was like."

But there is no going back.

Bugas shuffles along knee-deep in water, the river streaming around him. He looks for the lies he would prefer if he were a trout—in a depression in a riffle, in front of a midstream boulder, beside an undercut ledge. All the places he casts to when he fishes. He puts a trout, scaled to the spot, in each good lie.

"Godspeed," he says, as he returns the last fish to the river.

# PERFECT COVER

Ten miles west of the cornfields and peach orchards that surround Gettysburg, Pennsylvania, the Blue Ridge modestly takes shape as South Mountain, a recumbent green ridge that gives the surrounding countryside, east and west, a marked horizon. Small streams flow to small towns that once saw what is called history come and go. From Oak Hill, you can see the bluish mountains in the distance beyond McPherson's barn, around which war flowed red one summer morning. I know for a fact that they still bale hay on McPherson's land in early July, but the land is not the same.

If you have never lingered to watch the sun set on these fields from which the Blue Ridge rises, you owe yourself a vigil. If you have spent the day around Little Round Top and Devils Den, you will have recognized the Catoctin greenstone, perfect for cover, behind which men fought for their lives for three days. You may remember reading how they named the stream that ran between them Bloody Run. You may imagine they thought of other streams when the fighting stopped at night, wished themselves elsewhere and the land at peace.

Afterward, if you have the heart for it, you can fish the East Branch of Antietam Creek above the old stone bridge east of Waynesboro in the twilight. Swallows and then bats lace the silver air with flight. In early summer this pretty river will be warm and low, but you may find a stocked rainbow holding at the head of the first deep riffle to distract you. The flash of pink and the pull of life at the end of the line may help take your mind off the awful silence that rises from the fields west of Gettysburg in the evening, a silence that stills the rustling corn stalks at dark and hushes the cries of the mallards that nest on the creek.

"The merely political aspect of the land is never very cheering," Thoreau once noted. There is enough history in the Blue Ridge to remind you that nature is always hostage to politics. Not all the history is as remote as the Civil War. One day a few years ago an F-14 came out of nowhere, flying terrain over South River in Shenandoah National Park. The stocky jet bottomed out a shallow dive a few hundred feet overhead, nose up, flaps spread like tail feathers, and dropped a sonic boom into the river. After the shock wore off I could not help but admire the thing. For the rest of the day I felt exposed and foolish to be fishing.

If the Blue Ridge has its gentle beauty, the resemblance of its terrain to the mountains of Southeast Asia was not lost on men who needed a place to practice for war. One of the U.S. Navy jets lost in the Vietnam war went down in the Blue Ridge, crashing near the Pinnacle in Shenandoah National Park between the Hughes River and Brokenback Run. And fifteen years later, when the woolly mountains on the evening news once again resembled the Blue Ridge, I was not entirely surprised to look up from a campsite on Basin Creek, in North Carolina, to see two fighters tracing the canopy of the cove ahead of their own shattering noise headed—the pilots might have been thinking—for Central America.

The jets don't come often to the Blue Ridge, but their appearance doesn't surprise me any more than finding a minié ball in an embankment along a road down which Jackson marched his men from the Valley. What does surprise me is the long record of how poorly the land is treated once the wars are over, as if in peacetime the political process can't take care of what has been protected at such great cost.

# VI

# STILL POOLS

By July the North Fork of the Moormans has turned an unappealing tea color. A good deal of the river has dried up, and what water is left barely flows. The whitewater is gone; riffles have shrunk and slowed, showing the holes where trout had been when the water was full of oxygen and the streambed covered with caddis cases and stoneflies. The river looks suffocated. Runs where spring currents had dug deep into bed and banks, bringing mayfly nymphs to waiting trout, are pockets of dead water. Pools sit clear and slack, their surfaces featureless except for wisps of eddies stirred by a barely audible flow that trickles from upstream. Trout fry swim circles in miniature algae-strewn oxbows. Cut off from what is left of the main river, the fry make easy prey for water snakes and raccoons.

Trout cruise aimlessly in the absence of the logic of

flowing water. All afternoon they can see me coming.
They feel my steps in the streambed from fifty yards
away and see the shadow of the leader rope thickly across
the bright brown and yellow stones over which they swim.
Even the small, delicate midges and the tiny ants I cast
into what is left of discernible feeding lanes seem to hit
the water like pebbles, bouncing the dusty-looking surfaces of pools and spooking fish. All day trout vanish
ahead of me upstream.

There is no blue in the mountains, which are covered
by a thick white haze, a woolly blanket of muggy heat
that the nights can't dissipate. A constant buzz of insects, rising and falling like a mantra, seems to make the
heat pulse warmer through the long afternoon. Not a
wisp remains of the cool air that played above the river
during spring. Where the river still drops over ledgerock
with any insistence, the diminutive rushing sound seems
to be absorbed by the dry woods.

I fish poorly all day, clattering up the river and hanging backcasts in trees. I move too quickly, trying to get
ahead of the insects that swarm about me. I can't establish a pace and a rhythm that works in the heat. There is
no way to get inside of the hot summer days in the mountains. I can't shake my awkwardness and aggravation.
For the first time since the slow-motion fishing of winter,
I feel out of synch with the year. Spring is gone, and I
no longer feel like a part of the river.

I was midway through a long, uninteresting pool
before I recognized it as the place where I caught the
first good trout of the year. Of course, it wasn't that pool
any longer. Water that had been at my thighs was at my
shins. The fallen sycamore that in February helped to
dam the back of the pool was now a foot out of the water.
The large boulder in the center of the pool, against which
trout had hid, was now baking in the sun. The wedge-
shape, mottled forms of suckers schooled in the tail of the
pool while sculpin vacuumed the vegetation on the tops of

submerged rocks. Brook trout fry hung at the margins just out of reach of crayfish, whose red-tipped claws gave them away.

I sat on the boulder over which I had cast in February to the first good trout of the year. A faint current gathered just in front of me—a narrow, rippling band of water that defined what was now the only good lie in the pool. Two dace worked the current side by side just ahead of where it pillowed against a rock and formed a small, midstream pocket. The graceful undulation of the black lateral bands of the dace were synchronized by the slight flow in which they held. They watched the current carefully, like trout, and rose to something in the film I couldn't see, making minuscule riseforms.

Then the dace were gone. Two trout took the lie, the smaller behind and to the side of the larger fish. The trout did not rise but fed sedately beneath the surface, more intent than the dace and less inclined to waste energy. Neither moved more than a fraction of an inch to the side to take whatever was in the water. Each trout held in the slight current with gentle tail movements, planing its fins as it gathered itself precisely every twenty seconds or so.

I backed off the boulder and crept to the rear of the pool. I came back to the trout at the end of a long, gossamer 8× tippet in the form of every tiny midge and nymph I had to offer. For the first time all day I fished well. I cast accurately and unobtrusively, drifting to them as a part of the river, a convincing accident of the current, I thought. I rested them between flies and never spooked them. Finally I seined barely visible mayfly nymphs out of the current with a hand net and matched them with an olive pheasant-tailed nymph, a slender, delicate tie I love to fish. I drifted the nymph to the trout near the bottom of the shallow flow and carefully lifted it into that small zone of water on which each trout was focused.

Nothing I could do moved those trout. Holding in the sluggish river, far more a part of the season than I was, they seemed, for all their visibility, as distant as winter trout.

I fished the mouth of the river at the reservoir when I got down the mountain, just to do some easy, unencumbered casting. I waded out on the cobbles that form a shallow tongue of land at the mouth of the river. I cast a sink-tip line with a heavy, slow rod I use for bass fishing. After seeing so many trout I could not catch, casting blind into stillwater was an unusual pleasure. Here, at least, I would not see all my mistakes darting away. The evening did not get much cooler than the day had been, but the long, slow casting helped me get a purchase on the stillness of summer and the change of season.

I waded as far out into the reservoir as I could, cool and buoyant chest-deep in the water, and cast right to left in a lengthening semicircle. The water was so still, emerging insects made what looked like small riseforms as they popped from beneath the surface. Bream cruised stumps in the shallows and were easy to catch, hooking themselves on a nymph their pouty mouths could barely get around. Their translucent colors were beautiful to see, glowing blue and green and yellow in my hand, but the zest of their deep circular charges through the water was lost in the heavy fly rod.

I cut the leader back and tied on a streamer too big for the bream to be able to fool with. I cast into the dark drop-off along the north bank of the reservoir, let it sink toward the ledge I knew was there, and stripped it lazily through the water. I caught some stocked fish—pale, poorly marked brook trout with stubby, ragged fins— trout that looked and acted as if they had been nurtured en masse in a concrete raceway on food pellets and then hauled in a truck and dumped in water the nature of which most would never survive long enough to understand. There was no river in these fish. You could feel

that in the purposeless way they thrashed at the end of
the line when hooked and you could see it in their form
and color, both of which had devolved into something unremarkable. They had not been honed from egg to fry to
adult by the chancy life in a river, knew nothing of either
predators or prey, and had no feel for the rhythm of the
year. I had no appetite for mushy, unmuscled fish flesh,
so I let them go.

Just before full dark I caught a smallmouth bass—a
sleek, green, ornately finned creature with a will as fine
as a wild trout's will, a river-formed fish that did not lose
its beauty or its fight in stillwater. I was pleased to catch
it. When I was a boy, I spent years of summer vacations
fishing with my father for smallmouth bass in a cold,
rocky Maine lake at just this time of year. The fishing
was as fine as the pursuit of trout in the Blue Ridge
mountains, full of clear sights and sounds and odors in a
world that seemed unspoiled. Released from the suburban
round of work and school, we dutifully fished the edges
of each day, dark to first light and dusk to dark, covering
coves and weed beds and the rip-rapped shorelines of forested islands with wordless casts from the bow and stern
of a wooden rowboat.

The fishing was exciting in the uneventful way of
such things, but what I remember most clearly was how
eagerly we adapted for two weeks each year to the odd
times of the day when the fish were active—waking up i
the dark and moving purposely through the predawn s
lence, which no one else was awake to hear and then co
ing off the dock in the late evening with the pleas
sensation that the day on shore had ended without u
did not think it at the time, but I had a sense that
were witnessing something, that something import
happened when you subordinated your own routines
the circuit of another creature's existence and looked, a
dawn and dusk, into the open secrets of an unfamiliar
place.

I released the smallmouth more reverently than I had released the hatchery trout. I had been still for a long time, and when I turned to wade back to shore in the near dark the sound startled two geese that honked in alarm and clambered gradually into the air. When they gained flight, their honking smoothed into distinct calls, a sustained all-is-well and a brief answering affirmation from out of the graying air. It wasn't until my truck roared to life and the headlights ruined the woods that I realized how late it was and had a pleasant feeling the day had ended without me.

Summer destroys the illusion I try to cultivate during winter and spring that there is an inexhaustible back-country in the Blue Ridge. Like most fishermen, I nurse a misanthropy that grows another ring when flocks of featherless bipeds take to what the Sunday supplements announce each June as "The Great Outdoors." The care-fully wrought mystique of the fly fisherman, an anachro-nism despite its current high-tech gloss, pales before this onslaught.

Frat boys from UVA pad around the lower Moor-mans in flip-flops and surfer jams, dates and Heinekens in hand. They look around vacantly, grinning at nothing n particular, talking some coded patter and sticking lose to silver BMWs and cream Saabs. The locals sit in eir pickups and pitted-out Galaxies draining cans of d Milwaukee, watching intently the perfect blondes the t boys parade by them. Young families steer them-ves through the beery, undefined tension in the air king for places to picnic.

Dirt bikers and ATV aficionados roar up and down e Rapidan fire road, lost in an unfathomable reverie of noise and blue smoke. Swimmers float around the plunge pools of Whiteoak Run. Tour buses from Washington, D.C., off-load squads of day hikers at overused trailheads in Shenandoah National Park. Pods of backpackers clink along trails, staring with hatred at their stiff boots and looking a little desperate under Himalayan loads of new gear. Troths are plighted with Krylon on granite and greenstone boulders. *Mike loves Tina.* Or did, one summer on the Rose. Bud cans thrive as if they had evolved in the Southern Appalachians. Everywhere a spoor of trash adds an industrial brightness to the understory. It is a strange migration.

North of Shenandoah National Park, the Blue Ridge is a thin ridge two thousand feet high, flanked by a hilly green country laid out in prosperous-looking horse and dairy farms separated by cornfields and orchards. As I drove north this July into northern Virginia and Maryland looking to escape the crowds and find new rivers to fish, I thought there must be a few remnant trout streams flowing through the corridors of hardwoods I could see back on those farms. I was tempted to stop and ask, but if I was a farmer I'd save those precious streams and their trout for my kids to fish.

I crossed the Potomac at Point of Rocks and stopped to watch fishermen in johnboats working their way along the small islands in that beautiful stretch of river. They had the right idea. July was for poking around the edges of big brown rivers, lazily zipping a crankbait at bass lairs. But I continued north into Maryland, keeping the Blue Ridge on my left, zigzagging on local roads that kept me as close to the long, low ridge as possible.

The Appalachian Trail hugged the Blue Ridge, but there was barely enough forested land for it to squeeze through. "Blue Ridge Acres" was, in various guises, sprouting up all over. Most of the northern Blue Ridge is destined for the housing developments, county malls, and industrial parks county supervisors everywhere insist on calling "growth." I quickly lost hope in finding native trout in increasingly unlikely terrain. The farther north I drove, the more unlikely the quest became, and I was tempted to continue on to Carlisle around which flowed the great limestone spring creeks of central Pennsylvania. But, true to my mission, I stopped at the northernmost point of the geographical Blue Ridge, not far from Lincoln Lanes, Mr. Ed's Elephant Museum, and the Gettysburg Game Farm, whose billboard boasted live monkeys and llamas.

Because I was on a symbolic search, I concocted a symbolic method. If beyond the elephants, monkeys, and llamas featured now in central Pennsylvania there was just one native trout left in the northern Blue Ridge, it would be holding in a small pool in the northernmost stream in the mountains. If I held to the strict definition of the Blue Ridge, that would be Carbaugh Run, which flowed from the north side of South Mountain through part of the Michaux State Forest. My map showed that a scant mile of the stream was protected as a special Natural Area, a good sign. Beyond the Natural Area, Carbaugh flowed through a golf course, presumably losing there whatever virtue it had to lose.

I badly wanted to cheat. Just ten miles beyond the range of what could be considered the Blue Ridge proper flowed one of the finest Pennsylvania spring creeks on which you could wish to float a dry fly. This sweet meadow stream was full of the descendants of Shasta River rainbow trout that would be sipping windblown ants and hoppers along its grassy banks, or tipping up to suck down tiny *Tricorythodes* or small *Baetis* from the river's glassy surface. I could close my eyes and see heart-stopping riseforms on Falling Spring Run. But the rules of questing are medieval, and the object of a quest cannot be changed to suit the terrain, or the fishing. So, Carbaugh Run it would be, upstream of the golf course.

In mid-July the patch of Michaux State Forest south of Route 30 is a brave affair as would-be forests go. A perpetual haze of brown dust hangs in the air, kicked up by the considerable traffic zooming around on its gravel

roads. The Appalachian Trail tries hard to find a dignified way through its burns and clear-cuts and generally
sorry state. Orange timber sale flags bloom everywhere,
helping the bull thistle and ironweed put some color into
the struggling woods. The remains of a few small streams
simmer in dusty riverbeds. It does not look like trout
country.

I spooked two furtive lovers in a Bonneville at the
trailhead into Carbaugh Run. Wildlife. Their angry surprise turned to astonishment when they saw me pull a
fishing rod from the truck. I think the sweaty red-faced
man wanted to shoot me, not for breaking up the rendez-
vous but for walking off confidently into the dry dusty
world around them with a *fishing* rod. I doubt if he noticed that it was a fly rod, which is just as well.

A jeep track quickly became a pleasant trail; scraggly
new growth was replaced by older trees. The small enclave became something like a forest—cooler, deeper,
darker than the surrounding woods—with an understory
that aspired beyond weeds. Moss-covered logs, shelf fungus, club moss, and a complex mix of plant life spoke well
for the Natural Area. It was, in fact, a colony of large
purple fringed orchids that led me to the stream.

Humble as it was, Carbaugh Run was all good signs.
It was cold and fast, full of small pools and cover, and
well shaded by hemlocks and some stunted rhododendron
rooted in its boggy banks. The stream was too overgrown
to fish, but as I walked along it for a quarter mile looking
for trout, I saw suckers, dace, and raccoon tracks. There
were nymphs in the river, though I couldn't tell what
they were. One or two stoneflies made their way into the
air as I moved along. I had no proof, but I decided there
were native trout in Carbaugh Run, upstream of the golf
course.

On my way back south I stopped at the Potomac
where it slices through the Blue Ridge downstream of
Harpers Ferry. I contented myself with wading through

the trash along the banks and hopping rocks out into that magnificent river. I spent an hour casting for small-mouth bass and catching chubs in the deep, green water. Brightly colored fleets of kayaks threaded their way through a few hundreds yards of whitewater that stretched, from bank to bank, across the river.

When I had my fill of casting into the big river, I drove on a few miles to Harpers Ferry. I made my way slowly through a throng of vacationers and climbed the stone steps to the upper town. From a churchyard there you can see the confluence of the Potomac and the Shenandoah rivers that Thomas Jefferson boasted was "one of the most stupendous scenes in nature" and itself "worth a voyage across the Atlantic." Perhaps Jefferson was exaggerating for his French readers, whose art and architecture he knew America could not, in the 1780s, compete with. He suggested throughout his *Notes on the State of Virginia* that the American landscape was a kind of art, and he implied that it should be preserved for the value of the thoughts and feelings that could be gained by looking on it.

People waited and jostled a bit for a brief view from the rock Jefferson had stood on.

This summer I doggedly returned to the mountains every few weeks, backpacking away from the crowds along Skyline Drive and the Blue Ridge Parkway, traveling slowly from watershed to watershed with a minimum of gear. I searched for a river worth fishing, a stream with headwater springs that hadn't failed or one in a watershed that was catching evening thundershowers with enough regularity to keep its currents flowing.

But river after river was a disappointment, each one a bleached watercourse nursing a ribbon of brown water that did not flow at all. Pools were stranded, connected only by an underground flow fed from the aquifer in the mountains. Here and there springs trickled a bit of cool water into the tepid streams. Days were scorching, and the muggy heat hung on doggedly after sunset. The cool curtain of air that made spring nights in the mountains so pleasurable never descended. The night heat broke a bit an hour before dawn, and the change in temperature and the slight breeze that stirred were usually enough to wake me. Most mornings I would break camp in the dark and move through the relative coolness of the early-morning hours to the next river.

Without rivers flowing through them, giving them a center and a direction, watersheds emptied of significance. Hiking up Big Run along a half mile of dry riverbed, I had an eerie sense of catastrophe. Not only was most of the river gone—I was used to dry riverbeds by then—but even the idea of a river seemed to lay dismantled in the heat. At one point I stood in the whitened riverbed and tried to visualize April flows washing white over the jumble of bleached sandstone and quartzite boulders, filling the dusty watercourse with blue water, but I couldn't imagine a river in the meaningless scree. Aquatic vegetation had died or disappeared into some imperceptible dormancy. The red oak, basswood, hemlocks, and sycamores that had sought out the once moist banks looked betrayed; their twisted roots gripped dry rock and crumbling soil.

The trout in Jeremys Run were bunched up uncharacteristically in what pools were left in the upper half of the river. Individualists forced to school, the trout looked more like captives than creatures of the river. The interesting behavior of a wild trout warily managing its fate in a fast-flowing stream was reduced to a group instinct to fretfully mill about a shrinking habitat. The year seemed stalled at high noon, and the trout were left exposed.

Below the falls halfway down from Elk Wallow, a thin spume of cascading whitewater gave the river a slight sound of life, and I made camp there. You could sit on the wet rocks where a few asters and Chinese day-flowers hung on in the heat and get a faint sense of late-spring coolness from the mist. The effect was purely local. The sound barely penetrated to the plateau on the south side of the river where good-sized hemlocks spaced them-selves out in an inviting campsite that, shaded by the evergreen canopy, at least looked cool. In spring this camp would be dominated by the sound of the river. As it was, you had to stop what you were doing—staking out the tent or hoisting a food bag into a tree—to pick up a hint of a stream not thirty feet away.

I had lost most of my desire to fish, but I did my best on what flowing water I could find. There was no chal-lenge to catching trout out of the pools. You could not help but spook the fish, but either out of stress or hun-ger, a few would still take any gnat or ant you put on the water. I left the crowded pools alone and moved along slowly in the heat, hunting for the best spots left in each reach of stream. If there were any good-size trout left in the river, I ought to be able to see where they would be.

As I fished along, all the life left in the watershed seemed driven out into the open. Common water snakes crawled all over the riverbed, their splotchy brown mark-ings looking enough like the copperhead's hourglasses to keep me a bit on edge. I flushed grouse all day, surprised each time they fluttered off at my approach. I watched a rat snake move through the canopy over the river, grace-fully carrying itself from tree to tree. Deer clung to the river, drifting in and out of view. Two does walked the riverbed ahead of me for awhile, browsing as they went. When they spied me over their shoulders, they quickened their pace a bit, but they would not desert the water.

In midafternoon, as I hid behind a broad hemlock to watch for trout, I saw a black bear walking downstream. I had never spotted a bear before it saw me, although I have had numerous glimpses of them disappearing—bear sightings are typically a blur. But this bear came down the opposite side of the stream unaware of my presence, flipping rocks and pawing for grubs and insects as it went. Perhaps it was distracted by the heat, or scarcity of food. The bear was large and rotund—a two hundred-fifty pounder, I would guess—but it looked like everything else I had seen that day on Jeremy's Run, a little desperate, a little put out by the extremes of the season.

When the bear was almost opposite me, I stepped from beside the hemlock. I thought it would look at me and stare—that is the image you have in your mind of a confrontation with a large wild animal. But I cannot say I saw the bear react to me at all. I did not even see it turn its head in my direction. It simply broke into the woods, spooked by my motion, and disappeared like all the others in that odd split second animals have access to but which the human eye cannot quite catch.

I hunted the river hard, but I found no decent trout. I found a few enticing spots and worked them carefully as the only possible reward for dog-day fishing, but no big brookie broke the heat or the annoying insect buzz that seemed to taunt me all day.

I hiked downstream after dinner, too restless to stay in camp, too bored to fish. I sat on a boulder and watched the river without much interest when I got tired of walking. I had an itch for a cigarette, though I haven't smoked in years. While I thought about the irrational pleasure of drawing on a Marlboro again, I saw a trout being pushed up out of the water at the back of the pool. Two or three times an eight-inch trout seemed to lift itself out of the water, arched on its side. The white of its belly caught my eye. Then the trout let itself back in the water and lunged awkwardly toward the head of the pool.

When the trout rose out of the water closer to me, I saw the head of a snake, its mouth clamped as far around the meaty part of the trout's tail as it could reach. Its lower jaw was unhinged to widen the gape of its mouth.

The snake was not large, two feet long perhaps, blotched reddish brown, like the water snakes I had seen all day, and white underneath. It had a green eye. Held out of the water, the trout had no leverage, but in the deeper water where the trout had dragged it, the snake seemed at a disadvantage.

They struggled in the pool for twenty minutes, thrashing in and out of the water in a strange, purposeful dance. The trout tried desperately to right itself into a swimming posture, but the snake kept the fish on its side, so that the weight of the trout would work against its powerful tail muscle. The snake kept in motion around the fish, keeping the centripetal effect of its writhing centered on its death grip. The trout's lunging attempts to swim grew weaker and weaker. When it could, the snake coiled itself under the fish and lifted it out of the water, weakening it until the trout's struggling was purely formal.

On my way back to camp, I found a dead luna moth on the trail. Even in death, the luna moth is beautiful, pale diaphanous green, shaped unlike any other winged creature to fit its place and purpose. The eyes on its wings looked like oriental symbols. I was glad to find it.

The night was miserably hot, and I lay awake for a long time on top of my sleeping bag. Once I started listening to the jet traffic bound in and out of Dulles, I could not shake the sound until I heard a bear approach. I heard it first at the tree in which my food was rigged about fifty feet away. Then I heard it pad toward the tent, and stop, and walk around it, and stop again. The bear made little noise, and its steps were like a man's except softer, and heavier. A rank odor drifted in with its tread.

Bears usually come and go if they do not find food about, but this bear stayed. It went back to the food tree and then came back to the tent and stopped and circled again. I thought it was making a connection between the smell of food in the tree and the strange, odd-smelling object in which I lay—or sat bolt upright in. I remember that I silently put on my boots as the bear beat its path between the tent and the food. There was no point in doing this, but I felt better when it was done.

Then I realized there was nothing else to do beyond listening to the emphatic pounding of my heart and clutching a flashlight—clichéd responses that didn't embarrass me in the least at the time. The bear settled into a routine—shifting around the tent, cruising the campsite, and keeping me on a fine nervous edge, giving me a brassy taste of the wild. I knew that black bear rarely harmed anyone. And I was afraid.

After an hour of this, I took a look at my watch and saw it was only a few minutes past midnight. It would be a long night. I heard a plane and wished I was on it, headed for Dulles and city lights. I wished I was talking to someone. I tried to see humor in the absurdity of lying in a tent with a thousandth of an inch of nylon between myself and a curious black bear while I listened to a jet plane overhead. When I travel by plane, there is always a moment when I look down at the earth and flight seems wild and unpredictable, and I wish I were back on the ground.

Determined to survive at all costs, I set myself for a long, vigilant watch and fell asleep before I heard the bear walk away.

By morning, the night fears had vanished, leaving an unearned trace of self-confidence in their wake. The bear became a satisfying memory. After breakfast, I packed out of the Jeremys Run watershed and descended the next ridge to Overall Run. Overall Run is a spectacular watercourse in spring. The upper river does not so much flow as fall off the mountains through a narrow, precipitous greenstone gorge that sends the river tumbling west toward the South Fork of the Shenandoah River. In summer, a faucet's worth of water drops silently over the

whitened lip at the top of the falls. I followed switchbacks down a steep descent through stunted pine and laurel. The gentler watershed below the gorge simmered in
the heat, and a thick haze obscured the Shenandoah Valley to the west.

Overall Run was closed to fishing, but I wanted to see
if there were trout below the falls. The thin white line of
water that slid down the greenstone rock face for a hundred feet gathered without much fanfare in a shallow
brown pool. The first two or three pools below the plunge
pool absorbed what little momentum the falls passed into
the gorge. Fifty yards downstream from the base of the
falls, the river was motionless.

The steeper headwater streams like Overall Run,
which see such extremes in flow from spring to summer,
are marginal habitat. But the Southern Appalachian
brook trout is a remarkably tenacious species. During
years of severe drought and equally damaging flash
floods in the early 1950s, the wild trout in the Blue Ridge
were nearly extirpated from many watersheds. As much
as 75 percent of some streams in Shenandoah National
Park were completely dry for extended periods. Temper-
atures as high as 82° were recorded in some pools, well
above the brook trout's tolerance. Natural predation sky-
rocketed. One biologist reported that some trout were so
enervated by stress that they could be picked up by hand.
Trout and other fish and aquatic insect populations were
reduced to their lowest recorded levels.

Beyond closing the Park streams to fishing, to at least
eliminate angling mortality, there was nothing to do except wait out the weather. When rainfall patterns returned to normal, the forested streams in the mountains
quickly re-established their viability as habitat, and wild
brook trout populations restored themselves, as they undoubtedly had done many times in the past. An attempt
in 1955 to aid the recovery by dumping stocked fingerlings in the rivers failed, but did no harm. Tens of thou-

sands of stocked fish were unable to survive flash floods caused by two hurricanes in August of 1955 that the wild trout withstood. This seemed to convince Shenandoah National Park fisheries managers, who oversee more native *Salvelinus fontinalis* habitat than anyone else in the southeast, that if the integrity of watersheds is protected, native brook trout can survive the worst conditions that naturally arise to challenge them.

But I saw no trout in the upper reaches of Overall Run this summer. I couldn't spook fish out of hiding: no dark shapes bolted from the shadows beside boulders or from under ledgerock outcrops when I wet-waded through the biggest, coolest pools. No trout materialized over sunlit patches of streambed waiting for insects. None cruised the dead water, gambling their slim reserves of energy on the chance of finding food in a still, unpromising environment. Few insects emerged from the river; little life stirred along its banks.

But trout survive summer.

At the end of August I essayed one last summer river after a week of rain had broken the prolonged heat. I walked along a trail that followed the broad, flat crest of a forested ridge for two miles. For a mile I roamed through pine and then, having come over a rise that set the trail on a gentle slope down into the watershed, relatively young oak and hickory. A steady morning breeze blew over the ridge from the southeast like an impossibly long sea breeze from the ocean hundreds of miles away. I thought of the Outer Banks and saw cold blue ocean water behind a broad white line of surf. Images of surf casting for blues in late November came to mind. The air almost felt crisp, and for an hour I felt fall lapping at the mountains.

I followed bear sign all the way to the river, fresh scuff marks too broad for deer in the brown pine needles that carpeted the trail and recently overturned rocks, their depressions still dark and damp. At the bottom of the last tight turn in the trail, a young black bear sent broken branches clattering to the ground as it hustled down a hemlock and ran away up the slope. A good summer for bear.

A hundred yards further on I came to a river deeply shadowed by greenstone outcrops. The late-August rain had settled the summer's dust and softened the light in the woods. Pools were full, and the river flowed quietly, having pulled itself together. I unshouldered my backpack as soon as I saw it, and reached for the rod and vest. The revived river had enlivened the trout, which must have had some rudimentary sense that they had made it through the gauntlet of the year. Trout held and hid in predictable places as the current ribboned around them.

# HABITAT

Sooner or later, most trout fishermen find themselves on a trout stream with a cant hook, wrecking bar, or hammer in hand instead of a fly rod. This year I found myself with a dozen anglers corralled by the Virginia Council of Trout Unlimited. We met on Crabtree Creek above the South Fork of the Tye River one Saturday morning and headed downstream carrying an odd assortment of tools and material. Since there is barely enough flow left to get in the way, August is the best month for stream improvement work.

Crabtree Creek is on the George Washington National Forest. Much of the wild trout water left in the Blue Ridge is on National Forest land—the George Washington and Jefferson in Virginia, the Pisgah and Nantahala in North Carolina, the Sumter in South Carolina, and the Chattahoochee in Georgia. Little wild trout habitat has survived on private land, which is rarely managed for wildlife, so every mile of trout water on public land is important.

We spend the day restoring a streambed scoured, straightened, and channelized by spring floods—a river that has lost its structure as a trout stream. Check dams are built at the heads of blown-out pools. Deflectors put curves back in the river. Riffles and pocket water are reconstructed stone by stone, boulder by boulder. Old hands build bulkheads; new hands men shovel and roll rocks. Hikers stop and stare. All the activity looks strange—grown men and women mucking around in a near-dry riverbed trying to put a trout stream back together.

If wild trout water wasn't so scarce, and getting more so each year, such efforts would be purely symbolic. Such work is a muscle-wrenching reminder that the civilized world has not been kind to trout habitat. If the world was still full of trout streams, you could let upper Crabtree Creek repair itself over time. Most fishermen would prefer that—there is something less than pristine about a trout stream lined with hog wire and fortified with log bulkheads. But if you do it right, the artificial improvements get the hydraulics of the stream working in favor of trout again, and the river reforms itself more quickly than otherwise would have been the case.

The Forest Service sponsors such cooperative efforts, which are good public relations. Prodded by the National Forest Management Act of 1976, and by increasing concern about the use of public lands, the Forest Service has been attempting to change its image and, to some extent, its practices. The 1976 law called attention to concepts like biodiversity, mandating that forest management practices "provide for diversity of plant and animal communities" and pursue goals that "recognize the interrelationships between and interdependence within the renewable resource." The law implied that the intangible pleasures many people seek in undisturbed forests are as valuable as board-feet of lumber. Although, in practice, the multiple use principle has made a Solomon's baby out of public lands, recent legislation seems to recognize the fundamental—and rather striking—difference between using a watershed with a chain saw and using it with a fly rod.

Although the Forest Service often manages forests with an eye toward protecting the wild trout resource, its appetite for clear-cutting and road building remains disturbing to those who value rivers as part of complex, land-related ecosystems, and who think of public lands as belonging to the public. The Forest Service has a long way to go to live up to its redefined mandate to "be a leader in assuring that the Nation maintains a natural resource conservation posture that will meet the requirements of our people in perpetuity."

In the meantime, trout fishermen will rebuild streams like Crabtree Creek stone by stone and take it as a hopeful sign when the redirected water starts digging out trout habitat in a few hundred yards of stream.

# VII

# THE HEART OF
# THE COUNTRY

*Eeseeoh,* the Cherokee called it, river of many cliffs.

The river sounds closer than it looks. Even thirteen hundred feet above it, the rumble of the big river comes distinctly to the ear. Perhaps the shape of the gorge through which the river flows for ten miles amplifies the impression of its power to the listener at Wisemans View. Or perhaps the humbling visual impact of the long sweep of the mile-wide gorge somehow sensitizes the ear to the untamed life of the wild river at the heart of the most rugged country left in the Blue Ridge. Or perhaps to a small-stream fisherman a big river always looks unmanageable and sounds deafening. Even from a quarter mile away.

I first saw the Linville River from Wisemans View several years ago one rainy May afternoon. The insistent sound of the river, which seemed to be both far away and

at my feet, played off the tricky perspective imposed by
the deeply veed gorge through which it flows, a gorge
notched perfectly in the earth as if from the blow of a
gargantuan ax. The throbbing bass of the river's deep
water and the treble of its whitewater came intact to Linville Mountain in the heart of the North Carolina high
country, a meaningful sound full of structure and direction that kept itself distinct from the dull, purposeless
drizzle of the rain.

From Wisemans View the river winds in and out of
sight from north to south, tracing the jagged seam where
the eastern and western sides of the gorge meet. The
abrupt cut of the interior slopes of the gorge are softened
in appearance by virgin coves of hemlock, pine, poplar,
oak, and other southern highland hardwoods. From a distance the dense canopy of these trees softens the steep
pitch of the gorge's defiles and hides the underlying difficulty of the terrain. In those places where even the en-
terprising growth of an undisturbed cove forest cannot
gain a purchase, a complex maze of bleached cliffs, ledges,
chimneys, and outcroppings of bedded quartzite, granite
schist, and gneiss reveal the complex, adamant structure
of the land through which the Linville River flows.

The sweeping profile of the gorge is dominated by
three somber, haunting mountains, each cut distinctly
two thousand feet into the eastern horizon above the
river. The names of the mountains have long been trans-
lated into the quaint language by means of which the
American landscape has been made safe for snapshots—
Sitting Bear, Hawksbill, Table Rock. But the ancient
guardians of the river maintain an impassive, indigenous
beauty, as if some vestigial intransigence was embedded
in the stony heart of mountains the Cherokee once wor-
shiped as gods.

In spring the river has the look of a big western river.
Even from the rim of the gorge, the boulders and ledgerock of the riverbed look large, as if the river met the eye
undiminished by the intervening space.

Through the first six miles of the gorge the river descends more than two hundred feet per mile, and that gradient shows as whitewater where the river plunges until it reaches a pool large enough to absorb the heavy flow and hold it. The flats and margins of those big pools will catch the hopeful eye of any fly fisherman, particularly if he imagines himself on the river in the evenings when trout should be stirring under emerging mayflys, or grabbing stoneflies as they make their way out of the river, or slashing into a caddis hatch. Where the pools give out, fast but fishable currents slip and eddy among a complex of enticing rock structure that speaks, at every ripple and slick, of big wild browns and rainbows.

Five miles from Wisemans View, at the head of the gorge, I saw where the river got its wild nature. Upstream of the gorge the Linville River wanders southwesterly for twenty miles along the western side of the Blue Ridge. The Blue Ridge plateau sends the small, undistinguished river south just past the town of Altamont, where it meanders through a narrow, low-lying gap in the mountains. Once east of the crest, the river comes out of one of its gentle bends to spill over a ledge of ancient cranberry gneiss, a twenty-foot drop into a broad pool that, without warning or obvious cause, narrows to a twisting chute of oddly eroded bedrock.

The Linville funnels into the corkscrew fracture, rages white, and then roars down into the chute of bedded Linville quartzite, twisting and turning through the opening into which it disappears. The once-placid river booms loudly here in what sounds like a continuous sequence of small explosions. The chute ends on a resistant ledge where the river emerges at a window through which it jumps free of a cliff face in a broad, thunderous waterfall.

By the look of it, this great trout river is born between that anomalous ledge of gneiss over which the river spills and the incessant thunder at the base of the falls. Nowhere does a river plunge with such bright promise out of the Blue Ridge into such promising country. Nowhere is the visual relationship between the mountains and one of its rivers so precipitously clear, or so beautiful. Nowhere in the Blue Ridge does the country open itself so dramatically as at the head of the Linville Gorge.

Below the falls the river collects itself in a rectangular plunge pool that doles water generously downstream into the gorge. Eight miles after leaving the gorge, the Linville sloughs into the deadwater impoundment known as Lake James, which gathers the mountain-driven waters of the upper Catawba River drainage into a tepid, uninspiring reservoir.

I knew nothing of the Linville River when I admired it from the crowded tourist vistas that rainy May afternoon, but I thought it was auspicious that here at the heart of the Blue Ridge was a wild, free-flowing river running through ten thousand acres of preserved wilderness, a stunning landscape hard of access and full of wildlife and rare flora sheltered by an unperturbed cove forest.

By the time I got to the head of the gorge, the rain had stopped and dusk was filling the gorge evenly. I walked down one of the well-worn tourist trails the Park Service maintains around the photogenic falls and watched the river pour through the window in the cliff.

As I watched the river, wondering if there were wild trout in it, I saw two fly fishermen working their way upstream. A hundred feet above the river I had a hawk's view of them. Each waded carefully along the edge of the high water, one on each side of the river. They moved slowly, fishing the edges of the main current thoroughly. Occasionally they would lift their lines off the water simultaneously and cast in unison. The slow, synchronized beats of the fly rods and the tight, graceful loops of line imposed a formality on the scene. I watched them until darkness fell. I did not see either one strike at a fish, but their presence, and the studied way they fished, gave me confidence in the river.

I didn't have time to fish the river that May, but I often thought about those two fly fishermen skillfully casting and wading patiently toward the enormous plunge pool below the falls. The falls were managed by the National Park Service, but the gorge was part of the Pisgah National Forest and had been managed as wilderness since 1951, making it one of the oldest wilderness areas in the eastern United States. The Linville didn't, I learned, have much of a reputation as a trout river, but once I had seen it, the tug of possibilities at the bottom of the gorge continued to work on me.

This September found me in a campsite off a Forest Service road on the east rim of the Linville Gorge, purging gear on the tailgate of the truck in the glare of a Coleman lantern. Because I am a fly fisherman who backpacks, rather than a backpacker who brings along a pack rod and a few flies for fun, logistical problems at a wilderness trailhead are thorny and profound.

Gear reveals character. The fisherman with too many doodads is as morally suspect as the fisherman who cannot match an odd hatch in the boondocks with a fly that works. When you have to pare down to what you will carry on your back over demanding terrain, you define your essential self. An extra quart of water or felt-soled wading boots? Another dehydrated Chicken Tetrazzini or the extra reel? A comfortable sleeping pad or a backup rod? Such choices reveal the true dimensions of one's soul.

I had planned to take a seven-day trek, hoping to be in the gorge long enough to get a meaningful feel for it, to have—I may as well admit it—a wilderness experience. But many a journey into the wilderness is threatened by backcountry regulations that coil and rattle menacingly when you walk into a permit office and probe the substance of the friendliness proffered there.

Camping in the gorge was limited to two consecutive

nights, just long enough to lose your road ding and back-woods nervousness, but not long enough to be able to meet the country on its own terms, and certainly not long enough to be thoughtfully affected by it.

The permit office is not the place to expound ideas on the potential relation of a man to a landscape he admires. Brief discussion, tentative argumentation, exploratory wheedling did not avail. Even a polite telephone call to HQ—during which I pleaded the case of a single, low-impact backpacker, who wouldn't build fire rings and burn wood and who had just driven 350 miles to get to know a river he had been thinking about for three years—was to no avail. I knew the Forest Service people had their hands full managing increasingly popular wilderness areas, and I gave up when I began to feel like part of the problem.

I did pick up one last bit of useful information at the permit office. Don't drink the water. Not even if you boil it. I had iodine tablets. No good. I had chlorine tablets. Ditto. Pollution from upstream on the civilized stretch of river. Development. Sewage treatment. Pesticides. There were also hundreds, maybe thousands of tires in the river, which laced it with whatever chemicals decomposing rubber gives off. Don't drink the water.

I knew what it meant for me. A quart of water weighs two pounds. A seven-day trek would have been impossible anyway. I didn't have the heart to ask how the fish were doing.

On my way back to my base camp I stopped at the falls. The river looked as good as I remembered it, but I was beginning to understand why the Linville, as beautiful as it was, wasn't celebrated in trout fishing literature. The people who came in droves to view the falls and the head of the gorge for a moment were seeing a mirage: a wild river that boiling wouldn't purify. Still, I wanted to fish it, and I couldn't believe there weren't large wild trout down in that spectacular gorge. In camp I sat down to a late dinner after I finished my preparations. When the night noises came on and the stars came out, I stopped worrying about water quality and put my faith in the river.

Hints of early fall were in the air the next morning when I descended into the gorge. In mid-September the weather in the mountains begins to swing through the wider latitudes it enjoys in Indian summer. During the night a cool breeze had drawn the late-summer haze out of the air. Morning light was clear. No motes of dust or pollen rose in the shafts of sunlight that poked through the canopy and pointed, here and there, to bright specks of red and yellow in the hardwoods. Occasional bursts of birdsong broke what would have been silence were it not for the creak of my pack and the *thuck* of my walking stick on the trail. Two fly rods in their cloth bags, carefully lashed to the packframe, stuck up over my shoulders like antennae.

The trail quickly left the chestnut and scrub oak of the ridge and entered dense forest. The steep slopes of the gorge had defeated the otherwise rapacious ambitions of centuries of southern lumbermen. Plumb-straight yellow poplars and massive eastern hemlocks grew from deep defiles. When the French botanist André Michaux explored around the gorge in the summer of 1794, he found a yellow poplar, *"un Tulipier,"* twenty-three feet in circumference. And, according to one backcountry ranger, there is a hemlock in the gorge four men holding their arms outstretched cannot reach around. Oaks, ash, maple, and hickory grow tall and heavy-limbed where the soil and exposure favored them. Some of these approach the now rare dimensions Gifford Pinchot described and photographed in his survey of these forests in the 1890s, just before the final assault on the South's virgin timber began. Mountain magnolias and laurel and the ever-present rhododendron spread like a second forest below the big trees.

Each turn of the trail compelled me to stop, though when I looked into the old-growth cove, I could feel my senses grappling with a maze of life I had not seen enough of to be able to bring into focus. Fires have been the principal enemy of these forests, but fire was a natural process that did not destroy the chemical and biological fabric of the forest. Fire rarely extirpates a native species. I had a sense, walking into the Linville Gorge, that everything was still there. After a while it was not the size of the trees that was most striking, but rather the completeness of life there—thick beds of moss on rotting logs where colorful coronas of shelf fungus also grew; lichens draped on tree branches; a colony of mushrooms growing in the shade of a poplar; the odd, white forms of Indian Pipe peeking like small periscopes out of the leaf litter. The closer I looked, the more order I saw in the wildness of the forest. Everywhere, death was host to life, and life was so various no space or resource from the forest floor to the canopy went unused.

The trail to the river was wide and well worn. For a mile it curved and descended gently along a sizable creek I could hear but not see. I thought of trout fry growing unseen under broad-fingered fans of rhododendron leaves. There were well-used campsites along the way, perched just off the trail, outposts of some strange occupation of the woods. Oversize stone fire rings filled with half-burned tree limbs and stumps, beaten undergrowth, ax-scarred trees, eroded paths, and trash took the edge off my expectations.

A half mile above the river, the trail began to switchback steeply down into the rocky heart of the gorge, the rough seam of jumbled bedrock I had seen from the rim. The sound of the river came up to meet me, an insistent, unspoiled voice. The slopes of the cove pinched together just above the river, and the creek finally broke into view, cascading in white ribbons over a wide brow of moss-covered rock pitched too steeply to allow the creek to serve as a spawning tributary. The trail threaded the notch in the cliff through which the creek tumbled and dead-ended at a large, emerald pool that looked as if it might have been formed by the imagination of a trout fisherman.

The river was wild. It looked, in fact, as if it had not yet come to terms with its landscape, as if after however many thousands of years it had flowed in that place neither the gorge nor the river had ceded its individual nature to their shared circumstances. The river looked like a violent seam in the landscape. Wildlife, of course, is essential to wilderness, but the impression of wilderness is deepened where it is underwritten by signs of inanimate struggle so intense and subtle it tears the veil and affords a glimpse of otherworldly forces in play—a storm surf pounding a barrier island, a blizzard whiting out a mountain pass, or a river crashing through basement rock with a logic as yet unresolved by time.

The river did not so much have a bed as a gauntlet to run, a large, disordered field of room-size boulders and slabs of bedrock fractured out of the base of the gorge. The image of the gorge as having been formed by the blow of an ax was accentuated at the splintered riverside. Upstream from the emerald pool, the inner gorge looked as if it had been split and opened by some force other than the river. The bedding planes of the bedrock still in place tilted sharply up from the east to the west bank of the river. Gray and white striations in the sheer cliffs along the banks pointed diagonally across the river. The break in the diagonal through which the river ran was still so sharply defined that the separation did not look like the product of erosion. The east bank of the river looked as if it had been wrenched up and away from the west bank, leaving many once-connected fragments pointing at one another along the angle of the original diagonal.

The emerald pool was in the middle of a pronounced bend in the river, and perhaps the dramatic look of the landscape was only a product of the upturned strata at that bend in the river. Whatever forces formed the river there, they were still wildly at work. Downstream of the pool the river completed its turn in a steep descent through water that looked less accessible at the bottom of the gorge than it had on the rim.

The bottom of the gorge was barely wider than the river at that point, and so I backtracked to the plateau above. I left the trail reluctantly at a well-marked spot and made my way slowly into the cove, trying to stick to level, open ground. When I lost sight of the trail, I felt a subtle umbilical snap and felt, too, the appeal of camping beside the well-worn path.

However tame and tainted wilderness may now seem, the first step off a trail is still a step over a noticeable threshold. On the trail you pass by the forest; the trail frames and distances it. Beyond the established way, a dark tangle comes to meet you at every step. Far enough into the undifferentiated woods, and the mind begins to think, irrationally, it might be anywhere, that you are lost. Steps only seem to fall in a straight line. Actually, they follow the hidden bias of the terrain and your own pattern of avoidance: You step over a log or around a tree, and you never quite recover your intended course. Your way is deflected by obstacles and directed by forest fears—snakes under logs, bear in rhododendron thickets, falls on rocky slopes. Your thoughts stretch, taut with unrealistic apprehensions, back to the trail you shunned as tame.

I made camp a half mile into the woods, far enough to feel respectably beyond the pale. A solo camp is a pleasant constant: a one-man bivouac tent pitched on a thick bed of pine needles under a rhododendron, which serves admirably as an extra tent fly; one-burner stove and kitchen kit on a nearby stump; food hanging in a bear tree thirty yards away; site for a latrine staked out; pack leaning against a tree with essentials at the ready, canteens hung above it. The fly rods lean against a nearby tree; vest, waders, and boots hang on a branch.

In a remarkably short period of time I will wear a network of trails into the area and the oddities around the site which at first seemed intimidating—dark boulders leaning together to form a kind of cave, an enormous dead hemlock, a persistent rustling on the slope above—will become familiar and, finally, mundane. In a half day they will be welcome signs of home, and after a few trips back and forth to the river, the walk through the woods to camp will lose its fretful edge.

I fished the big river hard for two days. There is an old saw that circulates freely through fly fishing books that a small-stream fly fisherman can fish a large river successfully by breaking the river down into its parts and fishing bits of it as if they were the small streams he was used to. A big river is more than the sum of its parts, however, and the thick green currents that swirled around the boulders and disappeared into the pools of the Linville didn't break down into anything I recognized. But the river was as compelling as it was unfamiliar, and like all rivers, it imposed a discipline.

I gave up the delicate nine-foot three weight I prefer to cast for a stout eight-foot five weight, and gave up turle knots and dry flies for improved clinch knots and streamers. I cut back my leaders until they were short and stout enough to get big flies deep. I cinched my chest waders tight and waded into the dark water feeling my buoyant self almost lift off the riverbottom with the effort of casting. I enjoyed the combative feel of the fast water and took pleasure in the physical effort the river demanded. It was full of edges and eddies, depth and rocky cover. The streamside terrain forced me back and forth across the river. I perched gingerly on tilted slabs of bedrock and clambered along outcrops that overlooked the best water.

All day, I pulled offerings from the suede fly book where I keep the large flies my western friends send me—as if to say "Find a river in your southern mountains where you can fish *these!*" I thought I had and so fished

beautifully tied stoneflies, sculpins, and streamers wherever they might turn a trout. I tried to remember what I
had read about nymphing big water, but the Linville refused to take hold. I slowed my casting motion to accom-
modate a heavy, weight-forward line with a sinking tip.
But the deeper I got into the river, the more I felt my
limitations.

That first day I fished upstream under the shadow of
Hawksbill Mountain. The sun beat down between thun-
derheads that sailed slowly overhead all day. When I
stopped to sun myself on a rock, content as a lizard, hum-
mingbirds flitted among half-withered cardinal flowers
and bright-orange jewelweed that laced the edge of the
river with late-season color.

Above the spectacular bend in the river, the gradient
eased and the Linville became more prosaic. I went back
to fishing small nymphs on a long, light tippet. Although
I caught smallmouth bass and chubs and warpaint shin-
ers, the river seemed emptier than before. I saw no trout
rising, or holding, or even darting off at my approach.
September is not the time for prolific hatches, but there
seemed to be fewer insects about than there should have
been. In fact, it was easy to notice things on the river
because so little was happening. Occasionally a pale mayfly would come off the river, an olive perhaps. I found a
few stonefly shucks on boulders and dead mayfly nymphs
stranded in dried-up pools. In places, dispirited shallows
were ringed with a brown and white scum. I walked a
length of river deliberately trying to spook fish, but saw
nothing. There were dragonflies about, and bats toward
evening, and a few kingfishers flying reconnaissance with
strong, steady wing beats and their eyes cocked, like
mine, on the river.

The next day I fished downstream toward Table Rock.
It was overcast, cool and dark all day, and I thought this
might make the trout less shy of the surface of the river.
I caught a half-dozen hatchery browns for my efforts,

eight- to ten-inch fish that took my Hares Ear without
reservation and fought like chubs.

By noon the rim of the gorge was lost in clouds. By
late afternoon, when I had fished and climbed my way
back to the emerald pool, a light mist hung from the
cloud cover into the evergreen slopes. The mist softened
the violent look of the gorge and the day's intermittent
rain had turned the whitish rocks of the riverbed an appealing gray. Muffled thunder rolled downstream.

The river was rising and turning murky. I walked a
log back to the side on which I was camped and waited
out a brief downpour under an overhanging cliff alongside the emerald pool. The pool was now a dark, impenetrable green, faster in the throat and ruffled in the tail
because of the rising water. I had fished it the previous
afternoon with no success.

Sheltered under the cliff, I watched the river rise and
the pool darken and quicken with new currents. Water
funneled off the tilted slabs of ledgerock at the head of
the pool and rain riffled its surface gray.

When the rain eased, I fished the fan of current at
the throat of the pool, as I had the previous afternoon,
and hooked a good brown trout where one should have
been all along. I thought of the large brown trout in the
Smith River, in Virginia, which only seemed to come out
of hiding in high, roily water.

I had a hard time finding a place to land the fish along
the steep-sided pool, but when I did I was pleased with
what I saw—a sixteen-inch trout. It was raining hard
again when I knelt over the fish to release it, but I looked
at it closely. The trout had good color and markings, but
it was not a wild trout. It must have been in a river for a
few years, but its fins and tail still showed hatchery wear,
and the brown and red spots on its side were blurred
where they should have been finely drawn. Given time, it
would look more like a wild fish, but it had not been born
in the river.

The next morning I broke camp in a downpour and hiked out of the gorge, content to comply with the Forest Service's regulations.

Wilderness is, of course, long gone. True wilderness, "bigger and older than any recorded document," as Faulkner wrote of it in "The Bear," will never be revisited. Now it takes a recorded document—a federal law, in fact—to make a wilderness *area*. This is an appropriate, perhaps even a useful irony for a culture that seems unable to fully commit itself to preserving a few vestiges of its natural origins—the mountains, forests, and wild rivers from which an important part of its character sprang.

The language of the Wilderness Act of 1964 aspires to literature. The bureaucratic restraint and legalistic precision with which the law is phrased enhance the seriousness of its purpose and the beauty of its ideas:

In order to assure that an increasing population, accompanied by expanding settlement and growing mechanization, does not occupy and modify all areas within the United States and its possessions, leaving no lands designated for preservation and protection in their natural condition, it is hereby declared to be the policy of the Congress to secure for the American people of present and future generations the benefits of an enduring resource of wilderness.

According to this law,

a wilderness, in contrast with those areas where man and his own works dominate the landscape, is hereby recognized as an area where the earth and its community of life are untrammeled by man, where man himself is a visitor who does not remain. . . . an area of

undeveloped Federal land retaining its primeval character and influence . . . and which generally appears
to have been affected primarily by the forces of nature, with the imprint of man's work substantially un-
noticeable.

The 1964 law established the current National Wilderness Preservation System "for the permanent good of
the whole people." This law was also a promising act of
generosity toward the land and living resources that had
underwritten this country's prosperity for centuries and
that helped shape its consciousness and imagination. If,
as Frederick Jackson Turner wrote in the *Atlantic
Monthly* in 1896, "the very fact of wilderness appealed to
men as a fair, blank page on which to write a new chapter
in the story of man's struggle for a higher type of society," the Wilderness Act was an attempt to save a few
small, scattered fragments of that page. The law is a
rather noble expression of a mature culture's interest in
and reverence for its natural past. Passing such a law
was not easy.

Even a century and a half ago, when there was con-
siderably more potential wilderness left in the United
States than there is now, Henry David Thoreau noted
that it was "difficult to conceive of a region uninhabited
by man," free from his "presence and influence." The
"fresh and natural surface of the planet Earth, as it was
made for ever and ever" was, Thoreau knew, more a part
of myth than history. The 1964 Wilderness Act set out
some reasonable guidelines, but it did not solve the problem of where, in the middle of the twentieth century, wilderness was to be had—or *if* it was to be had outside of
Alaska and a few regions in the West. Such as they are,
places like the Linville Gorge do not constitute wilderness
in the sense that they measure up to an ideal derived
from an irrecoverable past, but only in the sense that
they embody a certain character of landscape and quality

of natural life that links each place to its pre-human past in meaningful ways.

I stayed in a pleasant motel in Linville Falls for two days, waiting for the rain to stop, enjoying a bed and a shower and home-cooked meals. I let my wilderness experience go. I went to the falls to watch the river, which was chocolate colored, full of mud and debris. All that egg-smothering silt helped explain why naturally reproducing trout were not abundant in the river. I made some phone calls to Forest Service and state Fish and Game people.

The state classified the river as a "low quality" trout stream, one that needed to be stocked regularly to make it a "sport fishery." They backpack fingerling brown trout in cans down to the river each spring. Everyone I spoke to agreed that there were siltation and water quality problems, but no one was aware of any attempt to study those problems or do anything about them. One thought the river a potentially excellent wild trout fishery; others saw little potential beyond the few large holdover brown trout that were caught each season. The structure of the river, its temperature profile, and its pH were all good for trout, but it was not especially productive of fish or aquatic insects. I got contradictory information about whether there were any wild trout in the river. It seemed unlikely, and most people I talked to were surprised at my interest.

So the Linville was an awkward case, a wilderness river in name but not a wild trout river—good to photograph but not to drink or fish. The word *wilderness* derives from the word *wildeor,* Old English for "wild animal." A wilderness, I thought, should be inhabited by its native species. How long had it been since brook trout spawned there? There should be stream-born native trout in the wild river at the heart of the Blue Ridge.

I renewed my permit and backpacked down to Conley Cove for two more nights on the river. The rain had broken the last few strands of summer, and I hiked a cool fall morning through the cove, in which I saw hints of yellow in the poplars and red in the dogwoods. Wildflowers waned along the trail, foxglove and harebell and others I didn't know. I made the river in an hour.

Conley Cove is an abused place. Enormous sites where dozens of people could camp have been established where the trail meets the river. A dead rattlesnake rotted in a big stone fire ring, its head blown off. I hiked downriver until I found a place I liked, a small grove of rhododendrons on a terrace overlooking the river.

When the river settled down I fished it, but not with the same intensity as before. I wanted to enjoy the Linville for what it was, a free-flowing waterway that had survived far longer than most rivers in the country. A turn-of-the-century map of potential water power in North Carolina shows thirteen possible hydropower sites in the gorge, thirteen red hatch marks across the blue line of the river. The accompanying report notes that "the power at this place is entirely undeveloped," but sadly admits that building factories in the gorge "would be entirely impractical." The report entertained the possibility of building a pipeline in the gorge to convey its water power downstream, so that the value of the place would not go to waste. Although silty and polluted, I knew the Linville was lucky to be flowing at all.

I spent two days fishing and exploring, taking the river and its country on their own terms. Good-size smallmouth bass took my nymphs and streamers as I worked my way downstream into the less frequently used part of the gorge. When I tired of fishing, I bushwacked up dark cul-de-sac coves where the dense life of hemlocks and rhododendrons gave way to magnificent cliffs that had lost none of their ruggedness—or their dark, brooding character—because of man's presence in the gorge.

I once attended a forum at the University of Virginia's Law School on National Forest policy. The conference was informative—a predictable mix of unresolved controversy—but what sticks in my memory is an impromptu debate between the manager of a small-scale timber company and a professional wilderness advocate. The logger made his pitch for subsidized timber cutting, explaining himself in rational social and economic terms. But as he explained his position, he worked his anger up about those people who were arguing for non-utilitarian uses of public lands. He would not be put out of business, he concluded, so that someone could go have one of these wilderness experiences he kept hearing about. And what exactly, he angrily challenged his opponent, *was* a wilderness experience? He had spent a lifetime in the woods and hadn't had one. His bluster drew some laughs.

The wilderness advocate, a well-known lawyer and administrator, undoubtedly knew the high road to take in response but wisely declined to start preaching. What was there to say in that situation that would have bridged, to the logger's satisfaction, the gulf between the economic and non-economic values that separate the timber man and the naturalist? That, as Thoreau wrote and Aldo Leopold repeated, wilderness was "the raw material of all our civilization?" That man should leave himself the opportunity of looking back on the stuff out which his culture—his religion and art, his wealth and political institutions—had been made? Such answers assume what they set out to prove. If you are not drawn toward and moved by wilderness—the old dark idea of it and the now pale fact of it—it has no demonstrable value that would parry the logger's angry derision.

But enough has been written about wilderness and the experience of wilderness to verify the presence of a back-country in the human spirit toward which some men and women at times aspire, a trace topography of origins, of health and primitiveness, of danger and magic, and of very fundamental kinds of solace and comprehension. There once *was* wilderness, and human culture, which was predicated on successfully overcoming it, seems neither capable nor desirous of forgetting it completely. The logger was right: the experience is difficult to share and is not completely explicable. But so are many things worth having, and keeping.

We will never again sense civilization as a clearing in a forest, as a tentative opening in wildly enclosed ground. But that is where we started. During the course of American history, the relationship between civilization and wilderness was reversed for the last time. The early European explorers of the New World often wrote about a sense of being surrounded by wilderness. They tread self-consciously within an unconquered otherness and keenly felt their subordination—as men, as a species—to an overarching natural world which clearly had no stake in their fate, or being. They moved through a world that was not theirs.

Now nature is surrounded. There is no place left where man can experience his proper relation to the world within which his character and capacities evolved. What wilderness remains has, at best, a kind of museum status. We can never return to the wilderness, or ever know what it meant to walk within it, compelled by curiosity and ambition even as our steps were slowed by fear. What wilderness remains is a small forest in a great, insatiable clearing. It does not seem unreasonable to want to save what little is left.

The night before I left the gorge, I waded out into the middle of the Linville to watch the evening. The woods were dark, but there was light around the river, which was silver, and a pale blue sky overhead. To the east, high above the opposite bank, broad cliffs glowed gold with sunlight. Something flew downriver in the dark, twilit air, and when it rose into the light at the top of the gorge, I saw its long blue wings and its tucked neck and I knew it was a heron. It flew along the plane of receding daylight, dipping down into the darkness and rising back into view. I watched it until it flew out of sight.

The Cherokee named the highest mountain in the Blue Ridge after the animal it most resembled. The bare, cragged peak was Tanawha, Fabulous Hawk. The name recognized, as many Cherokee names do, the mutuality of being shared by animals and things, as well as the visible embodiment of spirit in land. A perched hawk is as still as stone. A mountain has the vantage of a hawk. A raptor's head and a quartzite scarp might share the same form. Understanding such relations was, the Cherokee thought, an important part of the spiritual business of life. Spirit included but was not coextensive with human being. A man who could hunt like a hawk was a better hunter than the man who did not study the spirit and practice of hawks. He was of more use to himself, his family, and his culture because his imagination ranged beyond his own identity, like a hawk hunting. So the highest mountain, beaked-shaped and poised over all, was named Tanawha, Fabulous Hawk. The idea is neither primitive nor picturesque.

Then the name was changed. The hawk flew. That was history.

The early white settlers, who wanted not only to own the land but to impose their image on a landscape they intended to alter radically in their own behalf, renamed the hawklike mountain Grandfather Mountain. This, too, was a spiritual gesture, biblical in fact, but it reduced the spirit of the land to the narrow scope of some men's sense of their own history and destiny. And their history had not completely prepared them to appreciate and understand the value of what their destiny had brought them to. They thought, as some of their descendants continue to think, that they had inherited the land—that was the implied myth created by the change in the name of the mountain—and so could reduce their new world's spiritual value to its cash value until they could plausibly deny that the land had ever meant more than the money for which it, or its bounty, could be exchanged. When they had achieved that, they could easily ridicule any man, woman, or child who thought they saw a hawk in the mountain and who suggested there was a spirit in the land worth not selling.

The Linville River, which once flowed from the slopes of Tanawha, now flows from Grandfather Mountain.

The heron was gone, and the cliffs glowed red. They reminded me of the greenstone cliffs on the top of Pasture Fence Mountain above the North Fork of the Moormans River. But the scene was larger here, and more deeply drawn. The river and the gorge and the light on the Cherokee cliffs presented a wilder image. I felt more alone in the wilder place, and more at home. For a few uncanny moments I felt lost and content, as if I were within a wilderness, a stranger in a familiar place. Then the shadow cast by the west rim of the gorge crept up the cliffs, turning them gray.

I waded back to shore filled. The sound of the river. The silver sky. The wind. The heron somewhere. The changing cliffs. Forest sounds rose around me as I walked back to camp. Night came through the woods. Camp was dark, but I recognized the odd shape of the tent. Landscape untrammeled by man. A cold wind blew downriver and spilled by me. A branch snapped. I hadn't shivered so since March. I felt smaller, more humane. I lit a fire.

# WATERSHEDS

The Cherokee called the Blue Ridge "the unending mountains." Looking out from the Pinnacles, northeast of Asheville, you can see how they got that name. All you can see, in fact, is an ocean of blue, forested mountains: the fir-darkened slopes of the Black Mountains to the north, Mount Mitchell across the head of the South Toe River watershed to the west, the Craggies beyond that. The Blue Ridge spreads itself as far as you can see to the north, south, and east. Each ridge and cove has a creek, or a stream, or a river running through it.

Much of the best land left in the Blue Ridge is in the hands of the National Forest Service, whose plans for the Southern Appalachians are disturbing. According to the Wilderness Society, logging in the Southern Appalachians will double by 1995 and increase by more than 350 percent by 2030. The Forest Service plans to build 3,300 miles of new, permanent logging roads, bringing the average road density on the southern forests to two miles of road for each square mile of land. These plans for the forests in the southeast mirror the Forest Service plans for the entire country.

Almost a century after the first National Forest Commission reported, in 1897, "on the inauguration of a rational forest policy for the forested lands of the United States," virulent, sometimes irrational debate on what constitutes the best use of public lands continues. Since its inception, the Forest Service has built 340,000 miles of logging roads, eight times the mileage of the interstate highway system. It has clear-cut most of the public's forests at one time or another and proposed during the

1980s to double its annual timber cuts and build 580,000 more miles of roads on which to haul out that timber. This is often done at the expense of the taxpayer, who is routinely asked to subsidize the timber industry's operations on public lands.

I have learned much from and admire the hard work of the Forest Service people I have met in the field, but I have not yet found one who can explain to me how the policies under which they are forced to do their forestry "meet the needs of the American people." Some get angry when I ask; some are embarrassed.

Each individual wilderness bill passed by Congress, which adds a specific area to the National Wilderness Preservation System, contained a Trojan horse, its so-called sufficiency and release language. The 1984 bills that created new wilderness areas and wilderness study areas in many states also released the remaining roadless areas for Forest Service "management activities," most notably road building and logging. This legislative compromise, which was necessary to pass the wilderness bills against bitter opposition, served to put at risk as potential wilderness most of the remaining land under Forest Service jurisdiction. The release language stipulates that the Forest Service is not required to protect the wilderness qualities of the released acreage—which was in every case far more than the acreage set aside as wilderness.

For example, although the Virginia Wilderness Act of 1984 created 56,000 acres of wilderness, it simultaneously released back to the Forest Service for multiple use management 157,000 acres of land that had been proposed for wilderness study. Speaking in support of the compromised legislation, Virginia's Senator John Warner seemed pleased to note that "we are thus returning to multiple use roughly three times the amount of land being placed in wilderness." It was only this kind of trade-off, and not legislative dedication to the common good, that enabled the wilderness bills of the 1980s to be passed against the strenuous opposition of special interests like the timber and mining industries, which have historically been inclined to look upon public resources as private inventory.

A cynic might interpret the Forest Service's ambitious road-building and timbering plans as its way of permanently ensuring that no more public land will be preserved in a relatively untouched state, even though it has become clear that the amount of wilderness we now have is inadequate. Wilderness areas are already so overused that, unless more land is set aside for such use, the ideals of the 1964 Wilderness Act will go unrealized forever.

# VIII

# AUTUMN BROWN
# ON THE ROSE

I doubt it will happen again. But every autumn I fish a certain stretch of the Rose River very carefully. Just to make sure.

After two years the picture in my mind is clearer than my effusive field notes or the oddly restrained narrative in my journal. Like most fishing stories, this one is simple enough, as much a matter of image as event.

A small Adams disappears in the middle of a pool. No splash. No orange flash of autumn brook trout. Just a tiny bubble, which replaces the fly, and a slowly expanding riseform. I set the hook by reflex against the angle of a line that is already suspiciously tight to the river. The dark bulge which replaced the fly quickly becomes a weight at the end of the line.

I remember the unusually heavy surges of the fish when I tried to set the hook. I thought I could feel the long, light tippet stretch, as if it were tied to something I could not move. I knew I wasn't snagged. Rock doesn't strain upstream, strumming the line against the current. And a sunken tree limb, though it will pulse in a lifelike way when hooked, doesn't mill sullenly in tight half circles at the bottom of a pool. I thought I could feel something shaking its head slowly from side to side, as if saying no.

In retrospect, that first instant seems full of details and decisions. I remember how the rod bowed parabolic each time I tried to set the hook. I remember sensing the weight of the invisible fish digging deep into the butt section of the fly rod. I remember tightening my grip on the cork and feeling a slight strain creep up my forearm.

The subtle disappearance of the fly, the extreme arc of the rod, the sullen, determined weight I could feel in my hand all registered together. As I got tight to the fish, I stepped up to the back of the pool and stood in the narrow channel that was the trout's only way downstream.

My move to block the channel was instinctive, though the instinct was learned. I knew not to give a large trout the river behind me.

One rainy spring I lost the two biggest brook trout I have hooked in the mountains when I let them get downstream of me. The first grabbed a bushy dry fly the current led under a log that arched over the back of a deep run. I had no choice but to play the fish on a short line at my feet. While I tried to keep the trout out of the tangle of branches from which it had emerged, it got into the fast water to one side of me and jumped past me over the ledge below which I was standing.

A week or two later another big brook trout passed me, this time in pocket water. This fish never showed, except as a tactic that worked. The trout sucked in a nymph in front of a boulder upstream of me. By the feel of it, the trout was large for the water, which was still running high, and I was still green. After an upstream surge the fish turned, putting slack between us. By the time I got the line tended, the trout was twenty yards downstream of me, winding its way among undercut boulders through which it neatly threaded a leader that came pinging back in my face when I tried to clamp down on its modest run.

I can still see both fish as clearly as if I had photos of them on the wall—one flashing away in the air, flanks bright with color against a background of cold spring whitewater—a fly hung in the roof of its mouth, a tippet draped over its back—and the other invisible except as a tight, sharply angled line cutting through the water downstream toward the freedom of a broad riffle.

Those two large brookies, far better fish than I was fisherman, seemed to take the fishing hopes of the young year with them. For a month I pored over the water where I lost them and lost the best part of the spring fishing trying to hook them again. But I never found them. Even in my mind I can't hold them upstream of me. They are always over my shoulder, going away with the river.

So when I felt the big trout in the Rose turn at the end of its first upstream run, I stepped into the narrow channel of fast water at the back of the pool and took the river away from it.

I don't know how I knew it was a brown, but I remember I wasn't surprised when, after its first run upstream to the head of the pool, it came back to midpool and showed itself, an angry yellow arc in the olive water. It *was* shaking its head. The small gray fly hung in a corner of the trout's mouth, where it lodged when the fish rose and turned to take it. I watched the trout's eye, a large black pupil ringed with an amber iris that glowed as if backlit. That eye watched me from the head of a foot-and-a-half-long swirl of dark, red-flecked brown lathered with yellow. In ten years of fishing in the mountains, I had never encountered a trout big enough to return a stare. In motion, the fish looked golden.

Brook trout are sprinters and jumpers, strong for

their size and energetic, if not particularly cunning, in
the first few seconds on the end of a line. They go
through their moves quickly, too quickly to follow with
much more than a generalized response. You catch them,
fairly easily in most cases, or you lose them in the irre-
trievable instant when, by instinct or luck, they jump
your complacency or inexperience.

But the big brown in the water in front of me was in
no hurry. Once hooked, the trout made three passes back
toward me, showing its broad, dark back more clearly
each time, as if to distract me either with the unexpected
beauty of its presence or with its bulk. The trout must
have had some sense that it was large for the river and
had grown to be a creature worth reckoning with. So the
fish swam at first in circles that brought it in and out of
view, a strange and wonderful sight in the small stream.

During ten years of fishing in the mountains, I had
dreamed of jumping a large trout, a fish big enough to
throw the brook trout fishing I had grown to love a little
out of focus. And I had heard rumors of big browns in
the Rose. This one seemed to have come out of the back of
my mind. So I wasn't altogether surprised by the large
trout slowly swimming circles in front of me, shaking its
head confidently from side to side, as if to say no.

I was in no hurry either. I knew what I was doing.
The brown had come out of one of those promising places
in a small stream a fly fisherman learns to see. Over the
years you casually study and studiously cast to thousands of such spots, until you come to understand the
possibilities for life the river has created on its way down
out of the mountains. You get an eye for where your luck
might lie. In a small stream the trout are not hard to
find, but for some reason the appearance of a trout of
any size from beneath a log or a boulder, or from the
depths below the only eddy in a stillwater pool, never
ceases to confirm something best not taken for granted.
When a drift brings such a spot alive, and you hook the

trout you made appear, the mountain up which you were wading seems revealed.

The trout had three moves, and it played them in different combinations, trying to unlock the invisible force that denied it the river.

When it returned under the deep shadow of the undercut boulder along the left side of the pool, where for years it had held while feeding, something was wrong. It now took effort to hold in the secure place where it had watched for insects struggling in the bright flowing film above it. A thin, sunlit diagonal cut across the pool from downstream. The fly in its mouth was attached to another world.

When the trout surged upstream, it could not find a way through the shallow riffles above the pool. It did not seem to tire, but it sensed how its strength was pointlessly eroded by the effort of swimming against the river. The force that pulled at it from downstream followed it. It could not slip the current to suddenly take cover, or drop to the layer of dead water on the bottom of the river to dart to new ground.

The right side of the pool deepened under a greenstone ledge the river had sculpted into a cavernous recess of deep stillwater. Here at the bottom of the river, under the ledge where the water was dark, the trout had hid and waited out the worst dangers. No natural predator could reach it there. No kingfisher or wandering heron could break into the depth of the place. No raccoon could reach it or water snake surprise it. But now when it sought this refuge, the force that controlled it followed.

The trout ranged around the pool, resting at times near the bottom fifteen feet in front of me, sullenly shaking its head. Every move was a waste of energy. The pool seemed undone. Something had taken the river away.

I played the trout for nearly ten minutes, giving it line when it insisted, but never giving it back the river. I had little to do but stay tight to the fish, hold the rod angled high to tire it, and keep the leader from catching on the rocks between us.

Several times toward the end the trout came straight back to me, not in a rush, but as if to check. It must have had some sense of the long river behind me. The way out was downstream, but the threatening, controlling shape stood *there,* just where it needed the river most.

Finally the trout charged the spot. I stood there awkwardly, holding the rod as high as I could trying to get some line into play, but only managing to get part of the long leader out through the tip top. When the fish came close I waved my left arm to scare it back into the pool, a graceless tactic that worked. I hoped no one was watching.

The trout made a few more circuits of its former havens, trying to regain its place in the river. But the threatening shape kept pressuring it from a distance.

The trout came back once more, fatigued but composed. There was no thrashing about, no gill flaring. It swam in front of me again, shaking its head and making the graphite tip of the fly rod dance. The water stirred all around it. The trout knew where the freedom of the river was: there where the water funneled downstream, white and fast into other pools.

I beached the fish in the leaf-choked slack water just downstream of the lie where it had been rising. The trout had grown too large for the food available to it, a fact that showed in the disproportion between its head and body. For all the beauty of its color and markings, which mimicked more accurately than a brook trout does the oncoming colors of autumn, that deformation and the fish's size betrayed it as out of place in the small mountain stream.

This was undoubtedly a fish that had first come to the river miles downstream in a hatchery truck, pale and slack-muscled, with ragged fins and no sense of the world of greenstone and blue water, of fat mayfly duns that a

river might offer it or of predators that might eye it in
turn. The brown escaped the first season of fishing in the
warm and silty stocked water that flows through the
farmland bordering Shenandoah National Park, and that
first fall started to move upriver. Eventually it passed
through the little Rose River valley, a hundred-acre
floodplain where an appealing ramshackle hamlet has established itself, and made its way into the dark hollow
through which the river flows.

At some point in its unnatural history, the trout
crossed the boundary into the national park. The trout
must have adapted quickly to the change in jurisdiction.
Silt and strange metallic and plastic refuse were no longer in the river. The bottom seemed a natural, undisturbed course of boulders and rubble, small stones, and
sand distributed by the current. The river made sense:
There were places to feed and hide and spawn; pools were
shaded; even in summer, when the water warmed, there
were deep holes with sunken layers of cool water.

The river was full of life. Brook trout swam in and
out of view, keeping a wary distance. Dace and sculpin
and other forage fish schooled defensively in the shallows.
Crayfish crawled about. Snakes swam through pools.
There were shadows along the banks at dawn and dusk
that bent to the river and stirred the water. Insects
moved along the bottom, and in the drift, and hatched in
the sunlit film at the surface. After a year, the trout
must have sensed in some rudimentary way the propor-
tion, regularity, and fitness of things in the cold, clear
water. You could live forever, it might have seemed, in
such a place.

As the trout grew, it changed. Its muscles were
strengthened by the constant play of current, and the fish
took on the lean, efficient shape of a salmonid. Its bruised
pectoral, pelvic, and anal fins grew out, repairing themselves into strong but delicately scalloped muscles that
caught and released filaments of currents with impercep-

tible precision. The trout's caudal muscle strengthened and its damaged caudal fin grew out. The natural color of the fish emerged during its seasons in the mountain stream, and although it never acquired the final brilliance of a stream-born brown, this trout had become, by the time I surprised it, a wild autumn brown in all but name.

I killed the trout with a blow on the head with the handle of my fishing knife and opened and cleaned the fish on the leaves against which I had admired it. Its stomach was nearly empty. I found a few unidentifiable, half-digested nymphs and one bright green katydid, still alive, lodged in its gullet. I cleaned the white interior of the trout carefully, picking blood out of the vertebrae with the point of my knife, and rinsed the scum and blood off the fish and my hands in the stream. It was still early in the afternoon, and I tried to keep fishing, but I had no expectations left with which to fish.

I found the vague fishermen's trail and followed a spur of it back up to the fire road that follows the Rose, one of the old transmontane pikes that leads west up over the Blue Ridge and down into the Shenandoah Valley. By the time I got back down to the steel bridge, a mile above where I was parked at the national park boundary, the colors of the big brown were fading and its skin was starting to blotch, as if the beauty of the fish had been held in place by its life in the river.

Two days later I blued the trout for friends in dry white wine. The bluing took the death pallor off it. The big fish had to be supplemented with small, mushy supermarket rainbows, but the entrée was buttressed with new potatoes, steamed broccoli, and hot biscuits. Everyone had a taste of the big fish and too much wine. Nothing was wasted. I must have told some version of the story about catching the trout.

I would like to have a painting of the two of us, rendered impressionistically, showing a fly fisherman deliberately blocking that narrow channel at the back of the pool, holding a dark parabola over the water, a bright line cutting down across the scene toward where a large brown trout shook its head from side to side, as if saying no. The scene would look like the beginning of the end of the year.

The painting would have to imply that the trout was being played to death in the early afternoon, and that the fisherman, who loved the lives of trout, felt no guilt about the killing. The painting would not be about death but about life, about early autumn on the Rose and years of fishing in the mountains. The painting would imply all that trout and fly fishermen learn about rivers during their lives, as well as render the graceful and awkward moves they make when they confront one another across the gulf between their natures and assert, for better or worse, the prerogatives of their species. Somehow the way the artist rendered the dark, greenstone landscape, softened by the pale yellow and bright green of October in the Blue Ridge, against which fish and fisherman appear together, would put all that in perspective.


Of course, the following year the pool was empty. I passed over that stretch of river in the spring, self-conscious about the trout that wasn't there. But I fished it the following fall, approaching the spot far more carefully and dwelling on it with far more ingenuity than I did the day I stumbled onto the big brown. But nothing I could do brought another such rise. Last spring I greedily fished big nymphs and woolly worms through the pool when the blue water started to subside, but nothing stopped the leader in the water.

This autumn I came up the Rose on a day much like that day two years ago. Driving through Criglersville and Syria, where the fall fruit markets were in full swing, I tried to tell myself to treat the river evenly and not plan the day's fishing around the pool where the

brown had appeared. But the memory of it was now a
hole in the river, and the big trout haunted my autumn
fishing as surely as those two lost brook trout haunted
my spring. The brown, too, had somehow gotten away.

By October, Indian-summer days with a hint of autumn have become autumn days with a vestige of summer. Even though the woods are still full and green, an
intermittent breeze flickers the yellow beech and hickory
leaves that start the turn of the hardwoods and rustle
slowly to the ground all day. The reds of sumac and ivy
catch the eye. You see the turn before you feel it, spawning colors unmasked in the hardwood canopy that has,
since June, been an undistinguished forest green.

This October the clear, distinct sound of the Rose
came to meet me through the woods, fairly ringing over
its stony bed. Its insistent current seemed to stir the
changing landscape. As I watched the Rose through the
yellow and green foliage, I thought of trout all over the
Blue Ridge moving out of the pools where they had con-
gregated during the dog days of summer, reoccupying
the rivers and beginning to search out spawning sites.
The cool, steady currents of autumn, which re-create the
spring character of rivers in miniature, seem to ensure
the continuity of life in the Blue Ridge. While deer and
bear increase their browsing range, wandering steadily
through the camouflaged woods, river creatures, for
whom stillness is exposure, take a cue from the motion
around them and prepare for the end of the year.

The diminished autumn rivers scale the eye to details
and slight movements. The exposed streambed of the
Rose, now full of tiny ponds and oxbows and the flora
that takes brief hold in the moist niches left by the contracted river, is full of life again. I walk along, fly rod in
hand, eyeing the river's interesting banks. A salamander
poises for insects on a wet stone. The pale brown stripes
along its back seem to emanate from its dark, protuber-
ant eyes. It tolerates my close inspection at first, but then

turns to crawl partway under a rock. It takes a touch of my finger, however, to send the salamander completely into hiding.

A hundred yards farther on, a dark brown snake with a bright orange ring around its neck is more visibly skeptical of my intentions. The foot-long reptile bunches its muscles and freezes, almost hidden on the dark stones and leaves. It keeps pace ahead of me as I follow it upstream along the edge of the river, turning toward me and tensing when I approach it too closely. While I am stooped over the ringneck snake, a kingfisher, chattering and swooping in shallow arcs over the river, flies past me headed downstream. When I turn back to the ground, the snake is gone.

The trout, too, sense my presence and move away as I approach. The Rose has been fished hard. My footfalls warn the bigger trout, which tuck themselves out of sight under rocks. My shape or shadow freezes some trout in the tails of pools until I move too close and send them fluttering upstream.

Although early autumn brings the rivers to life, I am still hung between seasons, and I fish most of the day in a fashion far too halfhearted for the demands of autumn water. The big pools on the Rose feel like empty rooms. The scant insect life fails to interest me—a smattering of caddis and stoneflies, and a few late-season mayflies. I have let my fly boxes deplete without sitting down at the vise and replenishing them for the season. My fishing instincts seem awry. Although I keep meaning to tie some well-balanced twelve- and fifteen-footers, I have been fishing with the same jerry-built leader for weeks, a leader that has grown, by fits and starts, to some odd, unbalanced length. The split upper of my left wading shoe is bound with duct tape. The tip of my fly line is cracked and stripped of finish and waterlogs quickly. I forget things, leave them in the truck or, worse, at home. In the autumn of a year I've fished hard, I'm content to be the kind of fisherman I wouldn't be caught dead with in April.

Where the gradient of the river increases, I scramble up and climb a greenstone staircase, sometimes pushing my gear on ahead and then boosting myself over a ledge to the brink of the next pool. Here the Rose is a series of short, deep pools joined by the spouts of pouring water that give the river its mellow autumn voice.

Trout are tucked under the lip of bright leaves log-jammed at the back of each pool. If you nose carefully over the ledge you can get close enough to touch them, but they are almost impossible to fish to. The large pools are beautifully lit and perfectly still, except at their throat and tail. I cast dry flies into openings the current makes between the endless stream of leaves.

In these weeks before spawning, when adult trout seem to hide, the juvenile trout are more noticeable than they are at any other time. Even the normally aggressive dace subordinate themselves to the young trout and parr which are warier and more predatory than they have been all year. Instead of milling about in schools, they stake out worthwhile holding positions. They hover under leaves like adult trout holding in the shadows of boulders. They hang effortlessly in the current, and have picked up up the habit of drifting back to insects in the film rather than darting forward for them. They seem to have found both a sense of themselves and the rhythm of the river.

Along one stretch of the river I catch more of these young trout than anything else for my trouble. Lying in the palm of my hand, each parr is a clear impression of a trout, formally perfect, grown already to be what trout evolved into long ago, the shape of parted water. The bodies of the tiny trout are completely formed, concave and convex by turns, their weight feathered by a delicate array of tiny fins. These young trout are pale—a soft, watery green—but all the markings of an adult are clear and distinct. Each parr seems like the idea of a trout in hand.

I work my way through a bright stretch of river, nymphing carefully through the brown's old pool. But the spot is less important than I thought it would be. The Rose is becoming a river again. When the afternoon begins to slip quickly away, as autumn afternoons do, I fish harder, especially the deep, sheltered runs. But except for a few small trout, the river flows blankly around me.

An oval pool below a long cascade offers me the day's last chance. The pool resembles a muted version of a spring pool. The river splashes into it, flushing the fallen leaves from its surface. A well-defined current rumples the throat of the pool below the whitewater, broadening into a tongue of turbulence that reaches to its center. Eddies slowly circle toward its banks. I lean against a cool brow of greenstone and work out line over the pool downstream of me. I cast a fur ant above the tip of the tongue of turbulence at mid-pool, below which I know a trout waits.

Brook trout are not prolific. Relatively few—say several hundred—fertilized eggs will begin to chance life in the river from a pair of spawning trout. Some of these eggs will settle properly into their redd, a bowl-shaped nest of gravel. If the eggs remain undisturbed and are properly filtered by the river, they will produce eyes; some eyed eggs will become alevins, wisps of trout. A handful of fry will come of this, and of these a half dozen will become the parr that bide their time in the marginal places in the river, as much prey as predators. Finally a trout or two will swim into adulthood out of the austere, beautiful mating of *Salvelinus fontinalis* that took place three years before and sent a small cloud of milt and eggs to the bottom of the river.

Throughout the year a brook trout is a compromise between camouflage and display. In autumn, in preparation for spawning, the natural definition of the male is enhanced to overstatement, and the trout becomes in fact what it often is in impression, a beautiful exaggeration.

The olive and black vermiculation on its back becomes more highly contrasted, as if it had been redrawn with a firmer, heavier hand. What from above should hide the trout borders on becoming a badge of identification, especially when the fish holds above the new-fallen leaves that have sunk to the bottom of a pool and not yet lost their bright colors. The vermiculation melts into a field of pale green contoured with yellow ovals that evolve into circles toward the midline; the yellow circles give way, on the flank of the trout, to scarlet spots surrounded by blue aureoles.

All year long, there is a splash of orange with a hint of fluorescence along the pearl white belly of the trout. But in autumn that orange darkens and spreads toward the gill covers and toward the tail, bleeding into the fins, reddening them at their base, and putting a hint of rose in the end of the tail. The white line along the tips of the fins and the bottom of the tail become wider and brighter, and the black line that finishes the tip darkens and thickens. Finally two thick black lines, which seem to have been quickly stroked on with a coarse brush, form a startling border between those orange flanks and what is left of the white belly of the trout.

The trout I hooked in the flatwater just beyond the tongue of current in that perfect autumn pool never left the water. I slipped the fly from its vomer and admired the way the fish glistened like an animated jewel in my loose grip. An autumn brook trout in its spawning colors is perhaps the clearest sign of the beginning of the end of the year. The beauty of the fish is difficult to convey. Releasing one such trout, I want to see another immediately. Photographs can capture their form, detail, and color, but not the impression of the fish in the field—the strange, otherworldly life in it. On the other hand, impressionistic renderings sacrifice the actual appearance of the trout to some inadequate idea of it. There is so much artifice in the brook trout's natural appearance that most representations are defeated by inaccurate stylization.

The trout dropped to the bottom of the pool when I released it and darted away when I straightened up. The amber afternoon light, which had given the river an appealing olive cast, had drawn away while I fished. A cool breeze chilled my wet hands.

During October I try to revisit the rivers I fish in early spring. October is like March, a time of year with a foot in each season; the days run backward, from fall to summer. In the morning you can see your breath; by midafternoon you have worked up a sweat. Evening comes quickly. The nights are cold, and that more than anything changes the rivers and the trout. The shortening days warm the rivers less and less, and the year runs on.

The unfamiliar calls of migrating birds counterpoint the breezy rustling in the woods, which each day seems more insistently stirred by the winds that turn the pleasant uncertainty of autumn into the long gray stasis of fall. The woods are rich with mast—acorns, hickory, and beech nuts. Hurried change is everywhere. This is the season of camouflage, of shifting patterns that conceal form. An unseen fox squirrel, blanked somewhere along the branch of an oak, chatters a warning through the canopy. The graying flank of a whitetail slides into a stand of ash. A dark bear-shape merges into granite shadows.

Cool mornings laced with autumn gives way to warm afternoons, but by the end of the day, when dusk sends me down a trail strewn with another day's layer of bright, dead leaves, I can feel the missing minutes in the air and sense the insistent flow of the year around the deadfall of spent days. The sun slips behind the southern ridge of the watershed too soon. I look up for the missing daylight as I try to tie on a fresh fly so I can fish one last quiet pool. The shadows that hover around my cold hands make me wonder where the year has gone. I sense, not without regret, the season of long evenings coming on. Rivers still hold the afternoon light longer than the woods, but I end the days fishing a little in the dark.

When I see so many irreversible signs of the season slipping away, I fish more attentively, combing each river for one last good trout. Although the hard-fished pools are usually deserted, the small, dark mayflies of autumn stir some trout out of hiding. To fish well in late autumn, you have to fight the sense of hurry in the woods around you, the change suggested by the constant rain of leaves and the chill autumn winds and the weakened warmth of the bright October daylight. The pace of bringing good trout to hand is one-tenth of what it was in spring, and it feels strange to move along so slowly and studiously when the year seems to be hurrying away. I play each good fish I hook a little longer than I should.

As I make this autumn circuit of my spring rivers, final signs appear, each one of which brings the fishing to a halt. On the North Fork of the Moormans, I stopped to watch a female brook trout build her redd. Vigorous white winks in the tail of a pool called my attention to the laboring trout. Even from fifty feet away, I knew instantly what the odd flashing in the river meant. Digging a redd is the most strenuous thing a brook trout must do, and its instinctual exertion in behalf of the next generation is as solemn an event as the spawning run of salmon. The nest building dramatizes, perhaps better than anything else a fisherman sees all year, the intimate relation of a wild trout to a river. From a distance, I could only see the fish when it turned on its side to fan the fine gravel at the tail of the pool. When I crept closer, I could see the bowl-shaped depression forming underneath its solitary efforts. The male trout was nowhere in sight, but the female swam in circles around the redd, as if to mark the site as claimed, and then twisted over on its side to work the gravel into shape with its tail. When I tried to get closer, I spooked the trout and put it off its task.

As autumn lost its luster and fall came on, I seemed to move too clumsily to stay close to what I wanted to see. I came on two spawning trout in a little side pool in the Chapman Mountain stretch of the Rapidan that I fish through carefully every spring—they might have been trout I caught and slipped back into the river in April. I crawled to within five feet of them. The female held over the redd without moving anything but her fins and tail to steady herself in the slight flow. She was so still and so intent, I wondered what kept kingfishers from gathering more noticeably over the rivers this time of year. The male poised himself next to her, almost brushing her with his fins. He might hold in the same position for as long as thirty seconds, and then, without apparent cause, swim to the other side of her and hold there. At times he would switch sides more frequently, as if to establish his presence everywhere. Several times he held at right angles to her, almost touching her side. These ceremonial gestures continued until I turned my head to glance at the large pool adjacent to their spawning alcove. When I looked back, they had disappeared.

On the Staunton a few days later my presence also seemed to do more harm than good. Toward the end of a day on what was left of the river above its long cascades I came on a brilliantly colored trout. I got within arm's length of it before it noticed me. When it did, it swam to the leaf-choked head of the run it occupied. As I approached closer the trout jumped out of the water onto a mat of sodden leaves. The spawned-out trout thrashed on the leaves as it tried to bore ahead, intent on surviving another year. Its desperation and lack of cunning in trying to escape were startling. I wanted to photograph the trout, but its thrashing there on the leaves made me ner-

vous. I thought I would put it back in the deep water at
the back of the run from which I had driven it, but when
I reached for it, the trout jumped violently at my uncertain touch and was gone.

If by the end of May I have had enough of trout fishing, by the end of October I am tired of watching the life
of rivers. A year of mountain fishing will wear itself
down. The vest and waders and fly rod begin to feel like
props, and I'm not sure what I am looking for. The few
bright, colorful weeks of autumn, which I distinguish
from the bare woods of fall, compose an odd, fifth season
in my mind. And in the field during those two weeks
when an uncanny, almost unnatural light filters through
the dying hardwood canopy in the afternoon, events in
the field seem odd, as if they had happened in a brightly
illustrated story.

Even so, this year I took one last autumn hike along
the Rose River fire road, unencumbered with gear of any
kind. I left the road at the trail that goes into Dark Hollow, a well-named, haunting place with a trickle of
stream running through it that eventually flows into the
Rose. I hiked the stream for a few miles just to spend the
time and started back down as I began to lose the light.
Along the way I stopped to watch reddish mayfly spinners laying eggs in a riffly stretch of the small stream.
They had prominent yellow thoraxes and heads. I didn't
remember ever having seen them before. I watched one
hold six or eight inches over the river, which flowed
quickly through the shallow riffle. I could see the yellow
egg mass at the end of its abdomen and its delicate, elongated tails. I wondered if the tails lengthened during its
egg-laying stage in order to help it sense the surface of
the river from a safe distance. I wondered if it felt the
water rushing under it.

The mayfly danced uncertainly over the river, eventually swooping suddenly to the surface and seeming to rest
there, for perhaps as long as a second, while a portion of

the egg mass broke off and drifted quickly to the bottom of the riffle. The mayfly did this several times in the same place and then flew off downstream. Other mayflies were performing this same hypnotic ritual.

It was, I wrote in my field notes, a common but wonderful thing to see. I have seen it before, as have all fly fishermen, and have often noted what a poignant picture of contingency is etched on the mind's eye by the sight of a lone insect mated for a moment to a river, finishing the work of its life with such strange ceremony.

Like the fire road along the North Fork of the Moormans, the Rose River road is a familiar way home, and on the way down the river in the evenings that familiarity comes to meet me halfway, like a friend. As I reached the road from the Dark Hollow trail, I remembered the large brown trout from two years before. I would not have mentioned the Rose by name, except that I suspect it will be years before another hatchery brown makes its way up river to grow large and wild among the native brook trout. Ten years, maybe, if ever, before another fly fisherman wades unaware into an early-autumn afternoon on the Rose to find himself tethered to a strong golden swirl with a black and amber eye.

However long it takes for that hole in the river to be filled with such life, I don't think I'll need to harass such a trout again. I won't need to come back down that old mountain road strewn with yellow beech and hickory leaves, feeling with strange, undeniable satisfaction the slack heft of the end of the year in the dead weight at my side.

At the end of October, I put in on the James River below Buchanan and floated north toward Natural Bridge.

The river slid quickly through the cattle pastures that stretched to the burnished mountains. The well-watered sugar maples and sycamores along the riverbank were still green, but except for umber and russet oak crowns and a few flames of hickory, the autumn color had bled from the mountains while the brook trout spawned. Now the gray open slopes in the distance looked like November, and the year seemed to lay fallen in the woods.

Despite rain, the river was low, tea-colored along its banks, brilliant blue in its channel. A handful of exposed boulders was strewn across the river, giving the long, slow flowing pools some visible character. The blue pools alternated with broad white reaches of river. As it flowed north, the river bent gently east and west, undercutting the banks on the outside of each curve, dropping discreetly in easy riffles that chattered their resistance to descent. When I looked into the sunlit water for the dark backs of smallmouth bass, I saw instead empty eelgrass waving downstream, as if the year were flowing toward the pronounced gap in the mountains below Balcony Falls where the James neatly halves the Blue Ridge.

The river is older than the mountains. Its bed limns a snaky old inclination that the rising of the mountains never argued out of the earth. Below Balcony Falls you float by the folded sandstone down through which the river wore as the mountains wrinkled upward. In the heart of the gap, where the water flows beneath the cliffs

called the James River Face, the warped bedding planes
of the exposed rock testify to the antiquity of the place.
The river seems most beautiful there where it reaches
most deeply into the mountains. When you float the year-
end flow of the James in the fall, you can feel the three-
hundred-mile-long heart of the river beat against the
mountains as it tilts ten thousand square miles of drainage easily toward the sea.

But flowing past Gilmore Mills, the river looked distinctly local. Cows watched me stupidly; pickups bounced
by kicking up dust. Norfolk and Western tracks glinted
out of the weeds in the right of way where migrating
sparrows flocked, nervously rising and falling en masse.
Silent silhouettes of paired ducks flew upriver, wings
chopping quickly.

A great blue heron guided me downstream all afternoon, carefully keeping its distance. When I loomed too
close, it gathered itself and drew its fragile legs from the
river with one slow wing beat, then folded itself and flew
ahead.

Summer refuse littered the muddy beaches opposite
good fishing holes. Styrofoam bait containers floated aimlessly in the shore weeds near abandoned log seats.
Empty forked sticks stuck in the mud were a sign on this
blue and amber Saturday that the easy fishing on the
river was over.

And the fishing was poor. One smallmouth for the
day. Nothing availed my windblown casting. I paddled
downriver slowly, hanging up on ledges, sensing the season was already ahead of me, hurrying downstream.

The afternoon turned cold, and the river went gray
from bank to bank. A head wind picked up, and evening
reached out from the mountains. I overshot the take-out
in the dusk and had to paddle the last short leg of the day
upstream.

# IX

# OLD FIRES

There were always people here.

All year as I fish I pass signs of lives, vestiges of the culture that took hold in the mountains, flowered as modestly as serviceberry in April, and then largely disappeared. When the fishing slows and fall rustles around me, I am likely to break down the rod and follow a game trail toward an old stone chimney revealed by the open November woods. Each year I have to look more closely to see what was once there.

A stone fence charts a neglected boundary. The remains of a dogtrot cabin hide in the understory, its rooms full of hemlock seedlings and its breezeway choked with gooseberry. Graying chestnut timbers, light as balsa, disappear by degrees. Stone walls are betrayed by doorways and window spaces. Time reaches in like a hand and takes a stone or two each year until a wall is a pile of rubble where copperhead hide. Pastures have become meadows. Orchards are crowded by black locusts. Barberry and bull thistle thrive randomly in old fields still vaguely fenced with rotted posts and rusted barbed wire. Woodbine closes trails.

Along one of my favorite late-season trout streams there is a log house that I have watched slump a little more into the rocky soil each year. The white-oak shingle roof is long gone, as are most of the walls, the remaining timbers splayed chaotically in a heap except where they are still fingered together at the corners. The square timbers were not mortised neatly like the round logs of the cabins Norwegian immigrants brought to the American frontier in the eighteenth century and which form most people's notion of what a log cabin should be. Roughly hand-planed with a draw knife and crudely notched with a hatchet and chisel, the construction indicates a lack of time, or skill, or better tools. The clay or plaster that once chinked the gaps between the logs has long since dried and fallen out, leaving a drafty skeleton. Wood fern have taken root in the fireplace. The chimney is largely intact, though it leans inward as if drawn, like the canted timbers, toward the center of the empty house. Loosestrife thrives around the threshold.

I stop for lunch at this house whenever I fish the river. My counterpart of fifty years ago who sat at his doorway would not have had much patience with the pretensions of fly fishing. A funnel trap fashioned of white-oak splints served his fishing needs admirably. Once set in a natural or contrived bottleneck in the river, he would only have to let his children stampede the trout into the trap from upstream to have all the fish he needed. The most unschooled whooping and arm-flapping would have the three-foot-long trap wiggling full of fish. A hooped flour sack would do almost as well.

The hollow folk, living as they did on the lean side of sustenance, kept their streams fairly empty of what they called speckled trout. They grabbed the yearly bounty of tasty pink-fleshed fish in the spring, when the getting was good, and weren't very discriminating in their tactics.

The large plunge pools might have brought out the fisherman in the mountain man. No fish trap or whooping kids would catch the good trout that appeared each spring beneath the cascades and waterfalls. So he fished for them with worms and crayfish, swinging a heavy line out into the current with an alder or birch branch that jumped violently when a large trout took. Then he might have sensed the sport in his dinner.

Undoubtedly the man recognized the mayflies and stoneflies that fluttered out of the river. Each year he saw trout rise with abandon in April and May, particularly in the evenings when helpless spinners fell into slow-flowing pools where trout waited for them to finish mating and laying eggs. On a whim or out of hunger he might have fashioned some kind of surface bait, perhaps even a crude fly from deer hair, fox fur, and turkey feathers. But I think that is unlikely. The mountain man lacked time, shot, and powder to waste, as well as any inclination to play at food gathering. The white-oak fish trap hung just inside the door, and the meat from the game from which flies could be tied would satisfy his hunger far better than a few small mountain trout would. Hardscrabble farming left little room for sport. However well its anachronistic rituals now seem to blend with Blue Ridge rivers, fly fishing has little past in mountains. In fact, it is a leisurely affectation much at odds with the difficulties people found in trying to make a living there.

The steeply pitched mountain defiles were not what people came to this country for. Those who eddied out of the mainstream for centuries and lodged in the hollows and coves of the Blue Ridge were marginal folk, resigned to subsistence farming and content with isolation. If you lived in the mountains, beside the headwater streams, something had probably gone wrong with your first dream. In soil too poor to grow tobacco, mountain folk grew corn and potatoes, raised livestock and families, nurturing a strain of Scotch-Irish intransigence that seems, in retrospect, to have grown out of the stony landscape they scraped each year with bull-tongue plows. As resources dwindled, they hung on like weeds, adapting to the deprivations their environment inflicted on them, enjoying its pleasures. A portion of their skills and stubbornness served well in wartime every few generations—at King's Mountain with Seviers, with Jackson in the Valley, sharpshooting across no-man's-land in France—but between times mountain clannishness sustained an independence predicated largely on withdrawal and so doomed to be overwhelmed eventually by the world beyond the hollow.

There are, of course, still mountain folk in the Blue Ridge, but their lives are more a function of a changed world than of their mountain past. I have seen satellite dishes in apparently impoverished surroundings hopefully scanning the night skies for whatever it is that entertains the rest of the world. The Appalachian frontier, which lasted longer than any other in the country, has disappeared. Like the native brook trout, mountain lives were buffered from a changing world for a time, left alone in an enclave protected only by its apparent lack of value.

Before they were moved out of the land that was to become Shenandoah National Park in the 1930s, the last of the hollow folk in that part of Virginia were surveyed and interviewed. Reports with austere titles were compiled: *Shenandoah Inspections and Investigations,* the *Evacuation and Subsistence Homestead Survey.* A sketchy picture emerges from this written record of who the mountain people were and what their lives were like. Lists and tables were compiled in the bureaucratic spirit of government documentation. Questionnaires were filled out by social workers, a census of the remnants of two centuries of mountain life. Strangers came into the hollows asking questions: How large is your family? How much land do you work? Do you own the land? What do you grow? What livestock do you raise? What tools do you use? How far did you go in school? How much money do you have? Are your parents alive? Are your children healthy?

Mountain culture was largely played out by the 1930s, its slender back finally broken by the chestnut blight. The ghostly white trunks of dead chestnuts stood like tombstones over the hollows where lifeways had coevolved with them. Chestnut trees meant lumber to sell to the railroads and bark to sell to tanneries, as well as chestnuts to sell for cash. When the trees died, a way of life was doomed. The almost biblical sustainer of the mountain folk's quiet ways and slender means vanished within a decade and left them just destitute enough to expose them to charity and caricature. Lives paced to the slow ticks of mountain time were exposed as thinly clad and apparently shiftless in public view. An image of Appalachia staring vacantly into the middle distance was fixed in the documentary black-and-white photography of the 1930s and 1940s. Children seem blighted, women worn, and men as though they were resigned, if asked, to march again toward Gettysburg, or Chancellorsville, or some other public disaster in which they had little obvious stake.

Ultimately the lists and tables in the resettlement reports are as drafty as the unchinked walls of the ruins in the field. Little seems illuminated by these attempts to quantify the lives of people for whom numbers were almost always a measure of lack. It is as hard to measure their poverty and ignorance as it is to value what they did have and understand what they knew. I doubt if either the deprivation sociologists are trained to see or the idyll folklorists are prone to create gets very near the true nature of their lives, which was left largely unexpressed. Their dreams have gone to ground like the walls of their homes.

There is, I think, more of the past in the field—in the tilt of an illegible tombstone shifting slowly on a hillside with each year's thaw or in the soft, peaty hump of a moldering woodpile—than in the written records I have seen. Along a stream, pieces of the past—a shard of milk glass or a rusted blade from a draw knife—sometimes come to hand, significant as trout. In November, when I walk back out of the woods to concentrate on the last good fishing of the year, maybe catching a brief hatch of *Baetis* out of a sunny patch of river, an important part of the past seems to hang like woodsmoke around those old homesites.

Beyond the ruined habitations, dirt roads wend back. Follow them far enough into the past and the ruins become homes, surrounded by well-tended gardens and small plowed fields. Blue smoke drifts from chimneys. Keep going back and the homes disappear and the clearings are swallowed by large trees that throw a cool, dark cast into the hills. Blazed trees mark a crude road recently widened from a buffalo path. One day I walked such a road to Wood's Gap along the South Fork of the Moormans River while botanist John Bartram rode beside me, his saddlebags full of seeds. It was autumn 1738.

We cross the Moormans below the confluence of its two forks. Bartram walks his horse easily across a broad riffle, calling encouragement as I hop rocks, unjointed fly rod in hand. We follow a narrow road that leads, at first, away from the river.

Bartram is full of talk. He is traveling alone; eleven hundred miles in five weeks. So much to see. Philadelphia to Annapolis to Gloucester Court House. Then to Williamsburg and up the James River, "thence travelling to your Blue Mountains."

Bartram has been wined and dined. Custis. Gooch. Where had Clayton been? Then with Byrd at Westover, William Randolph at Tuckahoe. He wore the fine drugget Collinson sent. *Pray go handsomely dressed to Virginia.*

Byrd offered good Madeira and showed him his books, told him about the survey from the coast to the mountains ten years before, complained about the awful Carolinians. Byrd warned him about endless briars and rattlesnakes, laughed about the bears. He had been glad to get home. Never crossed the mountains. Rivers everywhere. And haze from Indians fire hunting.

Last night Bartram stayed at Peter Jefferson's. At dawn he watched daylight cross from the Southwest Mountains toward the Blue Ridge, leading him on.

*In Europe they want to know what we have got,* he says with a laugh. *We are exotic. They plant our wildflowers in their gardens. Our forests grow in Sussex.*

A serious man, he laughs often, full of energy and curiosity. His dark eyes never stop moving, his long visage alert, radiant with the pleasure he takes in traveling through new country. His head is full of children and botany. He sees in Latin names, genus and species, thinks of his God as he rides along until he spies something he recognizes, or does not know.

We stop where everyone stops, at the top of the first long rise in the road where the river bends into view again, a silver bow in the forest. He dismounts and we walk to where the river flows at the base of a solemn brow of greenstone. Enormous hemlocks create a cool, dark cove.

*Peter Kalm's laurel.* He points.

Some stunted mountain laurel persist in the shade of the hemlock. *Kalmia latifolia.* A hundred miles south *Rhododendron maximum* would grab hold and make the understory impossible.

*I want much to come to Carolina, to observe the curiosities toward the mountains. There must be wonders among the Cherokee.*

He stoops. Close inspection halts his talk.

*These ferns. . . .*

He must remember.

*Hard to get books,* he complains, straightening up. *Collinson says,* Look, don't read. *Still. . . .*

Had I seen the Linnaeus? Bartram is full of the new system, laughs and says he counts *stamina* and *styles* in the spring. Male and female. He smiles.

*Makes sense. Collinson thinks there's money in ginseng.*

Ben Franklin also makes much of ginseng, but Bartram knows it's overrated. *Panax,* for panacea. Nature is not as simple as that. Besides, he is not in business.

Bartram shakes his head, remounts, and we move on.

Beyond the first ford I show him where there is a field of mayapple bordered by Christmas fern, a beautiful spot in April where, not long after he is gone, a settler will build a home, windows on the wildflowers, front door facing the river. It has been a warm fall, and there are still wood asters and harebell to see. He will write to Collinson. *The settlers say that the ground is covered with delicate beautiful blossoms in the spring.* Later he will see an Appalachian spring for himself and write to his sons with enthusiasm: "The variety of plants and flowers in our southwestern continent is beyond expression."

The road crests again, pinched between Middle Mountain and the Blue Ridge where the river slices between them, falling thirty feet over what is left of the broken spur hunched between the two ridges. You can see where the bedrock has been tilted and folded, as if a great hand in Burnthouse Hollow had shoved Middle Mountain west. Big boulders and outcrops line the river below the falls. Spring whitewater has carved deep blue pools. The plunge pool already has a name. The Blue Hole, Wood and his son call it. They say the biggest trout in the mountains are there.

Bartram stops to admire the tumult of the riverbed and cocks an ear to the subdued boom of the small river. He sees continuity in the mutability of nature. *This earth was made of the ruins of another, at the Creation,* he says, remembering Lewis Evans's talk when they went to see the Iroquois. He does not preach. The world looks like that to him. He detests the clownish Calvinists. *Mystery mongers,* he snorts. He will hold with no dark notions. *These great mutations need not perplex. Catastrophe can lead to another world. New rivers carve new pools. Life sorts itself out.*

There was, he knows, an ocean east of the mountains. The shells show that. There are, he conjectures, mountains and valleys in the depths of the oceans. He sees a deep past in "the beds and banks of our rivers . . . manifest by viewing the wide passages through the mountains, where the violent currents have for ages past washed and worn away all the soil to the bare rocks." Although a believer, he knows life is not biblical, his own thoughts "a confused heap of broken links." After Creation, life "hath since been maintained by particular matrices, fecundated by their respective seeds; which order, 'tis like, may continue until another great change."

Perhaps. I want to tell him about Lyell, about Charles Darwin. The books he won't read.

He gently shakes off his long thoughts and looks at me and at the fly rod I've forgotten I'm carrying. He smiles broadly, gesturing down at the long blue pool thirty feet below us.

*I like to watch them at home, casting on the Schuylkill.*

I come up the river slowly, shooting loops of line into the tail of the Blue Hole under John Bartram's watchful gaze. I put a small dry fly over all the stillwater, then work a nymph beneath the frothy chop at the head of the pool.

Nothing.

When I look up, Bartram has disappeared.

Back up on the road I find him taking a patch of cushion moss off some greenstone.

*They followed your fly, the floating one. I saw them, large trout. They did not believe it. The casting, though, that is something. Very mollifying.*

He reaches for the fly box sticking out of my jacket pocket, pokes a stubby finger around the dry flies and picks one out. He holds it by the hook up to the light to see it from below like a trout and laughs.

*Very good, very good. May-flie. A strange likeness. This works? I saw them with big trout last spring on the Schuylkill. Fishermen with baskets and long greenheart poles.*

Fly fishermen, I say.

He laughs again, tucking the fly back in its compartment, and hands me back the fly box.

*Of course,* he nods, clapping me on the shoulder, *fly fishermen. I have seen* Libellae—*Dragon-flie—swarming over the river thick as bees. Laying eggs. Up and down over the water. Beautiful to see. And smaller flies. Your* Ephemeroptera. *There is a black one in April.*

*Epeorus,* I tell him, Quill Gordon.

He seems pleased to know its common name, says it aloud to remember.

We cross the second ford, above which the South Fork of the Moormans becomes a nearly silent stream. There is a series of wide ledges fringed with rows of falling water above the ford that I would like to fish, but Bartram is moving on. A homesite is half cleared on a table of land opposite. Flat stones are piled for a hearth and chimney. White oaks and chestnuts are felled nearby. An acre of trees has been girdled beyond the clearing.

The road is rough but clear—hard-packed red clay in which rocks seem to grow. The rocks Michael and Archibald Wood and Ben Wheeler have pried out of the road are forming a fence on either side. We clear windthrows as is the custom, leave an open road behind us. The price of passage.

We flush a dozen deer at Turk Branch. There is bear scat full of undigested seeds everywhere. The bison have left the country east of the mountains. We watch for elk, which straggle after them in diminishing numbers, and think about catamount in the close, rocky places.

*Men have been attacked on horseback,* he tells me evenly, as if that were as unfair as it is startling.

There is no bravado in Bartram, but no fear either. No fear for himself. But just as he grew to love it, he saw the country receding before his eyes. Wherever he went twice, he saw changes. He worried species would disappear before he had collected their seeds, that he would miss something forever, never see what once was. The older he got, the more he traveled, trying to catch up, going "over and between the mountains," as he wrote to the collector Collinson about this trek, "in many very crooked turnings and windings." He would be more dramatic with Catesby, who drew the specimens that sprouted in Collinson's garden from Bartram's seeds: "the most desolate, craggy, dismal places . . . where no mortal ever trod . . . entirely to observe the wonderful productions in nature."

On foot I have a better vantage, but his eyes are sharper, quicker.

*There.*

Rattlesnake plantain at the foot of a pine, half buried in needles. Soft, velvety green leaves scored with a snakeskin of white lines. The long stem is brown, hairless now, but there are still seeds in the dry flower head.

*Here.*

Bartram hands me a small envelope.

He takes the packet of seeds from me, nodding thanks.

He mumbles as he writes on the packet.

*Collinson wants to know about rattlesnakes. I watched one last spring, stared at it for a good long time to see the emanations from its eyes. There were none. It did not charm me.*

He laughs, leaning down toward me to tell his story.

*I poked it with a stick—a long one, mind you—but it would not strike.*

He is thinking of the rattlesnake.

*I let it be. They're killing all the snakes, you know.*

And everything else, he thinks, frowning.

*The wood pigeons can't last the shooting. Six for a penny in the city. Have you seen the wolves they bring to your Court House? Yesterday I saw them give a man twelve dollars worth of tobacco for a hide! Gray wolf. Beautiful beast.*

The land, he has observed sadly all along his way, is poorly used.

*The soil. Tobacco burns it up. A quick return for a fool's future. Hard money for the gentry. And the trees. . . .*

We are above the tulip poplar and hemlock which limn the river. We pass the healthy, uneven-aged mix of a mature southern hardwood forest, wood too tempting to stand for long. Enormous oaks and chestnuts. Maple and walnut, cherry and hickory. Yellow birch and black ash. Masts and hull ribs for British shipping. Wood for the city on the hill. Flooring and fence posts, spokes and singletrees, gun stocks, ax handles, light and warmth.

Bartram breathes deep in the forest, listens to the stream.

*I still can't fathom all the oaks and hickories. So many kinds.*

Two miles farther on the road curves to the west toward a saddle in the Blue Ridge—Wood's Gap. The road is mud where two springs seep a constant trickle to start the river on its way, the watershed an oval bowl dipping down the mountain to the northeast. We watch a she-bear with two cubs traverse the opposite slope a hundred yards distant, shuffling quickly away into the dusk.

We rest and break bread where the road reaches the flattened crest of the Blue Ridge. Beyond the Great Valley, the mountains begin again, seem endless, as Evans had it on his map. Bartram knows he will not be able to travel far and long enough. He will tell Franklin that a western survey must be made, before the country is settled and changed. Franklin will pass the idea along to the younger Jefferson. Years later Thomas Jefferson will urge John Bartram's son William, at age sixty-three, to join Lewis and Clark, headed west up the Missouri. "You are not too old," friends encourage. But William declines. The son's fatigue will end the father's journey.

John Bartram finds that the seeds have jumped their packets on the rough way and are mixed up at the bottom of his saddlebags. He shakes his head. He cannot send them straight off to Collinson in London, identified in Latin in his neat hand. Bits of the New World for the Old, germs of American nature to be commented on in the patronizing way of the Royal Society.

He will plant them first in his garden, let the Blue Ridge sprout in Philadelphia. Then he will see what they are. Harvest them again. The stubborn mountain angelica won't sprout, and he will have to search again.

There is an hour's light on his side of the mountains, where the road dips west into Shenandoah Valley. The way I must retrace is dark now. Bartram mounts. His horse clops in place on Wood's Road. He senses my apprehension.

*You'll have a hunter's moon before you. Godspeed.*

John Bartram salutes and rides toward Staunton where he will stay the night.

Going home with the Blue Ridge on his right hand, the beauty and fertility of the Great Valley affects him deeply. He will write of a "terrestrial Paradise." He finds a new genus of cyclamen, a shooting star, that had eluded even Clayton. Collinson will send it to Linnaeus, from "beyond the first mountains in Virginia." He makes friends among the hardworking Alsatians and Ulstermen. They are better to the land than the impatient English, he notes. No tobacco, no slaves. They fertilize fields, rotate crops, plant cover, stay put and tend. Grow slowly. He promises to return.

I turn back and descend Wood's Road back toward Sugar Hollow through the thin, aspiring woods that now stand where John Bartram's unbroken forest stood. His shadow might have crossed the largest hemlocks. The terrain is much the same. The river sounds large in the dark. A deer, I think, edges back into the woods as I approach the meadow at the fire break. Rustling stills as I pass. Bats dart over the road and the river. I smell bear. The heavy flight of an owl dips from a tree. I pass empty, ruined habitations.

Moonlight reaches me at the rise above the Blue Hole. The road glows underfoot. I think of John Bartram riding toward South River on the other side of the mountains, listening to the night sounds and eyeing the shadowy lay of the land, a pious Quaker bearing witness to his country.

Godspeed, Friend. I wish I had your eyes, your world.

Thanksgiving weekend I made the year's last camp on Paine Run, where I went to photograph white-tailed deer. Near the head of the river there are dependable springs and dense stands of red oak and chestnut oak which provide good late-season browse. The area is generally full of game. The river flows southwest from Blackrock Gap for a few miles through a dog-legged hollow until it debouches suddenly into Shenandoah Valley.

Paine Run is a temperamental affair. Judging from its deeply undercut banks and its unusually braided bed, the river frequently flows in spates that shift it around the gentle slopes of its upper watershed. I have never seen it as anything other than a slow-flowing stream you can jump across in many places. A poor to fair trout stream characterized by shallow pools where small trout hold without benefit of much cover, the river needs more riffles, a few cascades to get things moving, and some deep pools with boulder rubble.

But I like Paine Run. It was the first river along which I camped in the Blue Ridge. I don't remember why it became a destination the first spring I backpacked the mountains, but I do recall being startled by a dark patch of ground moving in the woods in front of me when I got to the bottom of the last switchback that leads you down to the river. It took me a few confused seconds before the dark patch resolved into a flock of wild turkeys scattering uphill and out of sight.

I backpacked two miles down the river that day and made camp on a triangular terrace of land above the confluence of Paine Run and another, nameless stream. There are inviting terraces all along the upper river, level and free of the dense laurel slicks and huckleberry bushes that choke the slopes of the watershed. I liked the site and stayed two nights, breaking in new gear and enjoying country that was new to me. I was very bear and snake conscious at the time and looked over my shoulder and down at the ground a good deal, but mostly I explored and loafed and fished for trout with a fiberglass pack rod that, assembled, was all ferrule and had the action of a broomstick. I fished with an odd assortment of wet flies a size too large, which amused the few trout I couldn't spook.

I knew I was botching the fishing, but I had no ego invested in it. I liked the watershed and that campsite, and to this day I will camp at such a confluence of small streams when given the chance. White-tailed deer and small game materialized in the late afternoon, enlivening camp until dusk when they disappeared. Because it faced southwest, the watershed has a long evening in spring— a full hour of pale blue twilight held in the air after dinner. Then the woods darkened in a shrinking circle until I threw the darkness back with lantern light for an hour.

Lying in the sleeping bag after dark, I could cock an ear to one stream or the other and compare the character of the sound each made. I fell asleep trying to distinguish exactly where the sounds came together. My sleep was bothered more by screech owls than bear, which never made, so far as I know, an appearance in camp.

This year I returned to that campsite, though it would be inaccurate to say I recognized it. I found the confluence of Paine Run with that smaller, steeper stream easily enough. The triangular terrace was there, and I probably pitched my tent within ten feet of where I pitched it ten years ago. But I did not remember the island around which the rivers joined, or the distinctive rock wall opposite the campsite that formed one side of a pool where spawned-out trout waited for winter.

The morning I made camp hunters were working the bottom of the watershed, driving game in my direction. Deer browsed nervously along the river, throwing their heads into the air frequently and covering more ground than they normally would. If I approached openly and moved along slowly with them, I could get close enough for tight head shots with a short telephoto I could use without a tripod. Their coats had turned from summer brown to the grizzled winter gray that sets off their dark eyes and muzzles and the white in their tails and the insides of their ears.

I shot complacent does and yearlings until I found an eight-point buck that slowly learned to tolerate my presence and the whir of the motor drive. I followed it for an hour hoping to catch a gleam of sunlight in its eye and get a perfect angle on the curvature of its rack— a crisp, head-up profile that would convey some worthwhile impression of the animal's presence in the field. When I tired of trailing, I hid alongside a white oak as if I were still hunting and studied the way deer came into view out of the maze of gray tree trunks and branches.

After lunch I hiked downstream. I didn't like walking into the morning's gunfire, but there hadn't been a shot since noon. Hunting wasn't legal along Paine Run, but that fact wasn't especially reassuring. When

I parked at Horsehead Overlook on Skyline Drive to view the watershed early that morning, I had disturbed a pair of would-be tourists glassing the open slopes intently, walkie-talkies tucked in their camo jackets. A lot of poorly coded chatter broke back and forth on the CB as I drove on. I guessed things would be quiet until late afternoon. The deer, at any rate, were all behind me.

However much the pursuit of game has degenerated in modern times, Paine Run has a long and noble history as a hunting ground. Had I been more attentive my first time in the watershed, I might have guessed that. The hollow has an unusual variety of mast-producing oaks along with dense stands of sheltering conifers. And there is the stream with its inviting terraces and the springs below Blackrock Gap, a convenient crossing point between the eastern and western slopes of the Blue Ridge. Less obviously useful is the unusual abundance of quartz, quartzite, and chert that comes to hand along the riverbanks and the adjoining slopes.

When the Wisconsin ice retreated, drawing the tundra off the crest of the Blue Ridge and spruce and fir up its slopes, Paleo-Indians harassed doomed Pleistocene megafauna—mammoths, musk ox, giant bison—into the cul-de-sac at Blackrock Springs where I had flushed the flock of wild turkey. When northern hardwoods replaced the spruce and fir thousands of years later, Archaic Indians drove moose and elk and lesser bison over the same ground. The forest continued to change with the shifting climate until Woodland Indians were pursuing deer, bear, elk, and modern bison through a world very like the one into which, wide-eyed and heavily armed, Europeans stumbled and announced the beginning of American history.

Where for ten or twelve thousand years they butchered game for meat, bone, and hides men left litter, a scattered mix of lithic tool kits from thousands of hunts—quartzite cores and blanks, blades and flakes, Clovis points and microblades, worked bifaces and honed drills, as well as scrapers, choppers, burins and ax heads. Men have always hunted along Paine Run.

It wasn't until I got near the bottom of the watershed that I understood why. Paine Run turns due west near where it leaves the mountains, picking up some gradient and a little respectability as a trout stream. At that point you can see a white sandstone tower and, just beyond that, a narrow opening between sandstone cliffs where the river leaves the hollow. You could not ask for a better bottleneck toward which to drive game. You could not build better cover for your cohorts. Two dozen of them could easily have hid among the sandstone shelves and quartzose boulders that surround the narrow slot through which the river runs. The fifty-foot sandstone tower gives you a view far up into the watershed, better even than the view from Horsehead Overlook. The logic of the topography must have been immediately clear to the first human hunters to come through the sandstone gauntlet.

As you come up the river into the watershed, there is a rock shelter on the right bank above a ford. A well-used trail connects the ford to the shelter, a ten-foot by twenty-foot overhang facing the river. Beneath the cigarette butts and beer cans that testify to the site's continued usefulness lie millennia of prehistoric fragments, bits and pieces of the deep past. If you cleaned up the trash and ignored the graffiti, it would still be an ideal campsite.

Afternoons seem long, but nightfall comes suddenly in November. This year no game gathered, and camp seemed bleak and empty as I cooked dinner. Bundled up with a cup of coffee in front of the uninspiring hiss of a Coleman lantern, I tried to imagine the fires of Holocene hunting camps burning along the river. I walked around the cold circle of light to keep warm, stopping to sift through handfuls of rock fragments that the root action of the larger trees had brought to the surface. Most of them were at least vaguely triangular. Some were shaped like blades. But I have no eye for the faint dimples of worked edges that, to archaeologists, are signatures of tool making. All the fragments looked like stones.

In camp at night, even in the Blue Ridge, you sometimes feel you might be anywhere. I felt that way at Paine Run this November. I watched the dark and listened to the night noises and wondered where man thought he was when he lit his fires along this small river for the first time. After the ten-thousand-year journey from Asia, across Beringia, and on into the North American continent, where was he headed? Once he crossed the last mountains he would face the eastern woodlands that sloped down toward the ocean, which would someday betray him.

It soon got too cold to stay out and speculate so grandly. Besides, my curiosity seemed academic. No fires blazed along the river. No chinking of hammerstones rang through the air. No odor of butchered game came to me. Beyond its remnant wildlife and singular topography, the depth of the place eluded me. The harsh zipping of the tent door spooked any potential illusion. I had come there to make camp as others had before me.

# RIVERS THAT GET AWAY

The Blue Ridge may be a slender country, but by December there are more rivers left to fish than I have days to fish them. Ideally, the rhythm of a fly fishing year follows a self-adjusting beat that alternates between old water and new. There are days I want to be where I have been before, backcasting for an experience on a particular river at a certain time of year. And there are days I want to be where I have never been: on a nondescript local stream I have never bothered with or a well-known river hundreds of miles away I'm tired of reading about.

The Smith River, which snakes out of the mountains and down off the Blue Ridge escarpment near the Virginia–North Carolina border, eludes both categories. It is arguably the finest brown trout river in Virginia. I've fished the Smith for years, in all seasons and under all sorts of circumstances, but I have never gotten a handle on the selectivity of its trout.

The Smith is a tailwater fishery downstream of Philpott Dam, where the river is turned on and off by the Army Corps of Engineers. When power is being generated, the river is a dangerous freight train of roily water, brown and swollen and unfishable. When the Corps closes the tap, the river settles down into something like its natural banks, which have an ugly, permanent high-water mark. Brown and rainbow trout have adapted with enthusiasm to the cold water that flows from the bottom of Philpott Lake. The river's insect life is rich and varied, a year-long sequence of hatches and superhatches that will bring out the entomologist and the discriminating fly tier in the fly fisherman or leave him muttering psychotically in a pool full of freely rising but selective fish.

One Friday evening in mid-December I got an itch to fish the Smith. Three hundred miles of driving for seven hours on a river is a powerful itch, but if you do not fish your hunches, you are not a fisherman. I drove the 150 miles to the river, fished hard all day, and moved nothing. I cast my arm off and peered at my strike indicator until I was stupid. I changed flies with uncanny ineffectiveness. Between bouts of casting, I stood on the pothole-studded ledgerock islands in the middle of the river stomping my legs warm and eating sandwiches and candy bars, trying to stoke back the warmth the river sucked out of me.

I was losing light and thinking about the drive home when the river opened up. Trout rose in a line along a seam of current in a long pool. They made beautiful, deeply furrowed riseforms in the dark water. They rose steadily, holding their lies, ten feet out from a shoddy bank of muddy shrubbery. I had no idea what they were taking. I copped out of the hatch with the smallest black fur ant I had and tied it on the end of the longest, lightest tippet I could handle in the twilight.

The moment was brief, a sweet twenty minutes when I was tight to the river. In memory I savor it in slow motion. I moved slowly upstream, hoping my legs would not go numb in the frigid water. I could see the leader unfurl at the end of each cast, but the tippet and the ant were lost to the dusk. I struck at the riseforms, setting the hook by luck, and played each trout in the center of the pool so as not to disturb the others. I brought each fish in a little green, gentling it against my chest waders while I removed the fly. They were stout fourteen–inch fish. I picked them all off, one by one, and turned them back to the river, where they belonged. Four browns and two rainbows, a limit of sorts.

# X

# LOOKING FOR
# THE END OF
# THE YEAR

Geese bring winter.

All December dark banks of clouds flow west to east over the mountains in long fronts that contract the days with cold. Every few mornings the sky seems lower, and flocks of Canada geese vee overhead trailing more cold behind them. Their unflagging flight calls seem to announce the end of the year.

And the year does seem out of breath, out of light and warmth. The brief days of winter come silently in just after the geese and seem, like them, to descend around the house and settle into the surrounding fields.

When I hear the geese moving overhead, I know the trout are disappearing from the streams, moving back into the mountains to spend their stony winter beyond the artificial reach of the fly fisherman. In the evening, when the strong calls of the geese undo the ragged ends of my concentration and bring me out into the darkening field in front of my house, I watch them beating by low overhead and then watch the empty sky until they are out of earshot.

The astonishing speed of geese in full flight seems as inexplicable as the ceaseless flow of mountain streams. The shadows in the sky remind me of trout.

Winter is gray in the Blue Ridge. The blueness that lies over the mountains during much of the year withdraws to their interior sometime in mid-December. The gray familiar to hunters occupies the land formerly held by the blueness. When the gray takes over, the days change. In the field it will seem like midmorning for a long time until, very suddenly, it is late afternoon. The empty crowns of the barren hardwoods throw haunting patterns into the sky. A diffuse, gray daylight waxes and wanes among the empty branches of oaks and hickories in hues difficult to describe. This continuous shift in light seems to search out critical differences: movement against the grain, some subtle motion that is a sign of life. The incoming cold keeps the inessential at bay, within and without.

The essential varies, of course, from season to season, year to year, and the seasons and years have uncertain boundaries. Each year has its odd, memorable days—a warm day in February, a cold day in May, a day in October that begins in frost and ends in the pale fire of Indian summer—days that eddy against the flow of the year and change one's expectations. And the years do not always flow easily from one to the other, but sometimes swirl in gray confusion at their confluence.

As a fisherman I pay close attention to eddies. Hunters and fishermen know you succeed or fail depending on how well you read signs, how close you come to knowing, and how good the guess is that covers the difference between what you know and what you don't. The guess might be figuring a drop or measuring a cast that would take advantage of what you had just seen. Seeing was where it started.

If you are a hunter, you look for movement against the grain, a muscle quivered in the cold, or you listen for a difference in the silence, a step toward further browse or an animation in the rustle of forest litter. If you are a fisherman, you watch the eddies patterning the surface of a river, eye where the water fights itself and reveals by implication the resistances beneath its surface. You learn and grow by working those tricky edges between fast water and slow water, between water moving upstream and water moving down. You learn, too, by fishing the difficult, edgy days when you're not sure which way your year is going, and by fishing through the winter when all the signs fail and the river looks meaningless.

By deer season, trout fishing slows to a formality, and I fish with a nagging feeling that I am backtracking into a year that's coming to an end, trying to cover the same ground twice. I explore less and return to familiar riffles and pools, perch myself behind boulders I have used for cover in the past. But the invading grayness over my shoulder puts a hitch in my casting and an awkwardness in my wading that spooks trout and eventually sends me home for the day, spooked too.

Walking fly rod in hand down the Rapidan fire road in December, I pass hunters headed up the mountain in pickups and 4×4s. The paraphernalia of fly fishing looks inconsequential next to a truckful of deer camp provisions, camouflaged gear, boxes of shells and gun cases. The faces of the hunters are at best amused, at worst break into shit-eating grins when they see me on the river at such an odd time of the year. Occasionally a vehicle stops, and some laconic talk passes about weather and game. No one asks about the fishing.

By mid-December a great deal of the invading grayness has settled into the river. The few trout I catch come slackly to hand to have a dark caddis removed from the side of their mouths. They are unremarkable, their colors no longer astonishing. Since their lethargy matches the forty-degree water they inhabit, it's difficult to tell when they are sufficiently revived to be released. Gills flaring slowly, they settle to the bottom beneath my hand and rest for a long time without moving.

That dark caddis is the last dry fly I can get the trout to take. It is hard to see in the shadows and in the dark swirls between boulders where I continue to believe the good trout are holding, but I fish the caddis hopefully because I know when it fails I have lost the surface of the river until spring. As winter progresses, the choice of flies becomes duller and duller. Necessity takes over. The trout won't rise to what pleases my eye or suits my theory or my attachment to the signs on the river's surface. The nymphs I fish look uninteresting in my hand, vague imitations of forms of life I never see. As I fish them, the rivers slip into winter. I wade until I'm cold and then start walking the fire roads again to get the warmth back in my legs.

The winter rivers work on me, slowing my thoughts until an uninteresting version of the year flows sullenly through my mind. I tell myself: *I fish for trout year round in the Blue Ridge, moving easily in the blueness from spring to fall until the year gives out to the grayness. Then I fish against the signs, within and without, eyeing the grayness until the blue comes back sometime in February or March, heralded by the sporadic emergence of Quill Gordons and by the reappearance of the dark green backs of brook trout in rivers that had begun to seem empty.*

If the mountains can be said to have a consciousness, it is to be found in these trout—brilliant glacial vestiges finning up-current into the cold, well-oxygenated water of higher elevations. They are an old sign. The rivers erode the mountains. The mountains become soil and vegetation, become insects and forage fish, become trout. The trout are the mountains' final idea. Hence their elaborate, indescribable color, for which even the stoic passion of spawning cannot account.

I do not know if the trout are threatened by the resolute grayness that sometimes troubles me in winter. I doubt that they are. Along with a few red spruce remaining in the higher elevations, these trout are part of the land's northern memory, vestiges of a deeper, arctic cold. Experienced over time, the trout and the spruce hold eons together. They winter well.

The years themselves, changing guard somewhere in the cold grayness of December and January, winter less well. The progression of days during the first half of winter seems to follow no order, and there is a deadly sameness in the hills. Often it is too cold to dwell on the landscape, which has shed its picturesque appeal. Most days I hardly look up from the river, which provides, at least, a familiar sense of direction through the apparent emptiness of the season. In late December the promise of the year seems outrun. Days in the field are cold and gray and uneventful, indistinct and somewhat threatening, as if the past and the present had not worked out the terms of their coexistence. The winter river sends me home early, defeated somehow. Grackles flap through the woods calling out with raspy, heartless voices, heralds of Emerson's dark thought that "there is throughout nature something mocking, something that leads us on and on, but arrives nowhere; keeps no faith with us." The days feel like that. In the rearview mirror, the grizzled watersheds look unimportant.

There is no dramatic boundary between one trout season and the next. I fish the short days of late December and early January without knowing whether one year is winding down or another beginning. I'm uneasy and don't fish well. I tell myself next season is beyond the white and gray haze that obscures the mountains.

As winter rimes logs and boulders with ice, you may sense within some weather-induced paranoia how profoundly a river may reject you, how the sluggish slate-gray surface may shut you out, cut you off from what you thought you knew well. In winter, the river conceals what you need to see and know, seems to carry it deep into the mountains, taking it north and back in time. The signs on the water's surface are no longer attached to the presence of trout. If you fish the river as winter deepens, you will find yourself going through the motions, wading stiffly around the imponderables left in the year and casting blindly, out of habit, a little unnerved by your poor purchase on a scene you thought you were a part of.

There are days on winter rivers I don't fish at all. Days I see no signs except for a few winter stoneflies clinging in the cold to the downstream side of boulders at the river's edge. These small *Plecoptera* are the only thing to emerge from beneath the river's intransigent surface during the heart of winter. And they don't emerge; they crawl. It's hard to know what they're a sign of—they have their niche in the order of things, and they are there to see at this time of year. Living as they do against the grain of the seasons, they elicit my interest and admiration. They keep the freezing river's pretense to being a source of life alive. In the dead of winter they take the place of the trout in my mind. I have learned to watch for them.

It's hard to tell when one year has ended and another begun. Signs in winter point backward as well as forward in time. The terrain is suspect and the weather stalls. You feel some changes from one trip to the next, imagine others as you eye the wall of white and gray. You read maps, overhaul gear, and tie leaders and flies for the coming season. You listen to the wintering geese shift around, and on warm, promising days you check the rivers close to home one by one, keeping the essential as portable as possible. You think about the trout in the mountains, the blue that surrounds the red. You see the ivory edges of their fins in the river. Their dark green backs ghost through your mind. At some point you've waded out of one year into another, crossed a gray ridge toward a blue one.

Woodsmoke and cabin fever. Fire thoughts and whiskey words.


Rick Webb was on the phone when I walked into his office in the basement of the University of Virginia's Clark Hall toward the end of December.

I don't mind waiting around Webb's office. The walls are covered with maps: USGS topos, colorful geologic and soil maps, as well as exotic computer projections of places I thought I knew like the back of my hand. The best of them is the state topographic map, a copy of which hangs in my own study. On Webb's version, black pins locate quarterly sampling sites for the ongoing Virginia Trout Stream Sensitivity Study. Webb has been choosing sites to sample on a weekly basis, to take yet a closer look at temporal fluctuations in stream chemistry in the Blue Ridge. The St. Marys is on the list for weekly sampling.

"Corvallis. EPA. You should call them," he says, nodding toward the phone. "They're doing interesting work."

He slides a hefty, two-volume report from the Environmental Protection Agency my way: *Chemical Characteristics of Streams in the Mid-Atlantic and Southeastern United States (National Stream Survey-Phase I).*

Webb's talk is typically peppered with names and acronyms of people and projects. There seems to be a lot of fruitful communication—people sharing data bases, comparing models, building up a picture of what's happening to streams and lakes. The political winds are shifting slowly back toward concern for the environment.

I am a little surprised to hear enthusiasm from Webb for the EPA. It hasn't been that long since disgruntled EPA employees were posing for the media in "Acid

Reign" T-shirts, back when budgets were being cut and policies undermined. That was in 1981 when, as the Canadian government tried to interest the American government in doing something about acid rain, the Reagan administration was attempting to suppress the 1981 National Academy of Sciences report on acid deposition because NAS's scientific conclusions flew in the face of the administration's political agenda.

The 1981 NAS report was unequivocal:

> Acid deposition, due to the further oxidation of sulfur and nitrogen oxides released to the atmosphere by anthropogenic sources, is causing widespread damage to aquatic ecosystems, including loss of bicarbonate, increased acidity, and higher concentrations of toxic metals. As a result, several important species of fish and invertebrates have been eliminated over substantial parts of their natural ranges.

The NAS was equally clear about what needed to be done: "Of the options presently available only the control of emissions of sulfur and nitrogen oxides can significantly reduce the rate of deterioration of sensitive freshwater ecosystems." Eight years later, reauthorization of the Clean Air Act with significant sulfur and nitrogen emission reductions was still up for grabs on Capitol Hill, a hostage of the political allies of the coal, auto, and utility industries.

Scientists, I've noted, have learned for the sake of sanity and objectivity not to care too much, on a day-to-day basis, about what politicians do or fail to do. If timely, rational appeals won't convince them, the eventual economic and social cost of a neglected problem will. It took a quarter of a century to legislate DDT from use, and the lesson summed up in 1962 in Rachel Carson's *Silent Spring* has yet to be fully implemented. The political reaction to the facts about acid rain has been no swifter.

In fact, the same tactics that were used by agribusiness from the 1940s through the 1960s were used by the opponents of reduced sulfur and nitrogen emissions: emerging facts are blindly denied until the denials ceased to be credible, at which point additional research is proposed as a way of delaying implementation of timely solutions to the problem. The public good gets lost in this predictable and transparently cynical political game.

Webb, in any event, is cautiously optimistic about the 1988 EPA survey. It provides a wealth of data, particularly about the mid-Atlantic and southeastern United States. But he can't help mentioning the bias of the National Stream Survey away from the small mountains streams he has set his mind on understanding. He goes to his map table.

"Look at the maps they based their survey on, these 1:250,000 scale projections." He roots around and pulls one out.

"Look at the blue lines, the rivers. Most of our trout streams don't show up on that scale. Just the tip of the main stem."

He draws in filaments that make each river look like a dendrite, circling the tiny branch filaments as he talks.

"We wanted to know what's happening to these thin blue lines, all these little feeder streams where the trout are, the whole catchment. Like those nine sites on the St. Marys we sampled last June."

What is happening is not good. In the short run, there is little new to see in pH and alkalinity readings. The upper reaches of the St. Marys, the tips of the dendrite, hover around a pH of 5.0, with alkalinities near zero or less than zero. Most of the main stem of the river has a pH less than 5.5 with low or negative alkalinity values. Most of the fish and invertebrate life associated with a trout stream cannot survive these acidity levels indefinitely.

But the St. Marys is only one river. More disturbing

are the predictions about the future of the rest of the trout streams in the Blue Ridge and the western Virginia highlands. Making predictions about what are technically known as nonsteady-state surface waters is difficult, given the matrix of interdependent variables in play, but there is enough data to project some expectations about the fate of life in the thin blue lines.

Ten years, thousands of man-hours, and hundreds of pages of research and analysis collapse into two sets of numbers: When the sulfate in the catchments finally reaches steady state with atmospheric deposition, at least 32 percent and as much as 88 percent of the native trout water in the Blue Ridge and Virginia highlands will be acidified. The lower figure represents a "conservative" estimate; realistic expectations lean toward the higher figure. Historically, no more than 3 percent of these streams were acidic; 10 percent already are.

Second, the median pH of nearly two thousand miles of remnant wild trout water in Virginia would drop from 6.7 to 5.6 in the best case and 4.4 in the worst. In either event, the future pH of most of the wild trout water in the Blue Ridge will be below the biologically critical level for the life of a trout stream. "A substantial change in the fisheries status of these streams would be expected," Webb and Galloway's first extended report concluded. The mountain streams of the Blue Ridge had become "a resource at significant risk from the effects of acidic deposition. The potential for deterioration of water quality (and concomitant damage to biological communities) appears to be large."

These changes will take place within the next fifty years, although the report warns that because of the "sulfate breakthrough" that occurs when the soils of these watersheds have soaked up all the sulfur they can hold, the loss of fisheries may come sooner rather than later, and be quite devastating and immediate in impact. Furthermore, prior to final, chronic acidification, most streams will become increasingly vulnerable to fish-killing episodic acidification from storms and snowmelts. In the end, only 7 percent of the streams are expected to be unaffected by atmospheric acid deposition.

So the data the skeptics in Congress and the Reagan administration said they wanted was in. It confirmed the reasonable suspicions of a decade before, when effective emissions reductions would have done much to head off or ameliorate the impending death of the wild trout streams in the mountains. But exercising prudence in such matters has not yet become part of the political process. Fifty years from now, few will remember all the trout that were in the mountains.

A few days after I talked to Rick Webb, I went to see John Kauffman at the Charlottesville office of the Virginia Department of Game and Inland Fisheries. During the past year Kauffman had been giving a paper and slide presentation about the St. Marys at fisheries conferences. He knows the river's biology as well as Webb knows its chemistry.

I got an impromptu version of the presentation. We sat on folding chairs in his office, and I listened to a steady stream of facts and carefully drawn conclusions as he showed slides on the wall. A few pleasing pictures of the river and its trout and benthic life quickly gave way to statistics, tables, and bar graphs.

Kauffman spoke quietly but earnestly, measuring his conclusions against the data that had been drawn from the river and against what was known about acidification effects from the existing scientific literature. The closer field researchers get to significant conclusions, the more carefully they choose their words.

"There is not a lot yet in the literature that documents actual changes from acidification in the field. You have to rely on differences between streams due to water chemistry. If you see those changes occur in *one* stream over time, then you are seeing the effects of acidification."

A trout stream is a complex ecosystem, and a drop in pH sets many variables in motion; their effects are manifold and interdependent. Many of the effects due to acidification that have been documented in laboratory and field studies are taking hold in the St. Marys. Kauffman's talk is a litany of changes.

Since 1976 both the variety of life forms and the populations of specific life forms in the river have declined. The lines and bars on the graphs, and the numbers in the columns and rows on the tables, all confirm the same trend. The data show fewer fish species in the river, fewer brook trout, fewer rainbow trout, fewer brown trout. Fewer forage fish. Less biomass of each species.

The most significant number is the near disappearance of young-of-the-year rainbow trout from all of the sampling reaches. Blacknose dace and rosyside dace have all but vanished from the four upper reaches, a fact that seems to correspond with the lower pH of the upper river. All invertebrate species, except those known to be acid tolerant, have declined significantly in the past decade; many have disappeared entirely.

The exact mechanism of physiological and ecological effects from acidification and stream chemistry changes are not fully understood, but the change in the river, the decrease in biodiversity, is clear.

"To me the pressing thing is not why, in each case, these species are declining, but the fact that they are declining. We need to keep looking more closely into the mechanisms of change, but the overall ecological change is clear. Look at the indices of species diversity. Generally, we are losing the distribution of species except for those that tolerate an acid-stressed environment. An across-the-board shift from a diverse to a nondiverse population indicates stress. In the St. Marys you are moving from a diverse stability to a nondiverse instability."

The slides end where they began, with an aerial shot of the St. Marys watershed, an innocent bird's-eye view with no numbers in it to mar the picturesque scene. The picture would make a nice postcard. Kauffman watches the St. Marys on the wall of his office and sums up.

"If we see all these changes in a stream over time, that's an indication of acidification. We see that in the fish and the invertebrate data—the rainbows, the dace, the resurgence of acid-tolerant species. All these things indicate that the St. Marys is acidifying."

Kauffman has been sorry to watch the river decline, but like Rick Webb he knows there are hundreds more like it in the Blue Ridge that will also become uninhabitable for wild trout in the coming decades. Too much has happened since Eugene Surber packed his gear up the river bent on understanding the nature of wild trout streams, thinking perhaps there was all the time in the world for that pleasant task.

Kauffman knew Surber and talks fondly of him. He has copies of his pioneering articles on the St. Marys on his desk. He pulls an old Surber square-foot sampler out of a storage closet.

"I liked him very much. I did some field work with him when he was near retirement. I remember him up on the St. Marys cussing the wind when he was trying to weigh small fish to the gram. He always talked about how actual field studies were the thing. Numbers. Data. Get to know what's happening in a stream before you do anything to change it.

"He cared about things. He helped set water quality standards for the U.S. Health Service in the 1940s and '50s. He did fish culture work in Iran and India for the UN—the Food and Agriculture Organization—after he retired. Then he came back to Virginia. He liked it here. I fished with him on the Shenandoah. He liked to pole a flat-bottomed boat after smallmouth. He was a good fisherman, with a fantastic memory for rivers, for details.

He thought if you knew enough, if you understood how the rivers worked, you could take care of them. He didn't know about all this."

Kauffman gestures toward the carousel of slides.

I ask if we can get Eugene Surber's St. Marys back.

Kauffman shakes his head no. "It's never going to go back to what it was. If the sulfur and nitrogen emissions controls are ever brought about, then we can probably preserve what's left by then. Otherwise, the river will continue to decline. When the final decline in the fish population comes, it will be a fairly rapid one. It's hard for the public, or the average fisherman, to see the decline in the fish population until it's too late, when the trout disappear."

A bleary-eyed evening with the June 1988 EPA report Webb lent me broadened the picture without brightening it. Although the report often veered toward elliptical, noncommittal language, some conclusions emerged. The EPA survey—which began as a pilot project in the southern Blue Ridge in North Carolina, South Carolina, and Georgia—confirmed the trends and extended the range of the Webb-Galloway findings. Because the EPA did not isolate the upper watershed reaches where acidification effects are most pronounced, their numbers are generalized compared to the University of Virginia's. Most notable in the EPA findings is the fact that 78 percent of the southern Blue Ridge is sensitive to the effects of acid deposition and that most of the nonorganically acidified stream reaches identified were in "forested upland drainages" in the northern and southern Appalachians—the remnant wild trout habitat—where the EPA also found relatively low pH values. Furthermore, low-alkalinity stream reaches were "abundant" in the interior Southeast, where extensive stream reaches had alkalinities less than two hundred microequivalents per liter, the widely accepted threshold of acid sensitivity.

Although the report tended to express some important implications in carefully guarded language—"acid deposition cannot be ruled out as the major source of acidity in this group of streams"—it did allow that "the predominant sulfate source appeared to be atmospheric deposition" for a significant number of extremely acid-sensitive streams "located primarily on upland, forested sites of the Allegheny Plateau, Valley and Ridge Province, Blue Ridge Mountains and Cumberland Plateau." The report mentioned though it did not stress the threat to fisheries represented by the large number of low-alkalinity stream reaches it documented, and the EPA acknowledged that even streams that were not yet acidic were "experiencing acidic episodes."

The EPA found the correlation throughout the Blue Ridge, and the Southern Appalachians, that Webb and Galloway had found in Virginia—"a strong positive linear relationship" between stream sulfate concentration and sulfate deposition from nonterrestrial sources in quantities and distributions that "corresponds well with sulfate deposition rates." They also documented the low alkalinity of otherwise undisturbed "pristine streams" that receive large amounts of acid deposition; regions with generally higher-alkalinity streams corresponded with lower atmospheric deposition rates. This corroborated the geologically-determined sensitivity of most native trout streams to high-sulfate deposition loads and the likelihood that they will eventually become acidified. The EPA also identified two significant populations of streams that had already been acidified: nearly 10 percent of the streams surveyed in the Valley and Ridge Province and 11 percent of the forested streams of the Allegheny Plateau, both areas west of the Blue Ridge which catch the brunt of the sulfur-laden air from the Ohio Valley. They noted that "there is no reason, however, to believe that most of the [acidified] upland forested reaches have always been acidified," implying that they must have been acidified by man-made emissions.

The EPA also recognized, without emphasizing the important fact, that the soils of the Blue Ridge and the Southern Appalachians—which had been buffering streams and stream life from the full effects of current levels of acid deposition—had become a sulfur time bomb with a fuse that shortened with every day of unabated sulfur emissions.

The parade of facts—the pieces of an unattractive puzzle—got wearying. Streams I thought I knew well seemed to get lost in numbers and terms. They became swollen with a Latinate vocabulary whose precision, unlike the formal names of mayflies and stoneflies, was mind numbing. When I mused over maps looking for new rivers to fish, I found myself cross-checking the list of alkalinity and pH I got from Rick Webb, which now hangs alongside my copy of the Virginia state topo map.

*"Nature,* in the common sense," Emerson wrote, "refers to essences unchanged by man; space, the air, the river, the leaf." By that definition, there is no nature left on earth. Very little space, none of the air, and few leaves and rivers have not been changed by man. What scientists call "anthropogenic effects" are everywhere and in every thing. No life form, no biological niche exists as it would, that is, unaffected by us. But we have known that for some time, and the knowledge has not made much difference.

In July of 1947 two researchers for the U.S. Department of Agriculture flew over the St. Marys River in a small biplane. They were conducting research in cooperation with the Federal Bureau of Entomology and Plant Quarantine and the Fish and Wildlife Service. As they flew, they dropped a dense swath of DDT into a mile-long stretch of the river at the highly toxic rate of one pound per acre. "This procedure," they noted, "insured that a maximum amount of spray was deposited on the stream." Three days later they hiked up the river and, with Surber square-foot samplers, sampled the riffles of the river for benthic invertebrates. The widespread die-off of the river's invertebrate population was, in the sometimes feckless language of the report published in the *Journal of Economic Entomology,* "tremendous," more severe than that of other rivers on which they had similarly experimented: 61 percent of the river's invertebrate life died immediately from the spraying. Downstream losses were as high as 90 percent.

Despite the immediate die-off, the researchers claimed that, a year later the benthic invertebrate populations of the St. Marys had returned to normal, at least in terms of average population numbers. They did note in passing that in one of the streams they had studied in this fashion "the species composition had changed, and some forms with a short life cycle had replaced others with a longer life cycle." These changes were not, apparently, of any further interest. Satisfied with what they had seen, the USDA researchers "summarized broadly" that "airplane applications of DDT at the rate of 1 pound of DDT per acre . . . cause no permanent damage to most forest- and stream-inhabiting animal populations."

What is most notable about this research, rather typical of attempts during the 1940s and 1950s to prove DDT harmless, is not so much its conclusions as its starting point. The USDA's researchers began their article by denigrating the growing concerns of those scientists who questioned the reigning broad assumption that DDT's long-term effects on ecosystems were benign. They were openly derisive about the nay-sayers who stood in the path of progress, "certain entomologists and others [who] condemned its use because they feared disruption of the so-called balance of nature, and painted vivid pictures of catastrophic losses."

Of course, the balance of nature turned out not to be

a figment of the imagination of malcontents, and the losses to fish and wildlife, as well as to water quality and human health, were catastrophic. But research driven by the primarily economic concerns of industry, or blinded by the often-compromised status of regulatory government agencies, fought a prolonged rearguard action that made the eventual environmental victory over DDT a typically Pyrrhic one. There are, similarly, stacks of research sponsored by the auto, coal, and utility industries during the the 1970s and 1980s that attempted, often with more sophistication than the DDT research conducted on the St. Marys, to mask the emerging truths about acid deposition. The scientific limitations of such self-interested research does not, unfortunately, diminish its political usefulness in the critical short term.

The lesson Rachel Carson tried to graciously set before the American people in 1962 is more widely accepted in theory but no more widely acted upon in practice more than a quarter of a century later. Her words about the world bear repetition:

> In some quarters nowadays it is fashionable to dismiss the balance of nature as a state of affairs that prevailed in an earlier, simpler world—a state that has now been so thoroughly upset that we might as well forget it. Some find this a convenient assumption, but as a chart for a course of action it is highly dangerous. The balance of nature is not the same today as in Pleistocene times, but it is still there: a complex, precise, and highly integrated system of relationships between living things which cannot safely be ignored any more than the law of gravity can be defied with impunity by a man perched on the edge of a cliff.

There are still those who are willing to pretend the cliff is not there. Their pretending does not make it so. But with each new environmental problem that rears its head—

acid rain, deforestation, ozone depletion, global warm-
ing—the same political battles must be fought over and
over again. Because environmental processes don't wait
on political brinkmanship, irrecoverable losses—like the
loss of a significant part of the remarkable native brook
trout population in the Blue Ridge Mountains—accom-
pany the long-delayed victories. Faced with such cynicism, land and wildlife inevitably lose.

If you look for the end of the year in the numbers the
scientists bring in from the field, you will see nothing but
vanishing points, each place and species sliding down an
asymptote whose slope is a function of the greed and stu-
pidity that have always been busy behind the cultural
myth of America's love of nature. In an increasingly
toxic world, facts crowd out metaphors. There is, at the
end of each year, less left to care about, less left to see.

Soon after that first massive grass-roots collection of
stream samples for the Virginia Trout Stream Sensitivity Study in April of 1987, the U.S. Supreme Court
upheld the Justice Department's right, under the 1938
Foreign Agents Registration Act, to label as "political
propaganda" three films produced and distributed by the
National Film Board of Canada. Two of those films, *Acid
Rain: Requiem or Recovery* and *Acid from Heaven,* were
about acid deposition; the third was the 1983 Academy
Award–winning documentary about nuclear war, *If You
Love this Planet.*

Although most civil libertarians and environmentalists saw the decision as having little practical impact,
*Meese v. Keene* stands out in retrospect as a curious but
telling example of the political instinct to substitute
words for deeds. Rather than turn to solve a problem its
own agencies had documented, the Reagan administration worked only to discredit credible information intended to enhance public recognition of the problem.
While the EPA's water-quality programs were losing 42
percent of their funding and 40 percent of their staff, the

Reagan administration spent five years of Justice Department time and effort establishing its legal right to label information about acid rain "the work of foreign agents."

Canadian propaganda notwithstanding, acid deposition continued to fall on the mountains, and sulfate adsorption continued unabated in the soils of the Blue Ridge and the Southern Appalachians during the 1980s. Undeterred by the sophistry of corporate lobbyists and the cynicism of the politicians they influence, the acid neutralizing capacity of Blue Ridge rivers declined. Stream biota, wild trout among them, struggled with chemical changes for which nothing in their long evolution had prepared them.

# CUSTOM AND
# CEREMONY

I felt eyes on me as I waded the mucky bottom at the mouth of the Moormans one April several years ago. I was fishing a small streamer among the drowned tree stumps hoping to find spawning crappie schooled in the shallow water. A warm breeze pushed little waves against my chest and ruffled the cold water around the tangled cover into which I cast. I tried to concentrate on stripping the fly toward me with a wounded zigzag retrieve, but I couldn't shake the feeling I was being watched.

I was twenty feet from her before I saw a female Canada goose calmly watching me from her nest. Given the intentness of her gaze, I was not surprised to have felt it. The goose had built the nest on a small island in the mouth of the river which gave it access to the reservoir. Three small sycamores grew at the margins of the island and the earth held by their tangled roots formed a space just large enough for the goose's work. Wood violets grew at the base of one of the trees.

The goose watched me without alarm or trust. I waded close. When she grew accustomed to my presence, she resumed feathering the nest, vigorously probing her bill into her chest, plucking tufts of down that she tucked under her to cushion the shallow thatch of twigs. When she stood to work things into place, I saw a soft gray bowl of down. The goose was large with eggs, and she settled heavily back into the nest, body and tail feathers spread wide. The male eventually sailed back from the perimeter he had been patrolling and drove me off, rearing on the water and flapping his wings, and then hissing and pursuing me slowly with his knotted neck outstretched and his beak opening and clamping shut menacingly. The pink tongue of the goose quivered with rage.

I came to the nest daily for weeks. Eventually the geese grew accustomed to my presence, and I was allowed to crouch unmolested nearby for long periods of time.

The female sat calmly on the nest throughout, turning her stately head to follow scents and sounds, never breaking silence. At the beginning of the second week, she rose and revealed five white eggs sitting in the down. They clicked like billiard balls when she turned them. As the days wore on, she rose more frequently to adjust them. One day she covered the eggs with leaves and twigs and, with one glance into the woods behind the island and one glance at me, swam off for an hour. I resisted a terrible impulse to uncover the eggs and touch them.

The male came and went, eyeing the woods and patrolling the open water, honking challenges in response to the calls of the other geese on the reservoir and occasionally coming back to stare me down.

Toward the end of my visits, the female turned the eggs every ten minutes and plucked down furiously. She fidgeted underneath her all the while, lifting her wings to peck at the cracked eggs with her stout beak. Finally one morning she stood up over a formless wet, black mass slumped in the down. By evening the black mass had gathered itself into five yellow goslings she had difficulty keeping clamped under her wing. The next day they were in the water, swimming in family formation.

A ceremony of innocence, I suppose. Everything the geese had done for weeks seemed formal. I had taken to bowing slightly when I approached the nest and again when I departed, an awkward, self-conscious gesture, but one I felt compelled to make. When they were gone, and the small island was empty except for the flattened twigs and down and one leathery eggshell, I missed their company and customs.

# XI

# RIVERRUN

Toward the end of March, while the Canada geese were building their nest at the mouth of the Moormans this year, eleven million gallons of North Slope crude spread over Prince William Sound on the evening news. As the slick billowed from the stranded *Exxon Valdez* toward the Gulf of Alaska, coating the pristine islands and choking the beautiful bays of the Chugach National Forest, a succession of Exxon executives appeared on television looking as if they had been forced to attend the funeral of someone they didn't know. Their language was as hard to grasp as the globs of oil on Prince William's beaches. One allowed that the spill was "a very unfortunate happening." Another announced that "at this point in time" Exxon regretted any "inconvenience" the spill may cause. Exxon would, the unruffled men kept repeating, pay for everything.

When it became clear that public relations would not vanquish the spill, President Bush dispatched a plane-load of officials to *Valdez* to assess the situation firsthand. The bureaucrats returned, said there was nothing to be done, and pronounced the accident a "tragedy." Meanwhile, wildlife biologists, who looked as if they understood the meaning of that word, held up oily fistfuls of dead sandpipers and guillemots for the television cameras and tried, within the attention span of the national media, to explain what was happening.

By the time this spring's goslings hatched out on the Moormans, there were twenty tons of dead animals on the shores of the Gulf of Alaska. Sea lions, gulls, cormorants, and other fouled creatures were stacked around Quonset huts awaiting autopsies; the biologists and small squads of volunteers had their hands full. Increasing numbers of migrating birds flew into the area, and seals came ashore to calve their pups. Bald eagles and bears died on the beaches from having ingested tainted fish. Commercial fishermen boomed the mouths of salmon streams and worried about herring, halibut, shrimp, and crabs. The unskimmed oil sank toward the fine-grained sediments at the bottom of the sound, which supported an elaborate food chain. No one knew what cold crude oil did to limpets and mussels, eelgrass and kelp. There isn't time to study everything. The biologists and fishermen would have to wait and see.

But most people were working for Exxon, rubbing rocks with paper towels, making good money, as the men on TV had promised. An extraordinarily beautiful and fecund ecosystem had become a symbol, a fund-raiser for environmentalists, who have grown used to bitter defeats. Another one of the last best places on earth had been irrevocably changed.

There are days when the mountain streams in the Blue Ridge look quite ordinary to me, and the idea of fly fishing for small native trout seems a poor use of time, an exercise in Romantic nostalgia that threatens to wear thin. Some days the beauty and value of these free-flowing streams and their wild trout seems merely a function of mood, or need. And the birth of half-wild Canada geese does not seem, every time I look back on it, so extraordinary either. When the Blue Ridge seems tame and ordinary, barely able to rise above its increasingly suburban surroundings, I search my maps for more exotic places where the land is wild and untouched and full of uncompromised life, places like Prince William Sound.

When William Byrd camped in the shadow of the Blue Ridge in the fall of 1728, he asked his Indian guide about his religion. "He believ'd," Byrd reported, that "God had form'd many Worlds before he form'd this, that those Worlds either grew old and ruinous, or were destroyed for the Dishonesty of the Inhabitants." Byrd discounted his guide's cosmology as quaint and primitive.

Two hundred sixty years ago, the Blue Ridge was Prince William Sound, remote and exotic and full of life. When Byrd and his men approached it, they could only conjecture about what lay beyond. They knew the names of the big rivers—the Potomec, the Sharantow, the Roanoak, the Mississippi—whose headwaters they could not place with accuracy on their crude maps. Some men thought the Appalachians marked the center of the continent and that an arm of the China Sea reached the western foot of the mountains. Byrd was reluctant to conjecture beyond his certain knowledge, but noted at the end of his journey that "our country has now been inhabited more than 130 years by the English, and still we hardly know any thing of the Appallachian Mountains, that are no where above 250 miles from the sea."

It is hard now to imagine the modest eastern mountains as capable of keeping the ambitious European adventurers at bay for more than a century, just as it is difficult to think of the Potomac, Shenandoah, Roanoke, and Mississippi as geographic mysteries. The maps have

been complete for a long time, and we have known for a
while the exact nature and extent of what Robert Frost
called, at John Kennedy's inaugural, "the gift outright."
Most of the gift, if gift it was, is gone. Given the facts of
history, and the empty rhetoric of politics, I am amazed
that any watershed, or stream, or wild trout has survived
in the Blue Ridge to this late date. When I watch what is
left of the natural world being squandered on the evening
news, the persistence of wild trout in the Blue Ridge
seems as miraculous as the return of salmon to rivers in
Alaska, and the nesting of geese at the mouth of the
Moormans in April as wondrous as it must be on the Copper River delta in June.

The news made me restless. While thousands of miles
away the hemorrhage of oil on Bligh Reef petered out, I
drove two hundred miles south toward one of the few
blank spots left on my map of the Blue Ridge. The green
and white signs flashed by: Lynchburg, Danville, Greens-
boro, Charlotte, Spartanburg, Greenville. After seven
hours of interstates I was in upstate South Carolina at
the foot of the Blue Ridge, drinking bad coffee in a Har-
dees in Seneca and trying, with a tattered paperback and
road maps, to trace an old journey.

In the spring of 1775 William Bartram set out from
Charleston, South Carolina, for what was then the Cherokee
nation. A botanist like his father John, he shunned the high
road for the richer land along the Savannah River, which
brought him through pine forests and savannahs to Augusta, the prospering head of navigation. That settlement
was about to become the seat of Georgia's government, and
Bartram watched slaves clearing the virgin forests around
the growing town. They pushed the downed pines and enormous hardwoods off the bluffs along the river and boomed the
timber to Savannah.

North of Augusta, the country grew wilder by the
mile. The Savannah River was one long, wild cataract
that split into tributaries that led back into the moun-

tains—the Broad, the Little, the Tugilo. The country was full of what for Bartram was a pleasing and instructive array of wildflowers, trees, and shrubs. Each mile toward the Cherokee confirmed his faith in the fecundity of the New World.

But as he made his way upcountry, he couldn't help but notice that there were more ancient Indian mounds than there were live Indians and more carcasses than live wild animals—"heaps of white, gnawed bones of the ancient buffaloe, elk and deer, indiscriminately mixed with those of men." "Purling rills and fleeting brooks, roving along the shadowy vales" are uncomfortably juxtaposed in his mind and prose with evidence of the ongoing war against both nature and the Cherokee, "transactions and events," he notes with considerable understatement, "perhaps not altogether reconcileable to justice and humanity." If the document to be signed the following year in his native Philadelphia was a rhetorical model of rational, enlightened eighteenth-century thought, life along the American frontier reflected an altogether different set of values. As Bartram rode toward the Blue Ridge in 1775, everything native to the country was already in retreat.

When history rears its head, Bartram turns his eye to nature—a hillside of "fiery Azalea," "a large, beautiful spreading Red Cedar," a new species of rhododendron all convince him that "the land hereabouts is indeed exceeding fertile and productive." Doused by daily thundershowers, he made his way through "an uninhabited wilderness, abounding with rivers and brooks," "an uneven country, its surface undulated by ridges or chains of hills, sometimes rough with rocks and stones, yet generally productive of forests." He then ascended the Keowe River to the Cherokee town of Seneca, where I sat reading his *Travels.*

The Keowe River is now dammed from the Savannah River to the mountains. The river and "the vale of Keowe" Bartram described in detail no longer exist, and he becomes difficult to follow after he leaves Seneca. I crossed Lake Keowe—haven for bream, bass, and water skiers—on Route 123, headed west. Bartram ascended the river north noting that the once-prosperous valley settlement, recently decimated, was a humiliating spectacle to "the once potent and renowned Cherokee." At some point he turned west, toward what is now the town of Walhalla.

In early April the worn storefronts of Walhalla are brightened by the dogwood and redbud trees that bloom along its broad main street. A mile west of town a two-lane blacktop leaps into the Blue Ridge and into the Sumter National Forest. For a few miles you have, in places, a view of something like what Bartram describes as he rode west from Fort Prince George toward the "extremely well timbered" slopes of Oconee Mountain.

I was now in a very elevated situation, from whence I enjoyed a view inexpressibly magnificent and comprehensive. The mountainous wilderness through which I had lately traversed down to the region of Augusta, appearing regularly undulated as the great ocean after a tempest; the undulations gradually depressing, yet perfectly regular, as the squamae of fish or imbrications of tile on a roof: the nearest ground to me of a perfect full green, next more glaucous, and lastly almost blue as the ether with which the most distant curve of the horizon seems to be blended.

Perched on the edge of the Blue Ridge, Bartram's imagination was absorbed in what for him was a "magnificent landscape, infinitely varied, and without bound."

Bartram proceeded down Oconee Mountain along a winding, rocky road, "shaded by incomparable forests, the soil exceedingly rich, and of an excellent quality for the production of every vegetable suited to the climate." He noted that the "magnificent high forests" were domi-

nated by northern species he had seen in his native Pennsylvania, and in New York and Canada. He crossed Chattooga Ridge and entered a narrow valley, "through which
flows a rapid large creek." Where Bartram turned south
along the Chattooga, looking for a way across, I turned
north.

The Chattooga River speaks in a buttery voice at the
bridge above Burrells Ford. The river there is quick and
deep, full of complicated ribbons of current mobile as the
minds of trout. At the Burrells Ford bridge, the quiet
pools and chattering riffles give no sign of the mayhem
twenty miles downstream at Bull Sluice and Woodall
Shoals.

I backpacked a few miles upstream into the Ellicott
Rock Wilderness and made camp where the East Fork
of the Chattooga joins the main river. I fished the
main stem for a week, slowly getting to know the
river, slowly getting to like it more and more. The
water was April high and cold, and many of the spots
I wanted to fish were still out of reach—isolated runs
and deep holes where the Walhalla brown trout grow
old and wary. I fished the riffles I could handle and
the pools I could approach properly. The river fished
slowly, but I did all right when I took my time short-
lining nymphs through the cold, quick water. The trout
were sluggish and early-season mayflies came out of
the river only grudgingly.

By the look of it, Ellicott Rock sees some traffic, but
the heavily used campsites are surrounded by a stately
hemlock-pine forest. Hardwoods are rare, and the understory is open and clear except for patches of laurel and
groves of large rhododendron. You are surrounded by
evergreen growth, which softens the signs of misuse. The
ground is soft with layers of pine and hemlock needles,
and I remember sleeping extraordinarily well there. The
watershed was a few weeks ahead of the season at home.
Trout lilies, sessile bellwort, and yellow violets bloomed

in the woods; bluets covered the riverbanks. Copperhead curled on sunlit rocks; the air seemed full of flickers. Between the river and its trout and the life emerging around it, the country looked good. I fished hard, glad to have a new river flowing around me and promising country stirring around the river. At night I built a fire after dinner and followed William Bartram.

Apparently Bartram descended the Chattooga a few miles until he came to a trading path along Warwomans Creek that led him northwest into the Blue Ridge through Rabun Gap:

> one of the most charming natural mountainous landscapes perhaps any where to be seen; ridges of hills rising grand and sublimely one above and beyond another, some boldly and majestically advancing into the verdant plain, their feet bathed with the silver flood of the Tanase, whilst others far distant, veiled in blue mists, sublimely mount aloft with yet greater majesty lift up their pompous crests and overlook vast regions.

However mannered his descriptions may now seem, Bartram's journey alone into the Blue Ridge and the Nantahalas is one of the finest moments in American history. A year before Jefferson drafted the Declaration of Independence, Bartram was exploring the natural character of the country. He crossed the ridges veiled in blue mists into the Nantahalas, "the highest land in the Cherokee country," from which he beheld "with rapture and astonishment, a sublimely awful scene of power and magnificence, a world of mountains piled upon mountains. . . . an expansive prospect, exhibiting scenes of mountainous landscape, Westward vast and varied, perhaps not to be exceeded any where."

Beyond the Nantahalas lay the Overhill towns, where Bartram was well treated and respected by the Cherokee for his interest in the natural world. They named him Puc-Puccy, Flower-hunter, and gave him safe passage through what was left of their lives and land.

On the Chattooga, the weather ran backward, as if the year were turning around. A week that had begun with summerlike days was back in March by Friday. I labored for a day up the steep and narrow East Fork. I was told there were native brook trout in the river, but I caught only browns. The river is in places so rugged and tightly thatched with rhododendrons, it often defeats any normal kind of fly fishing. But I bushwhacked slowly up a good part of it, dropping flies into small green pools where trout frequently swirled. I barely covered a half mile of stream in a day's fishing, but I liked the rough rush of cold water and the way the land seemed to fend me off. The terrain seemed to guard each good pool, but trout came out of hiding and charged flies hard, as if the wildness of the land gave them faith in the river.

By the end of the week it was too cold at night to read. So I put Bartram's book away and played the new rivers back in my mind as I huddled at a small fire.

The morning after fishing the East Fork I woke up in a half foot of snow, a little amazed at the new world around me. The air was stiff with cold. A bluish morning light hung over the river. The Chattooga glistened. I wandered about this strange, whitened world for half a day, disoriented by the change and mesmerized by the trackless look of things. I broke camp after lunch, carving a fresh trail out. What was it Bartram had written about the awful, reverential harmony of undisturbed forests? Inexpressibly sublime, and not to be enjoyed anywhere, but in native, wild regions.

I pointed my pickup toward Virginia and headed north on Route 107. I didn't get ten miles before I pulled over at a long view that opened to the east. The sky was gray in the mountains to the west, where I had been camped, but to the east the bad weather was already breaking. Bright tufts of clouds drifted between the ridges that descended in waves to the piedmont. The near slopes were whitened, but further east the mountains were blue. Pieces of Lake Keowe came in and out of view, glistening where sunlight reached it. The sky above looked like an undisturbed field of snow. This wasn't one of Bartram's "marvellous scenes of primitive nature, as yet unmodified by the hand of man," but you could see the native, wild lay of the land that underwrote the beauty of what remained. By the time I drove away, four other cars were stopped there. People got out, a little self-consciously, to look.

I stopped for gas and a hot meal in Cashiers, just over the border into North Carolina. The spring snow storm had put an unfocused excitement in the air. I dropped some quarters in the machine at the end of a diner booth and watched cars fishtail through the intersection. The waitress smiled when she heard Emmylou start singing "Blue Kentucky Girl." She brought more coffee and told me that there was a foot of snow in the Nantahalas. After the coffee I drove west to see it.


Thoreau, I'm happy to note, numbered fishermen among "all honest pilgrims, who come out to the woods for freedom's sake." Although he briefly considered making his Walden experiment along the trout brook at Baker Farm, he was a stillwater thinker at heart, and so settled for a time by the water that best reflected his intellect and imagination. I find him better company on wild water, and would rather paddle with him on the West Branch of the Penobscot, where he met the natural world on its own terms, than sit with him at Walden Pond, where he made of nature a studied still life, albeit a beautiful and thoughtful one.

For all his pond watching, Thoreau knew that the wild flow of a river was "a beautiful illustration of the

law of obedience," which is where its wildness comes
from. The deeper obedience of a river is the source of its
freedom. Left alone, a wild stream will be true to its nature, and so free. The cyclical regularity of the mountain
trout streams in the Blue Ridge, their mayflies and rising
trout, are proof of that. The freedom the fly fisherman
fishes for is that free order in the river. Wild trout are a
kind of truth.

I fish the same rivers too often to be much of a fly
fisherman. I carry fewer flies each year, and less gear.
Each year I watch a little more, fish a little less. My expertise with a fly rod, such as it is, fails to improve much.
But I like fishing along the folds in the blue horizon and
catching wild trout where wild trout have always been.

There is, finally, no field guide to the year. Memories
do not structure themselves into months or seasons. A
year never fits one's expectations, and the world always
exceeds our knowledge of it. But knowledge, Thoreau
also wisely noted, is not the quarry. As all fishermen
drawn to the life of rivers know, the company of rivers
over the course of years will shift some substrate within
the soul, and they all eventually flow together in ways
beyond accurate recall. Time itself seems to play over the
surface of the water while you fish, and the contours of
familiar horizons come to structure and shelter one's
thoughts.

When you are fishing well on a good river, it is hard
to stop at the end of a day, hard to turn your back on the
trout even after they have stopped rising, hard to walk
out of the darkening water. You keep casting with the
four-count rhythm that has disciplined the fly fisherman's expectations for centuries, casting silently into the
failing light to what you think are the faint sounds of a
rise, and casting, finally, to the twilight sheen of the river
itself, as if you are thereby paying homage to something
important. On the river some evenings, you feel you
could go on forever.

I believe Thoreau was right, that the fairest landscape

lies within, but I know too that we need real places in this world to traverse—wilderness and blue horizons and cold, unfettered streams with wild trout in them as quick as thoughts, or feelings. We need what undisturbed remnants are left of the natural world to help us shape our lives, inform our dreams, and enable us to become selves we can inhabit.

The traverse of a mind along its rivers leads on and on. The grammar of fly fishing prose flows naturally toward the promising, hypnotic parataxis a young, unspoiled Ernest Hemingway brought into the mainstream of American literature from the trout streams of a midwestern boyhood. That style, which Nick Adams borrowed from Huck Finn, who got it from the big river at the heart of the country, is nostalgic and hopeful and poised against man's tendency to destroy. In all its variants, the style, like the backward-seeming effort of casting a fly line, is an attempt to reach into the natural world and confirm its sustaining presence in the lives of men.

The North Fork of the Moormans flows silver at dusk in late April. There is a dim, vestigial brightness in the seams of its currents. You can just see a dry fly cast on the water.

I heard the trout take the fly and played it briefly in the waning light. I bent over to release it and then straightened up. I listened to the river and watched for the fish to dart away. As I leaned back toward the water, to see if the trout was still there, I might have seemed to be bowing.

# BIBLIOGRAPHICAL
# NOTE

A variety of texts and documents have informed my understanding of the Blue Ridge. For the purposes of this book, I have briefly quoted from the following material. The epigraphs: Roderick L. Haig-Brown, *A River Never Sleeps* (New York: Nick Lyons Books, 1974); Henry David Thoreau, *The Maine Woods* (New York: Norton, 1950). Chapter one: Captain John Smith, *A Map of Virginia* (1612) in Volume I of *The Complete Works of Captain John Smith (1580–1631)*, ed. Philip L. Barbour (Chapel Hill: University of North Carolina Press, 1986). Chapter two: Joseph Ewan and Nesta Ewan, *John Bannister and His Natural History of Virginia 1678–1692* (Urbana: University of Illinois Press, 1970); *William Byrd's Histories of the Dividing Line Betwixt Virginia and North Carolina* (New York: Dover, 1967). Chapter five: H. B. N. Hynes, *The Ecology of Running Waters* (Toronto: The University of Toronto Press, 1970); Eugene W. Surber, "Bottom Fauna and Temperature Conditions in Relation to Trout Management in St. Mary's River, Augusta County, Virginia," *Virginia Journal of Science,* Volume 2, New Series (July 1951); Eugene W. Surber, "Lost: 10,839 Fingerling Trout! An Appraisal of the Results of Planting Fingerling Trout in St. Mary *[sic]* River, Virginia," *The Progressive Fish Culturist,* No. 49 (March–April 1940); J. R. Webb, et al., "Acidification of Native Brook Trout Streams in Virginia," *Water Resources Research,* Volume 25, No. 6 (June 1989), pp. 1367–1377; J. R. Webb, et al., "Acidic Deposition and the Status of Virginia's Wild Trout Resource," *Wild*

*Trout IV: Proceedings of the Symposium*, ed. Frank Richardson and R. H. Hamre (Washington, D.C.: U.S. Department of the Interior, et al., 1989), pp. 228–33. Interchapter six: Henry David Thoreau, "Natural History of Massachusetts," *The Natural History Essays* (Salt Lake City: Peregrine Smith, 1980). Chapter six: Thomas Jefferson, *Notes on the State of Virginia* (Chapel Hill: University of North Carolina Press, 1955). Chapter seven: "Journal de André Michaux," *Proceedings of the American Philosophical Society*, Volume 26 (1888); William Faulkner, *Go Down, Moses* (New York: Random House, 1973); Frederick Jackson Turner, "The Problem of the West," *Atlantic Monthly*, Volume 78 (1896); Thoreau, *The Maine Woods*, cited earlier; G. F. Swain, et al., *Papers on the Waterpower in North Carolina*, North Carolina Geological Survey Bulletin No. 8 (Raleigh: North Carolina Geological Survey, 1899); Aldo Leopold, "Wilderness," *"A Sand Country Almanac" and "Sketches Here and There"* (New York: Oxford University Press, 1987). Interchapter eight: Laura E. Jackson, *Mountain Treasures at Risk: The Future of the Southern Appalachians* (Washington, D.C.: The Wilderness Society, 1989); Gifford Pinchot, *Breaking New Ground* (Washington, D.C.: Island Press, 1987). Chapter nine: Ernest Earnest, *John and William Bartram: Botanists and Explorers* (Philadelphia: University of Pennsylvania Press, 1940); Edmund Berkeley and Dorothy Smith Berkeley, *The Life and Travels of John Bartram: From Lake Ontario to the River St. John* (Tallahassee: University Presses of Florida, 1982); Josephine Herbst, *New Green World* (New York: Hastings House, 1954); "A Letter from Mr. John Bartram of Pensylvania, to P. Collinson, Esq; F.R.S.," *The Gentleman's Magazine and Historical Chronicle* [London], Volume 26 (1756), pp. 474–75; "Some Observations on the Dragon-Fly or Libella of Pensilvania, collected from Mr. John Bartram's *Letters,* communicated by

Peter Collinson, F.R.S.," *Philosophical Transactions* [Royal Society of London], Volume 46 (1749–50), pp. 323–25; "A further Account of the Libellae or May-flies, from Mr. John Bartram of Pensylvania, communicated by Mr. Peter Collinson, F.R.S.," *Philosophical Transactions* [Royal Society of London], Volume 46 (1749–50), pp. 400–402; *John and William Bartram's America: Selections from the Writings of the Philadelphia Naturalists,* ed. Helen Gere Cruickshank (New York: Devin-Adair, 1957). Chapter ten: Ralph Waldo Emerson, "Nature" (from *Essays: Second Series*), *The Selected Writings of Ralph Waldo Emerson,* ed. Brooks Atkinson (New York: Modern Library, 1950); National Research Council, *Atmosphere-Biosphere Interactions: Toward a Better Understanding of the Ecological Consequences of Fossil Fuel Combustion* (National Academy Press, 1981); P. R. Kaufmann, et al., *Chemical Characteristics of Streams in the Mid-Atlantic and Southeastern United States,* Volume I: *Population Descriptions and Physico-Chemical Relationships,* EPA/600/3-88/021a (Washington, D.C., U.S. Environmental Protection Agency, 1988); Ralph Waldo Emerson, *Nature, Selected Writings of Emerson,* cited above; C. H. Hoffmann and E. P. Merkel, "Fluctuations in Insect Populations Associated with Aerial Applications of DDT to Forests," *Journal of Economic Entomology,* Volume 41, No. 3 (June 1948); Rachel Carson, *Silent Spring* (Boston: Houghton Mifflin, 1962); Stuart Taylor, "Court Backs 'Propaganda' Label for 3 Canadian Films," *New York Times,* 29 April 1987, p. A28. Chapter eleven: *William Byrd's Histories of the Dividing Line,* cited earlier; *The Travels of William Bartram,* Naturalist's Edition, ed. Francis Harper (New Haven: Yale University Press, 1958); Henry David Thoreau, *Walden* (Salt Lake City: Gibbs Smith, 1981); Henry David Thoreau, "A Winter Walk," *The Natural History Essays,* cited earlier.

I referred to the following legislation in interchapters

seven and eight: The National Forest Management Act of 1976 (16 U.S.C. 1600–1614) and the Wilderness Act of 1964 (16 U.S.C. 1131–1136). In interchapter eight, Senator John Warner is quoted from the *Congressional Record* for 3 October 1984.

799.1758 Camuto,
C          Christopher.

    A fly fisherman's
    Blue Ridge

  $19.95

| DATE | | | |
|---|---|---|---|
| | | | |
| | | | |
| | | | |
| | | | |
| | | | |
| | | | |
| | | | |
| | | | |
| | | | |
| | | | |
| | | | |
| | | | |
| | | | |

JUN   1991

© THE BAKER & TAYLOR CO.